The Latin-English Bible – Volume XX

Lamentations
Ezekiel

The texts used in this edition are from the
Vulgate and the King James Version

Compiled by Timothy Plant

Cover picture
The Vision of Ezekiel
By Raphael

CHAPTER 1

CHAPTER 1

1. ALEPH quomodo sedit sola civitas plena populo facta est quasi vidua domina gentium princeps provinciarum facta est sub tributo

2. BETH plorans ploravit in nocte et lacrimae eius in maxillis eius non est qui consoletur eam ex omnibus caris eius omnes amici eius spreverunt eam et facti sunt ei inimici

3. GIMEL migravit Iuda propter adflictionem et multitudinem servitutis habitavit inter gentes nec invenit requiem omnes persecutores eius adprehenderunt eam inter angustias

4. DELETH viae Sion lugent eo quod non sint qui veniant ad sollemnitatem omnes portae eius destructae sacerdotes eius gementes virgines eius squalidae et ipsa oppressa amaritudine

HOW doth the city sit solitary, that was full of people! how is she become as a widow! she that was great among the nations, and princess among the provinces, how is she become tributary!

2 She weepeth sore in the night, and her tears are on her cheeks: among all her lovers she hath none to comfort her: all her friends have dealt treacherously with her, they are become her enemies.

3 Judah is gone into captivity because of affliction, and because of great servitude: she dwelleth among the heathen, she findeth no rest: all her persecutors overtook her between the straits.

4 The ways of Zion do mourn, because none come to the solemn feasts: all her gates are desolate: her priests sigh, her virgins are afflicted, and she is in bitterness.

5 Her adversaries are the

5. HE facti sunt hostes eius in capite inimici illius locupletati sunt quia Dominus locutus est super eam propter multitudinem iniquitatum eius parvuli eius ducti sunt captivi ante faciem tribulantis

6. VAV et egressus est a filia Sion omnis decor eius facti sunt principes eius velut arietes non invenientes pascuam et abierunt absque fortitudine ante faciem subsequentis

7. ZAI recordata est Hierusalem dierum adflictionis suae et praevaricationis omnium desiderabilium suorum quae habuerat a diebus antiquis cum caderet populus eius in manu hostili et non esset auxiliator viderunt eam hostes et deriserunt sabbata eius

8. HETH peccatum peccavit Hierusalem propterea instabilis facta est omnes qui glorificabant eam spreverunt illam quia viderunt ignominiam eius

chief, her enemies prosper; for the Lord hath afflicted her for the multitude of her transgressions: her children are gone into captivity before the enemy.

6 And from the daughter of Zion all her beauty is departed: her princes are become like harts that find no pasture, and they are gone without strength before the pursuer.

7 Jerusalem remembered in the days of her affliction and of her miseries all her pleasant things that she had in the days of old, when her people fell into the hand of the enemy, and none did help her: the adversaries saw her, and did mock at her sabbaths.

8 Jerusalem hath grievously sinned; therefore she is removed: all that honoured her despise her, because they have seen her nakedness: yea, she sigheth, and turneth backward.

9 Her filthiness is in her skirts; she remembereth not her last end; therefore she came down wonderfully: she had no comforter. O Lord, behold my affliction: for the enemy hath magnified

ipsa autem gemens et conversa retrorsum

9. TETH sordes eius in pedibus eius nec recordata est finis sui deposita est vehementer non habens consolatorem vide Domine adflictionem meam quoniam erectus est inimicus

10. IOTH manum suam misit hostis ad omnia desiderabilia eius quia vidit gentes ingressas sanctuarium suum de quibus praeceperas ne intrarent in ecclesiam tuam

11. CAPH omnis populus eius gemens et quaerens panem dederunt pretiosa quaeque pro cibo ad refocilandam animam vide Domine considera quoniam facta sum vilis

12. LAMED o vos omnes qui transitis per viam adtendite et videte si est dolor sicut dolor meus quoniam vindemiavit me ut locutus est Dominus in die irae furoris sui

13. MEM de excelso misit ignem in ossibus meis et erudivit me himself.

10 The adversary hath spread out his hand upon all her pleasant things: for she hath seen that the heathen entered into her sanctuary, whom thou didst command that they should not enter into thy congregation.

11 All her people sigh, they seek bread; they have given their pleasant things for meat to relieve the soul: see, O Lord, and consider; for I am become vile.

12 Is it nothing to you, all ye that pass by? behold, and see if there be any sorrow like unto my sorrow, which is done unto me, wherewith the Lord hath afflicted me in the day of his fierce anger.

13 From above hath he sent fire into my bones, and it prevaileth against them: he hath spread a net for my feet, he hath turned me back: he hath made me desolate and faint all the day.

14 The yoke of my transgressions is bound by his hand: they are wreathed, and come up upon my neck: he hath made my strength to fall, the Lord hath delivered me into their hands, from

expandit rete pedibus meis convertit me retrorsum posuit me desolatam tota die maerore confectam

14. NUN vigilavit iugum iniquitatum mearum in manu eius convolutae sunt et inpositae collo meo infirmata est virtus mea dedit me Dominus in manu de qua non potero surgere

15. SAMECH abstulit omnes magnificos meos Dominus de medio mei vocavit adversum me tempus ut contereret electos meos torcular calcavit Dominus virgini filiae Iuda

16. AIN idcirco ego plorans et oculus meus deducens aquam quia longe factus est a me consolator convertens animam meam facti sunt filii mei perditi quoniam invaluit inimicus

17. FE expandit Sion manus suas non est qui consoletur eam mandavit Dominus adversum Iacob in circuitu eius hostes eius facta est Hierusalem quasi polluta menstruis

whom I am not able to rise up.

15 The Lord hath trodden under foot all my mighty men in the midst of me: he hath called an assembly against me to crush my young men: the Lord hath trodden the virgin, the daughter of Judah, as in a winepress.

16 For these things I weep; mine eye, mine eye runneth down with water, because the comforter that should relieve my soul is far from me: my children are desolate, because the enemy prevailed.

17 Zion spreadeth forth her hands, and there is none to comfort her: the Lord hath commanded concerning Jacob, that his adversaries should be round about him: Jerusalem is as a menstruous woman among them.

18 The Lord is righteous; for I have rebelled against his commandment: hear, I pray you, all people, and behold my sorrow: my virgins and my young men are gone into captivity.

19 I called for my lovers, but they deceived me: my priests and mine elders gave up the

inter eos

18. SADE iustus est Dominus quia os eius ad iracundiam provocavi audite obsecro universi populi et videte dolorem meum virgines meae et iuvenes mei abierunt in captivitatem

19. COPH vocavi amicos meos et ipsi deceperunt me sacerdotes mei et senes mei in urbe consumpti sunt quia quaesierunt cibum sibi ut refocilarent animam suam

20. RES vide Domine quoniam tribulor venter meus conturbatus est subversum est cor meum in memet ipsa quoniam amaritudine plena sum foris interfecit gladius et domi mors similis est

21. SEN audierunt quia ingemesco ego et non est qui consoletur me omnes inimici mei audierunt malum meum laetati sunt quoniam tu fecisti adduxisti diem consolationis et fient similes mei

22. THAU ingrediatur omne malum eorum coram te et devindemia

ghost in the city, while they sought their meat to relieve their souls.

20 Behold, O Lord; for I am in distress: my bowels are troubled; mine heart is turned within me; for I have grievously rebelled: abroad the sword bereaveth, at home there is as death.

21 They have heard that I sigh: there is none to comfort me: all mine enemies have heard of my trouble; they are glad that thou hast done it: thou wilt bring the day that thou hast called, and they shall be like unto me.

22 Let all their wickedness come before thee; and do unto them, as thou hast done unto me for all my transgressions: for my sighs are many, and my heart is faint.

eos sicut vindemiasti me propter omnes iniquitates meas multi enim gemitus mei et cor meum maerens

CHAPTER 2

1. ALEPH quomodo obtexit caligine in furore suo Dominus filiam Sion proiecit de caelo terram inclitam Israhel et non recordatus est scabilli pedum suorum in die furoris sui
2. BETH praecipitavit Dominus nec pepercit omnia speciosa Iacob destruxit in furore suo munitiones virginis Iuda deiecit in terram polluit regnum et principes eius
3. GIMEL confregit in ira furoris omne cornu Israhel avertit retrorsum dexteram suam a facie inimici et succendit in Iacob quasi ignem flammae devorantis in gyro
4. DELETH tetendit arcum suum quasi inimicus firmavit dexteram suam quasi hostis et occidit omne

CHAPTER 2

HOW hath the Lord covered the daughter of Zion with a cloud in his anger, and cast down from heaven unto the earth the beauty of Israel, and remembered not his footstool in the day of his anger!
2 The Lord hath swallowed up all the habitations of Jacob, and hath not pitied: he hath thrown down in his wrath the strong holds of the daughter of Judah; he hath brought them down to the ground: he hath polluted the kingdom and the princes thereof.
3 He hath cut off in his fierce anger all the horn of Israel: he hath drawn back his right hand from before the enemy, and he burned against Jacob like a flaming fire, which devoureth round about.
4 He hath bent his bow like an enemy: he stood with his right hand as an adversary, and slew all that were

quod pulchrum erat visu in tabernaculo filiae Sion effudit quasi ignem indignationem suam

5. HE factus est Dominus velut inimicus praecipitavit Israhel praecipitavit omnia moenia eius dissipavit munitiones eius et replevit in filia Iuda humiliatum et humiliatam

6. VAV et dissipavit quasi hortum tentorium suum demolitus est tabernaculum suum oblivioni tradidit Dominus in Sion festivitatem et sabbatum et obprobrio in indignatione furoris sui regem et sacerdotem

7. ZAI reppulit Dominus altare suum maledixit sanctificationi suae tradidit in manu inimici muros turrium eius vocem dederunt in domo Domini sicut in die sollemni

8. HETH cogitavit Dominus dissipare murum filiae Sion tetendit funiculum suum et non avertit manum suam a perditione

pleasant to the eye in the tabernacle of the daughter of Zion: he poured out his fury like fire.

5 The Lord was as an enemy: he hath swallowed up Israel, he hath swallowed up all her palaces: he hath destroyed his strong holds, and hath increased in the daughter of Judah mourning and lamentation.

6 And he hath violently taken away his tabernacle, as if it were of a garden: he hath destroyed his places of the assembly: the Lord hath caused the solemn feasts and sabbaths to be forgotten in Zion, and hath despised in the indignation of his anger the king and the priest.

7 The Lord hath cast off his altar, he hath abhorred his sanctuary, he hath given up into the hand of the enemy the walls of her palaces; they have made a noise in the house of the Lord, as in the day of a solemn feast.

8 The Lord hath purposed to destroy the wall of the daughter of Zion: he hath stretched out a line, he hath not withdrawn his hand from destroying: therefore he

luxitque antemurale et murus pariter dissipatus est

9. TETH defixae sunt in terra portae eius perdidit et contrivit vectes eius regem eius et principes eius in gentibus non est lex et prophetae eius non invenerunt visionem a Domino

10. IOTH sederunt in terra conticuerunt senes filiae Sion consperserunt cinere capita sua accincti sunt ciliciis abiecerunt in terra capita sua virgines Hierusalem

11. CAPH defecerunt prae lacrimis oculi mei conturbata sunt viscera mea effusum est in terra iecur meum super contritione filiae populi mei cum deficeret parvulus et lactans in plateis oppidi

12. LAMED matribus suis dixerunt ubi est triticum et vinum cum deficerent quasi vulnerati in plateis civitatis cum exhalarent animas suas in sinu matrum suarum

13. MEM cui conparabo te vel cui adsimilabo te

made the rampart and the wall to lament; they languished together.

9 Her gates are sunk into the ground; he hath destroyed and broken her bars: her king and her princes are among the Gentiles: the law is no more; her prophets also find no vision from the Lord.

10 The elders of the daughter of Zion sit upon the ground, and keep silence: they have cast up dust upon their heads; they have girded themselves with sackcloth: the virgins of Jerusalem hang down their heads to the ground.

11 Mine eyes do fail with tears, my bowels are troubled, my liver is poured upon the earth, for the destruction of the daughter of my people; because the children and the sucklings swoon in the streets of the city.

12 They say to their mothers, Where is corn and wine? when they swooned as the wounded in the streets of the city, when their soul was poured out into their mothers' bosom.

13 What thing shall I take to witness for thee? what thing

filia Hierusalem cui exaequabo te et consolabor te virgo filia Sion magna enim velut mare contritio tua quis medebitur tui

14. NUN prophetae tui viderunt tibi falsa et stulta nec aperiebant iniquitatem tuam ut te ad paenitentiam provocarent viderunt autem tibi adsumptiones falsas et eiectiones

15. SAMECH plauserunt super te manibus omnes transeuntes per viam sibilaverunt et moverunt caput suum super filiam Hierusalem haecine est urbs dicentes perfecti decoris gaudium universae terrae

16. FE aperuerunt super te os suum omnes inimici tui sibilaverunt et fremuerunt dentibus dixerunt devoravimus en ista est dies quam expectabamus invenimus vidimus

17. AIN fecit Dominus quae cogitavit conplevit sermonem suum quem praeceperat a diebus antiquis destruxit et non

shall I liken to thee, O daughter of Jerusalem? what shall I equal to thee, that I may comfort thee, O virgin daughter of Zion? for thy breach is great like the sea: who can heal thee?

14 Thy prophets have seen vain and foolish things for thee: and they have not discovered thine iniquity, to turn away thy captivity; but have seen for thee false burdens and causes of banishment.

15 All that pass by clap their hands at thee; they hiss and wag their head at the daughter of Jerusalem, saying, Is this the city that men call The perfection of beauty, The joy of the whole earth?

16 All thine enemies have opened their mouth against thee: they hiss and gnash the teeth: they say, We have swallowed her up: certainly this is the day that we looked for; we have found, we have seen it.

17 The Lord hath done that which he had devised; he hath fulfilled his word that he had commanded in the days of old: he hath thrown down,

pepercit et laetificavit super te inimicum et exaltavit cornu hostium tuorum

18. SADE clamavit cor eorum ad Dominum super muros filiae Sion deduc quasi torrentem lacrimas per diem et per noctem non des requiem tibi neque taceat pupilla oculi tui

19. COPH consurge lauda in nocte in principio vigiliarum effunde sicut aqua cor tuum ante conspectum Domini leva ad eum manus tuas pro anima parvulorum tuorum qui defecerunt in fame in capite omnium conpetorum

20. RES vide Domine et considera quem vindemiaveris ita ergone comedent mulieres fructum suum parvulos ad mensuram palmae si occidetur in sanctuario Domini sacerdos et propheta

21. SEN iacuerunt in terra foris puer et senex virgines meae et iuvenes mei ceciderunt in gladio interfecisti in die furoris

and hath not pitied: and he hath caused thine enemy to rejoice over thee, he hath set up the horn of thine adversaries.

18 Their heart cried unto the Lord, O wall of the daughter of Zion, let tears run down like a river day and night: give thyself no rest; let not the apple of thine eye cease.

19 Arise, cry out in the night: in the beginning of the watches pour out thine heart like water before the face of the Lord: lift up thy hands toward him for the life of thy young children, that faint for hunger in the top of every street.

20 Behold, O Lord, and consider to whom thou hast done this. Shall the women eat their fruit, and children of a span long? shall the priest and the prophet be slain in the sanctuary of the Lord?

21 The young and the old lie on the ground in the streets: my virgins and my young men are fallen by the sword; thou hast slain them in the day of thine anger; thou hast killed, and not pitied.

22 Thou hast called as in a solemn day my terrors round

tui percussisti nec misertus es

22. THAU vocasti quasi ad diem sollemnem qui terrerent me de circuitu et non fuit in die furoris Domini qui effugeret et relinqueretur quos educavi et enutrivi inimicus meus consumpsit eos

about, so that in the day of the Lord's anger none escaped nor remained: those that I have swaddled and brought up hath mine enemy consumed.

CHAPTER 3

1. ALEPH ego vir videns paupertatem meam in virga indignationis eius

2. ALEPH me minavit et adduxit in tenebris et non in lucem

3. ALEPH tantum in me vertit et convertit manum suam tota die

4. BETH vetustam fecit pellem meam et carnem meam contrivit ossa mea

5. BETH aedificavit in gyro meo et circumdedit me felle et labore

6. BETH in tenebrosis conlocavit me quasi mortuos sempiternos

7. GIMEL circumaedificavit adversum me ut non

CHAPTER 3

I AM the man that hath seen affliction by the rod of his wrath.

2 He hath led me, and brought me into darkness, but not into light.

3 Surely against me is he turned; he turneth his hand against me all the day.

4 My flesh and my skin hath he made old; he hath broken my bones.

5 He hath builded against me, and compassed me with gall and travail.

6 He hath set me in dark places, as they that be dead of old.

7 He hath hedged me about, that I cannot get out: he hath made my chain heavy.

egrediar adgravavit conpedem meam

8. GIMEL sed et cum clamavero et rogavero exclusit orationem meam

9. GIMEL conclusit vias meas lapidibus quadris semitas meas subvertit

10. DELETH ursus insidians factus est mihi leo in absconditis

11. DELETH semitas meas subvertit et confregit me posuit me desolatam

12. DELETH tetendit arcum suum et posuit me quasi signum ad sagittam

13. HE misit in renibus meis filias faretrae suae

14. HE factus sum in derisu omni populo meo canticum eorum tota die

15. HE replevit me amaritudinibus inebriavit me absinthio

16. VAV et fregit ad numerum dentes meos cibavit me cinere

17. VAV et repulsa est anima mea oblitus sum bonorum

18. VAV et dixi periit finis meus et spes mea a Domino

19. ZAI recordare

8 Also when I cry and shout, he shutteth out my prayer.

9 He hath inclosed my ways with hewn stone, he hath made my paths crooked.

10 He was unto me as a bear lying in wait, and as a lion in secret places.

11 He hath turned aside my ways, and pulled me in pieces: he hath made me desolate.

12 He hath bent his bow, and set me as a mark for the arrow.

13 He hath caused the arrows of his quiver to enter into my reins.

14 I was a derision to all my people; and their song all the day.

15 He hath filled me with bitterness, he hath made me drunken with wormwood.

16 He hath also broken my teeth with gravel stones, he hath covered me with ashes.

17 And thou hast removed my soul far off from peace: I forgat prosperity.

18 And I said, My strength and my hope is perished from the Lord:

19 Remembering mine affliction and my misery, the wormwood and the gall.

paupertatis et transgressionis meae absinthii et fellis

20. ZAI memoria memor ero et tabescet in me anima mea

21. ZAI hoc recolens in corde meo ideo sperabo

22. HETH misericordiae Domini quia non sumus consumpti quia non defecerunt miserationes eius

23. HETH novae diluculo multa est fides tua

24. HETH pars mea Dominus dixit anima mea propterea expectabo eum

25. TETH bonus est Dominus sperantibus in eum animae quaerenti illum

26. TETH bonum est praestolari cum silentio salutare Domini

27. TETH bonum est viro cum portaverit iugum ab adulescentia sua

28. IOTH sedebit solitarius et tacebit quia levavit super se

29. IOTH ponet in pulvere os suum si forte sit spes

30. IOTH dabit percutienti se maxillam

20 My soul hath them still in remembrance, and is humbled in me.

21 This I recall to my mind, therefore have I hope.

22 It is of the Lord's mercies that we are not consumed, because his compassions fail not.

23 They are new every morning: great is thy faithfulness.

24 The Lord is my portion, saith my soul; therefore will I hope in him.

25 The Lord is good unto them that wait for him, to the soul that seeketh him.

26 It is good that a man should both hope and quietly wait for the salvation of the Lord.

27 It is good for a man that he bear the yoke in his youth.

28 He sitteth alone and keepeth silence, because he hath borne it upon him.

29 He putteth his mouth in the dust; if so be there may be hope.

30 He giveth his cheek to him that smiteth him: he is filled full with reproach.

31 For the Lord will not cast off for ever:

32 But though he cause grief,

saturabitur obprobriis

31. CAPH quia non repellet in sempiternum Dominus

32. CAPH quia si abiecit et miserebitur secundum multitudinem misericordiarum suarum

33. CAPH non enim humiliavit ex corde suo et abiecit filios hominis

34. LAMED ut contereret sub pedibus suis omnes vinctos terrae

35. LAMED ut declinaret iudicium viri in conspectu vultus Altissimi

36. LAMED ut perverteret hominem in iudicio suo Dominus ignoravit

37. MEM quis est iste qui dixit ut fieret Domino non iubente

38. MEM ex ore Altissimi non egredientur nec mala nec bona

39. MEM quid murmuravit homo vivens vir pro peccatis suis

40. NUN scrutemur vias nostras et quaeramus et revertamur ad Dominum

41. NUN levemus corda nostra cum manibus ad

yet will he have compassion according to the multitude of his mercies.

33 For he doth not afflict willingly nor grieve the children of men.

34 To crush under his feet all the prisoners of the earth,

35 To turn aside the right of a man before the face of the most High,

36 To subvert a man in his cause, the Lord approveth not.

37 Who is he that saith, and it cometh to pass, when the Lord commandeth it not?

38 Out of the mouth of the most High proceedeth not evil and good?

39 Wherefore doth a living man complain, a man for the punishment of his sins?

40 Let us search and try our ways, and turn again to the Lord.

41 Let us lift up our heart with our hands unto God in the heavens.

42 We have transgressed and have rebelled: thou hast not pardoned.

43 Thou hast covered with anger, and persecuted us: thou hast slain, thou hast not pitied.

Dominum in caelos

42. NUN nos inique egimus et ad iracundiam provocavimus idcirco tu inexorabilis es

43. SAMECH operuisti in furore et percussisti nos occidisti nec pepercisti

44. SAMECH opposuisti nubem tibi ne transeat oratio

45. SAMECH eradicationem et abiectionem posuisti me in medio populorum

46. FE aperuerunt super nos os suum omnes inimici

47. FE formido et laqueus facta est nobis vaticinatio et contritio

48. FE divisiones aquarum deduxit oculus meus in contritione filiae populi mei

49. AIN oculus meus adflictus est nec tacuit eo quod non esset requies

50. AIN donec respiceret et videret Dominus de caelis

51. AIN oculus meus depraedatus est animam meam in cunctis filiabus urbis meae

52. SADE venatione

44 Thou hast covered thyself with a cloud, that our prayer should not pass through.

45 Thou hast made us as the offscouring and refuse in the midst of the people.

46 All our enemies have opened their mouths against us.

47 Fear and a snare is come upon us, desolation and destruction.

48 Mine eye runneth down with rivers of water for the destruction of the daughter of my people.

49 Mine eye trickleth down, and ceaseth not, without any intermission,

50 Till the Lord look down, and behold from heaven.

51 Mine eye affecteth mine heart because of all the daughters of my city.

52 Mine enemies chased me sore, like a bird, without cause.

53 They have cut off my life in the dungeon, and cast a stone upon me.

54 Waters flowed over mine head; then I said, I am cut off.

55 I called upon thy name, O Lord, out of the low dungeon.

ceperunt me quasi avem inimici mei gratis

53. SADE lapsa est in lacu vita mea et posuerunt lapidem super me

54. SADE inundaverunt aquae super caput meum dixi perii

55. COPH invocavi nomen tuum Domine de lacis novissimis

56. COPH vocem meam audisti ne avertas aurem tuam a singultu meo et clamoribus

57. COPH adpropinquasti in die quando invocavi te dixisti ne timeas

58. RES iudicasti Domine causam animae meae redemptor vitae meae

59. RES vidisti Domine iniquitatem adversum me iudica iudicium meum

60. RES vidisti omnem furorem universas cogitationes eorum adversum me

61. SEN audisti obprobria eorum Domine omnes cogitationes eorum adversum me

62. SEN labia insurgentium mihi et meditationes eorum

56 Thou hast heard my voice: hide not thine ear at my breathing, at my cry.

57 Thou drewest near in the day that I called upon thee: thou saidst, Fear not.

58 O Lord, thou hast pleaded the causes of my soul; thou hast redeemed my life.

59 O Lord, thou hast seen my wrong: judge thou my cause.

60 Thou hast seen all their vengeance and all their imaginations against me.

61 Thou hast heard their reproach, O Lord, and all their imaginations against me;

62 The lips of those that rose up against me, and their device against me all the day.

63 Behold their sitting down, and their rising up; I am their musick.

64 Render unto them a recompence, O Lord, according to the work of their hands.

65 Give them sorrow of heart, thy curse unto them.

66 Persecute and destroy them in anger from under the heavens of the Lord.

adversum me tota die

63. SEN sessionem eorum et resurrectionem eorum vide ego sum psalmus eorum

64. THAU reddes eis vicem Domine iuxta opera manuum suarum

65. THAU dabis eis scutum cordis laborem tuum

66. THAU persequeris in furore et conteres eos sub caelis Domine

CHAPTER 4

1. ALEPH quomodo obscuratum est aurum mutatus est color optimus dispersi sunt lapides sanctuarii in capite omnium platearum

2. BETH filii Sion incliti et amicti auro primo quomodo reputati sunt in vasa testea opus manuum figuli

3. GIMEL sed et lamiae nudaverunt mammam lactaverunt catulos suos filia populi mei crudelis quasi strutio in deserto

4. DELETH adhesit lingua lactantis ad

CHAPTER 4

HOW is the gold become dim! how is the most fine gold changed! the stones of the sanctuary are poured out in the top of every street.

2 The precious sons of Zion, comparable to fine gold, how are they esteemed as earthen pitchers, the work of the hands of the potter!

3 Even the sea monsters draw out the breast, they give suck to their young ones: the daughter of my people is become cruel, like the ostriches in the wilderness.

4 The tongue of the sucking child cleaveth to the roof of

palatum eius in siti parvuli petierunt panem et non erat qui frangeret eis

5. HE qui vescebantur voluptuose interierunt in viis qui nutriebantur in croceis amplexati sunt stercora

6. VAV et maior effecta est iniquitas filiae populi mei peccato Sodomorum quae subversa est in momento et non ceperunt in ea manus

7. ZAI candidiores nazarei eius nive nitidiores lacte rubicundiores ebore antiquo sapphyro pulchriores

8. HETH denigrata est super carbones facies eorum et non sunt cogniti in plateis adhesit cutis eorum ossibus aruit et facta est quasi lignum

9. TETH melius fuit occisis gladio quam interfectis fame quoniam isti extabuerunt consumpti ab sterilitate terrae

10. IOTH manus mulierum misericordium coxerunt filios suos facti

his mouth for thirst: the young children ask bread, and no man breaketh it unto them.

5 They that did feed delicately are desolate in the streets: they that were brought up in scarlet embrace dunghills.

6 For the punishment of the iniquity of the daughter of my people is greater than the punishment of the sin of Sodom, that was overthrown as in a moment, and no hands stayed on her.

7 Her Nazarites were purer than snow, they were whiter than milk, they were more ruddy in body than rubies, their polishing was of sapphire:

8 Their visage is blacker than a coal; they are not known in the streets: their skin cleaveth to their bones; it is withered, it is become like a stick.

9 They that be slain with the sword are better than they that be slain with hunger: for these pine away, stricken through for want of the fruits of the field.

10 The hands of the pitiful women have sodden their own children: they were their

sunt cibus earum in contritione filiae populi mei

11. CAPH conplevit Dominus furorem suum effudit iram indignationis suae et succendit ignem in Sion et devoravit fundamenta eius

12. LAMED non crediderunt reges terrae et universi habitatores orbis quoniam ingrederetur hostis et inimicus per portas Hierusalem

13. MEM propter peccata prophetarum eius iniquitates sacerdotum eius qui effuderunt in medio eius sanguinem iustorum

14. NUN erraverunt caeci in plateis polluti sunt sanguine cumque non possent tenuerunt lacinias suas

15. SAMECH recedite polluti clamaverunt eis recedite abite nolite tangere iurgati quippe sunt et commoti dixerunt inter gentes non addet ultra ut habitet in eis

16. FE facies Domini divisit eos non addet ut respiciat eos facies

meat in the destruction of the daughter of my people.

11 The Lord hath accomplished his fury; he hath poured out his fierce anger, and hath kindled a fire in Zion, and it hath devoured the foundations thereof.

12 The kings of the earth, and all the inhabitants of the world, would not have believed that the adversary and the enemy should have entered into the gates of Jerusalem.

13 For the sins of her prophets, and the iniquities of her priests, that have shed the blood of the just in the midst of her,

14 They have wandered as blind men in the streets, they have polluted themselves with blood, so that men could not touch their garments.

15 They cried unto them, Depart ye; it is unclean; depart, depart, touch not: when they fled away and wandered, they said among the heathen, They shall no more sojourn there.

16 The anger of the Lord hath divided them; he will no more regard them: they respected not the persons of

sacerdotum non erubuerunt neque senum miserti sunt

17. AIN cum adhuc subsisteremus defecerunt oculi nostri ad auxilium nostrum vanum cum respiceremus adtenti ad gentem quae salvare non poterat

18. SADE lubricaverunt vestigia nostra in itinere platearum nostrarum adpropinquavit finis noster conpleti sunt dies nostri quia venit finis noster

19. COPH velociores fuerunt persecutores nostri aquilis caeli super montes persecuti sunt nos in deserto insidiati sunt nobis

20. RES spiritus oris nostri christus dominus captus est in peccatis nostris cui diximus in umbra tua vivemus in gentibus

21. SEN gaude et laetare filia Edom quae habitas in terra Hus ad te quoque perveniet calix inebriaberis atque nudaberis

22. THAU conpleta est

the priests, they favoured not the elders.

17 As for us, our eyes as yet failed for our vain help: in our watching we have watched for a nation that could not save us.

18 They hunt our steps, that we cannot go in our streets: our end is near, our days are fulfilled; for our end is come.

19 Our persecutors are swifter than the eagles of the heaven: they pursued us upon the mountains, they laid wait for us in the wilderness.

20 The breath of our nostrils, the anointed of the Lord, was taken in their pits, of whom we said, Under his shadow we shall live among the heathen.

21 Rejoice and be glad, O daughter of Edom, that dwellest in the land of Uz; the cup also shall pass through unto thee: thou shalt be drunken, and shalt make thyself naked.

22 The punishment of thine iniquity is accomplished, O daughter of Zion; he will no more carry thee away into captivity: he will visit thine iniquity, O daughter of Edom; he will discover thy

iniquitas tua filia Sion non addet ultra ut transmigret te visitavit iniquitatem tuam filia Edom discoperuit peccata tua

sins.

CHAPTER 5

CHAPTER 5

1. recordare Domine quid acciderit nobis intuere et respice obprobrium nostrum
2. hereditas nostra versa est ad alienos domus nostrae ad extraneos
3. pupilli facti sumus absque patre matres nostrae quasi viduae
4. aquam nostram pecunia bibimus ligna nostra pretio conparavimus
5. cervicibus minabamur lassis non dabatur requies
6. Aegypto dedimus manum et Assyriis ut saturaremur pane
7. patres nostri peccaverunt et non sunt et nos iniquitates eorum portavimus
8. servi dominati sunt nostri non fuit qui redimeret de manu eorum

REMEMBER, O Lord, what is come upon us: consider, and behold our reproach.

2 Our inheritance is turned to strangers, our houses to aliens.

3 We are orphans and fatherless, our mothers are as widows.

4 We have drunken our water for money; our wood is sold unto us.

5 Our necks are under persecution: we labour, and have no rest.

6 We have given the hand to the Egyptians, and to the Assyrians, to be satisfied with bread.

7 Our fathers have sinned, and are not; and we have borne their iniquities.

8 Servants have ruled over us: there is none that doth deliver us out of their hand.

9 We gat our bread with the

9. in animabus nostris adferebamus panem nobis a facie gladii in deserto

10. pellis nostra quasi clibanus exusta est a facie tempestatum famis

11. mulieres in Sion humiliaverunt virgines in civitatibus Iuda

12. principes manu suspensi sunt facies senum non erubuerunt

13. adulescentibus inpudice abusi sunt et pueri in ligno corruerunt

14. senes de portis defecerunt iuvenes de choro psallentium

15. defecit gaudium cordis nostri versus est in luctu chorus noster

16. cecidit corona capitis nostri vae nobis quia peccavimus

17. propterea maestum factum est cor nostrum ideo contenebrati sunt oculi nostri

18. propter montem Sion quia disperiit vulpes ambulaverunt in eo

19. tu autem Domine in aeternum permanebis solium tuum in generatione et generatione

peril of our lives because of the sword of the wilderness.

10 Our skin was black like an oven because of the terrible famine.

11 They ravished the women in Zion, and the maids in the cities of Judah.

12 Princes are hanged up by their hand: the faces of elders were not honoured.

13 They took the young men to grind, and the children fell under the wood.

14 The elders have ceased from the gate, the young men from their musick.

15 The joy of our heart is ceased; our dance is turned into mourning.

16 The crown is fallen from our head: woe unto us, that we have sinned!

17 For this our heart is faint; for these things our eyes are dim.

18 Because of the mountain of Zion, which is desolate, the foxes walk upon it.

19 Thou, O Lord, remainest for ever; thy throne from generation to generation.

20 Wherefore dost thou forget us for ever, and forsake us so long time?

21 Turn thou us unto thee, O

20. quare in perpetuum oblivisceris nostri derelinques nos in longitudinem dierum

21. converte nos Domine ad te et convertemur innova dies nostros sicut a principio

22. sed proiciens reppulisti nos iratus es contra nos vehementer

Lord, and we shall be turned; renew our days as of old.

22 But thou hast utterly rejected us; thou art very wroth against us.

CHAPTER 1

1. et factum est in tricesimo anno in quarto mense in quinta mensis cum essem in medio captivorum iuxta fluvium Chobar aperti sunt caeli et vidi visiones Dei
2. in quinta mensis ipse est annus quintus transmigrationis regis Ioachin
3. factum est verbum Domini ad Hiezecihel filium Buzi sacerdotem in terra Chaldeorum secus flumen Chobar et facta est super eum ibi manus Domini
4. et vidi et ecce ventus turbinis veniebat ab aquilone et nubes magna et ignis involvens et splendor in circuitu eius et de medio eius quasi species electri id est de medio ignis
5. et ex medio eorum similitudo quattuor animalium et hic aspectus eorum similitudo hominis in eis

CHAPTER 1

NOW it came to pass in the thirtieth year, in the fourth month, in the fifth day of the month, as I was among the captives by the river of Chebar, that the heavens were opened, and I saw visions of God.
2 In the fifth day of the month, which was the fifth year of king Jehoiachin's captivity,
3 The word of the Lord came expressly unto Ezekiel the priest, the son of Buzi, in the land of the Chaldeans by the river Chebar; and the hand of the Lord was there upon him.
4 And I looked, and, behold, a whirlwind came out of the north, a great cloud, and a fire infolding itself, and a brightness was about it, and out of the midst thereof as the colour of amber, out of the midst of the fire.
5 Also out of the midst thereof came the likeness of four living creatures. And this was their appearance; they had the likeness of a

6. et quattuor facies uni et quattuor pinnae uni

7. et pedes eorum pedes recti et planta pedis eorum quasi planta pedis vituli et scintillae quasi aspectus aeris candentis

8. et manus hominis sub pinnis eorum in quattuor partibus et facies et pinnas per quattuor partes habebant

9. iunctaeque erant pinnae eorum alterius ad alterum non revertebantur cum incederent sed unumquodque ante faciem suam gradiebatur

10. similitudo autem vultus eorum facies hominis et facies leonis a dextris ipsorum quattuor facies autem bovis a sinistris ipsorum quattuor et facies aquilae ipsorum quattuor

11. et facies eorum et pinnae eorum extentae desuper duae pinnae singulorum iungebantur et duae tegebant corpora eorum

12. et unumquodque coram facie sua ambulabat ubi erat impetus spiritus illuc

man.

6 And every one had four faces, and every one had four wings.

7 And their feet were straight feet; and the sole of their feet was like the sole of a calf's foot: and they sparkled like the colour of burnished brass.

8 And they had the hands of a man under their wings on their four sides; and they four had their faces and their wings.

9 Their wings were joined one to another; they turned not when they went; they went every one straight forward.

10 As for the likeness of their faces, they four had the face of a man, and the face of a lion, on the right side: and they four had the face of an ox on the left side; they four also had the face of an eagle.

11 Thus were their faces: and their wings were stretched upward; two wings of every one were joined one to another, and two covered their bodies.

12 And they went every one straight forward: whither the spirit was to go, they went; and they turned not when

gradiebantur nec revertebantur cum ambularent

13. et similitudo animalium aspectus eorum quasi carbonum ignis ardentium et quasi aspectus lampadarum haec erat visio discurrens in medio animalium splendor ignis et de igne fulgor egrediens

14. et animalia ibant et revertebantur in similitudinem fulguris coruscantis

15. cumque aspicerem animalia apparuit rota una super terram iuxta animalia habens quattuor facies

16. et aspectus rotarum et opus earum quasi visio maris et una similitudo ipsarum quattuor et aspectus earum et opera quasi sit rota in medio rotae

17. per quattuor partes earum euntes ibant et non revertebantur cum ambularent

18. statura quoque erat rotis et altitudo et horribilis aspectus et totum corpus plenum

they went.

13 As for the likeness of the living creatures, their appearance was like burning coals of fire, and like the appearance of lamps: it went up and down among the living creatures; and the fire was bright, and out of the fire went forth lightning.

14 And the living creatures ran and returned as the appearance of a flash of lightning.

15 Now as I beheld the living creatures, behold one wheel upon the earth by the living creatures, with his four faces.

16 The appearance of the wheels and their work was like unto the colour of a beryl: and they four had one likeness: and their appearance and their work was as it were a wheel in the middle of a wheel.

17 When they went, they went upon their four sides: and they turned not when they went.

18 As for their rings, they were so high that they were dreadful; and their rings were full of eyes round about them four.

oculis in circuitu ipsarum quattuor

19. cumque ambularent animalia ambulabant pariter et rotae iuxta ea et cum elevarentur animalia de terra elevabantur simul et rotae

20. quocumque ibat spiritus illuc eunte spiritu et rotae pariter levabantur sequentes eum spiritus enim vitae erat in rotis

21. cum euntibus ibant et cum stantibus stabant et cum elevatis a terra pariter elevabantur et rotae sequentes ea quia spiritus vitae erat in rotis

22. et similitudo super caput animalium firmamenti quasi aspectus cristalli horribilis et extenti super capita eorum desuper

23. sub firmamento autem pinnae eorum rectae alterius ad alterum unumquodque duabus alis velabat corpus suum et alterum similiter velabatur

24. et audiebam sonum alarum quasi sonum aquarum multarum quasi sonum sublimis Dei cum

19 And when the living creatures went, the wheels went by them: and when the living creatures were lifted up from the earth, the wheels were lifted up.

20 Whithersoever the spirit was to go, they went, thither was their spirit to go; and the wheels were lifted up over against them: for the spirit of the living creature was in the wheels.

21 When those went, these went; and when those stood, these stood; and when those were lifted up from the earth, the wheels were lifted up over against them: for the spirit of the living creature was in the wheels.

22 And the likeness of the firmament upon the heads of the living creature was as the colour of the terrible crystal, stretched forth over their heads above.

23 And under the firmament were their wings straight, the one toward the other: every one had two, which covered on this side, and every one had two, which covered on that side, their bodies.

24 And when they went, I heard the noise of their

ambularent quasi sonus erat multitudinis ut sonus castrorum cumque starent dimittebantur pinnae eorum

25. nam cum fieret vox supra firmamentum quod erat super caput eorum stabant et submittebant alas suas

26. et super firmamentum quod erat inminens capiti eorum quasi aspectus lapidis sapphyri similitudo throni et super similitudinem throni similitudo quasi aspectus hominis desuper

27. et vidi quasi speciem electri velut aspectum ignis intrinsecus eius per circuitum a lumbis eius et desuper et a lumbis eius usque deorsum vidi quasi speciem ignis splendentis in circuitu

28. velut aspectum arcus cum fuerit in nube in die pluviae hic erat aspectus splendoris per gyrum

wings, like the noise of great waters, as the voice of the Almighty, the voice of speech, as the noise of an host: when they stood, they let down their wings.

25 And there was a voice from the firmament that was over their heads, when they stood, and had let down their wings.

26 And above the firmament that was over their heads was the likeness of a throne, as the appearance of a sapphire stone: and upon the likeness of the throne was the likeness as the appearance of a man above upon it.

27 And I saw as the colour of amber, as the appearance of fire round about within it, from the appearance of his loins even upward, and from the appearance of his loins even downward, I saw as it were the appearance of fire, and it had brightness round about.

28 As the appearance of the bow that is in the cloud in the day of rain, so was the appearance of the brightness round about. This was the appearance of the likeness of the glory of the Lord. And

when I saw it, I fell upon my face, and I heard a voice of one that spake.

CHAPTER 2

1. haec visio similitudinis gloriae Domini et vidi et cecidi in faciem meam et audivi vocem loquentis et dixit ad me fili hominis sta supra pedes tuos et loquar tecum
2. et ingressus est in me spiritus postquam locutus est mihi et statuit me supra pedes meos et audivi loquentem ad me
3. et dicentem fili hominis mitto ego te ad filios Israhel ad gentes apostatrices quae recesserunt a me patres eorum praevaricati sunt pactum meum usque ad diem hanc
4. et filii dura facie et indomabili corde sunt ad quos ego mitto te et dices ad eos haec dicit Dominus Deus
5. si forte vel ipsi audiant et si forte quiescant quoniam domus exasperans est et scient

CHAPTER 2

AND he said unto me, Son of man, stand upon thy feet, and I will speak unto thee.

2 And the spirit entered into me when he spake unto me, and set me upon my feet, that I heard him that spake unto me.

3 And he said unto me, Son of man, I send thee to the children of Israel, to a rebellious nation that hath rebelled against me: they and their fathers have transgressed against me, even unto this very day.

4 For they are impudent children and stiffhearted. I do send thee unto them; and thou shalt say unto them, Thus saith the Lord God.

5 And they, whether they will hear, or whether they will forbear, (for they are a rebellious house,) yet shall know that there hath been a prophet among them.

6 And thou, son of man, be not afraid of them, neither be

quia propheta fuerit in medio eorum

6. tu ergo fili hominis ne timeas eos neque sermones eorum metuas quoniam increduli et subversores sunt tecum et cum scorpionibus habitas verba eorum ne timeas et vultus eorum ne formides quia domus exasperans est

7. loqueris ergo verba mea ad eos si forte audiant et quiescant quoniam inritatores sunt

8. tu autem fili hominis audi quaecumque loquor ad te et noli esse exasperans sicut domus exasperatrix est aperi os tuum et comede quaecumque ego do tibi

9. et vidi et ecce manus missa ad me in qua erat involutus liber et expandit illum coram me qui erat scriptus intus et foris et scriptae erant in eo lamentationes et carmen et vae

afraid of their words, though briers and thorns be with thee, and thou dost dwell among scorpions: be not afraid of their words, nor be dismayed at their looks, though they be a rebellious house.

7 And thou shalt speak my words unto them, whether they will hear, or whether they will forbear: for they are most rebellious.

8 But thou, son of man, hear what I say unto thee; Be not thou rebellious like that rebellious house: open thy mouth, and eat that I give thee.

9 And when I looked, behold, an hand was sent unto me; and, lo, a roll of a book was therein;

10 And he spread it before me; and it was written within and without: and there was written therein lamentations, and mourning, and woe.

1. et dixit ad me fili hominis quodcumque inveneris comede comede volumen istud et vadens loquere ad filios Israhel

2. et aperui os meum et cibavit me volumine illo

3. et dixit ad me fili hominis venter tuus comedet et viscera tua conplebuntur volumine isto quod ego do tibi et comedi illud et factum est in ore meo sicut mel dulce

4. et dixit ad me fili hominis vade ad domum Israhel et loqueris verba mea ad eos

5. non enim ad populum profundi sermonis et ignotae linguae tu mitteris ad domum Israhel

6. neque ad populos multos profundi sermonis et ignotae linguae quorum non possis audire sermones et si ad illos mittereris ipsi audirent te

7. domus autem Israhel nolent audire te quia nolunt audire me omnis quippe domus Israhel

MOREOVER he said unto me, Son of man, eat that thou findest; eat this roll, and go speak unto the house of Israel.

2 So I opened my mouth, and he caused me to eat that roll.

3 And he said unto me, Son of man, cause thy belly to eat, and fill thy bowels with this roll that I give thee. Then did I eat it; and it was in my mouth as honey for sweetness.

4 And he said unto me, Son of man, go, get thee unto the house of Israel, and speak with my words unto them.

5 For thou art not sent to a people of a strange speech and of an hard language, but to the house of Israel;

6 Not to many people of a strange speech and of an hard language, whose words thou canst not understand. Surely, had I sent thee to them, they would have hearkened unto thee.

7 But the house of Israel will not hearken unto thee; for they will not hearken unto me: for all the house of Israel are impudent and

adtrita fronte est et duro corde

8. ecce dedi faciem tuam valentiorem faciebus eorum et frontem tuam duriorem frontibus eorum

9. ut adamantem et ut silicem dedi faciem tuam ne timeas eos neque metuas a facie eorum quia domus exasperans est

10. et dixit ad me fili hominis omnes sermones meos quos loquor ad te adsume in corde tuo et auribus tuis audi

11. et vade ingredere ad transmigrationem ad filios populi tui et loqueris ad eos et dices eis haec dicit Dominus Deus si forte audiant et quiescant

12. et adsumpsit me spiritus et audivi post me vocem commotionis magnae benedicta gloria Domini de loco suo

13. et vocem alarum animalium percutientium alteram ad alteram et vocem rotarum sequentium animalia et vocem commotionis magnae

hardhearted.

8 Behold, I have made thy face strong against their faces, and thy forehead strong against their foreheads.

9 As an adamant harder than flint have I made thy forehead: fear them not, neither be dismayed at their looks, though they be a rebellious house.

10 Moreover he said unto me, Son of man, all my words that I shall speak unto thee receive in thine heart, and hear with thine ears.

11 And go, get thee to them of the captivity, unto the children of thy people, and speak unto them, and tell them, Thus saith the Lord God; whether they will hear, or whether they will forbear.

12 Then the spirit took me up, and I heard behind me a voice of a great rushing, saying, Blessed be the glory of the Lord from his place.

13 I heard also the noise of the wings of the living creatures that touched one another, and the noise of the wheels over against them, and a noise of a great rushing.

14. spiritus quoque levavit me et adsumpsit me et abii amarus in indignatione spiritus mei manus enim Domini erat mecum confortans me

15. et veni ad transmigrationem acervum novarum frugum ad eos qui habitabant iuxta flumen Chobar et sedi ubi illi sedebant et mansi ibi septem diebus maerens in medio eorum

16. cum autem pertransissent septem dies factum est verbum Domini ad me dicens

17. fili hominis speculatorem dedi te domui Israhel et audies de ore meo verbum et adnuntiabis eis ex me

18. si dicente me ad impium morte morieris non adnuntiaveris ei neque locutus fueris ut avertatur a via sua impia et vivat ipse impius in iniquitate sua morietur sanguinem autem eius de manu tua requiram

19. si autem tu adnuntiaveris impio et ille non fuerit conversus ab impietate sua et via

14 So the spirit lifted me up, and took me away, and I went in bitterness, in the heat of my spirit; but the hand of the Lord was strong upon me.

15 Then I came to them of the captivity at Tel-abib, that dwelt by the river of Chebar, and I sat where they sat, and remained there astonished among them seven days.

16 And it came to pass at the end of seven days, that the word of the Lord came unto me, saying,

17 Son of man, I have made thee a watchman unto the house of Israel: therefore hear the word at my mouth, and give them warning from me.

18 When I say unto the wicked, Thou shalt surely die; and thou givest him not warning, nor speakest to warn the wicked from his wicked way, to save his life; the same wicked man shall die in his iniquity; but his blood will I require at thine hand.

19 Yet if thou warn the wicked, and he turn not from his wickedness, nor from his wicked way, he shall die in

sua impia ipse quidem in iniquitate sua morietur tu autem animam tuam liberasti

20. sed et si conversus iustus a iustitia sua fecerit iniquitatem ponam offendiculum coram eo ipse morietur quia non adnuntiasti ei in peccato suo morietur et non erunt in memoria iustitiae eius quas fecit sanguinem vero eius de manu tua requiram

21. si autem tu adnuntiaveris iusto ut non peccet iustus et ille non peccaverit vivens vivet quia adnuntiasti ei et tu animam tuam liberasti

22. et facta est super me manus Domini et dixit ad me surgens egredere in campum et ibi loquar tecum

23. et surgens egressus sum in campum et ecce ibi gloria Domini stabat quasi gloria quam vidi iuxta fluvium Chobar et cecidi in faciem meam

24. et ingressus est in me spiritus et statuit me super pedes meos et locutus est mihi et dixit

his iniquity; but thou hast delivered thy soul.

20 Again, When a righteous man doth turn from his righteousness, and commit iniquity, and I lay a stumblingblock before him, he shall die: because thou hast not given him warning, he shall die in his sin, and his righteousness which he hath done shall not be remembered; but his blood will I require at thine hand.

21 Nevertheless if thou warn the righteous man, that the righteous sin not, and he doth not sin, he shall surely live, because he is warned; also thou hast delivered thy soul.

22 And the hand of the Lord was there upon me; and he said unto me, Arise, go forth into the plain, and I will there talk with thee.

23 Then I arose, and went forth into the plain: and, behold, the glory of the Lord stood there, as the glory which I saw by the river of Chebar: and I fell on my face.

24 Then the spirit entered into me, and set me upon my feet, and spake with me, and said unto me, Go, shut

ad me ingredere et includere in medio domus tuae

25. et tu fili hominis ecce data sunt super te vincula et ligabunt te in eis et non egredieris in medio eorum

26. et linguam tuam adherescere faciam palato tuo et eris mutus nec quasi vir obiurgans quia domus exasperans est

27. cum autem locutus fuero tibi aperiam os tuum et dices ad eos haec dicit Dominus Deus qui audit audiat et qui quiescit quiescat quia domus exasperans est

thyself within thine house.

25 But thou, O son of man, behold, they shall put bands upon thee, and shall bind thee with them, and thou shalt not go out among them:

26 And I will make thy tongue cleave to the roof of thy mouth, that thou shalt be dumb, and shalt not be to them a reprover: for they are a rebellious house.

27 But when I speak with thee, I will open thy mouth, and thou shalt say unto them, Thus saith the Lord God; He that heareth, let him hear; and he that forbeareth, let him forbear: for they are a rebellious house.

CHAPTER 4

CHAPTER 4

1. et tu fili hominis sume tibi laterem et pones eum coram te et describes in eo civitatem Hierusalem

2. et ordinabis adversus eam obsidionem et aedificabis munitiones et conportabis aggerem et dabis contra eam castra et pones arietes in gyro

3. et tu sume tibi sartaginem ferream et

THOU also, son of man, take thee a tile, and lay it before thee, and pourtray upon it the city, even Jerusalem:

2 And lay siege against it, and build a fort against it, and cast a mount against it; set the camp also against it, and set battering rams against it round about.

3 Moreover take thou unto thee an iron pan, and set it

pones eam murum ferreum inter te et inter civitatem et obfirmabis faciem tuam ad eam et erit in obsidionem et circumdabis eam signum est domui Israhel

4. et tu dormies super latus tuum sinistrum et pones iniquitates domus Israhel super eo numero dierum quibus dormies super illud et adsumes iniquitatem eorum

5. ego autem dedi tibi annos iniquitatis eorum numero dierum trecentos et nonaginta dies et portabis iniquitatem domus Israhel

6. et cum conpleveris haec dormies super latus tuum dextrum secundo et adsumes iniquitatem domus Iuda quadraginta diebus diem pro anno diem inquam pro anno dedi tibi

7. et ad obsidionem Hierusalem converteres faciem tuam et brachium tuum erit exertum et prophetabis adversus eam

8. ecce circumdedi te vinculis et non te convertes a latere tuo in

for a wall of iron between thee and the city: and set thy face against it, and it shall be besieged, and thou shalt lay siege against it. This shall be a sign to the house of Israel.

4 Lie thou also upon thy left side, and lay the iniquity of the house of Israel upon it: according to the number of the days that thou shalt lie upon it thou shalt bear their iniquity.

5 For I have laid upon thee the years of their iniquity, according to the number of the days, three hundred and ninety days: so shalt thou bear the iniquity of the house of Israel.

6 And when thou hast accomplished them, lie again on thy right side, and thou shalt bear the iniquity of the house of Judah forty days: I have appointed thee each day for a year.

7 Therefore thou shalt set thy face toward the siege of Jerusalem, and thine arm shall be uncovered, and thou shalt prophesy against it.

8 And, behold, I will lay bands upon thee, and thou shalt not turn thee from one side to another, till thou hast

latus aliud donec conpleas dies obsidionis tuae

9. et tu sume tibi frumentum et hordeum et fabam et lentem et milium et viciam et mittes ea in vas unum et facies tibi panes numero dierum quibus dormies super latus tuum trecentis et nonaginta diebus comedes illud

10. cibus autem tuus quo vesceris erit in pondere viginti stateres in die a tempore usque ad tempus comedes illud

11. et aquam in mensura bibes sextam partem hin a tempore usque ad tempus bibes illud

12. et quasi subcinericium hordiacium comedes illud et stercore quod egredietur de homine operies illud in oculis eorum

13. et dixit Dominus sic comedent filii Israhel panem suum pollutum inter gentes ad quas eiciam eos

14. et dixi ha ha ha Domine Deus ecce anima

ended the days of thy siege.

9 Take thou also unto thee wheat, and barley, and beans, and lentiles, and millet, and fitches, and put them in one vessel, and make thee bread thereof, according to the number of the days that thou shalt lie upon thy side, three hundred and ninety days shalt thou eat thereof.

10 And thy meat which thou shalt eat shall be by weight, twenty shekels a day: from time to time shalt thou eat it.

11 Thou shalt drink also water by measure, the sixth part of an hin: from time to time shalt thou drink.

12 And thou shalt eat it as barley cakes, and thou shalt bake it with dung that cometh out of man, in their sight.

13 And the Lord said, Even thus shall the children of Israel eat their defiled bread among the Gentiles, whither I will drive them.

14 Then said I, Ah Lord God! behold, my soul hath not been polluted: for from my youth up even till now have I not eaten of that which dieth of itself, or is torn in pieces; neither came there

mea non est polluta et morticinum et laceratum a bestiis non comedi ab infantia mea usque nunc et non est ingressa os meum omnis caro inmunda

15. et dixit ad me ecce dedi tibi fimum boum pro stercoribus humanis et facies panem tuum in eo

16. et dixit ad me fili hominis ecce ego conteram baculum panis in Hierusalem et comedent panem in pondere et in sollicitudine et aquam in mensura et in angustia bibent

17. ut deficientibus pane et aqua corruat unusquisque ad fratrem suum et contabescant in iniquitatibus suis

abominable flesh into my mouth.

15 Then he said unto me, Lo, I have given thee cow's dung for man's dung, and thou shalt prepare thy bread therewith.

16 Moreover he said unto me, Son of man, behold, I will break the staff of bread in Jerusalem: and they shall eat bread by weight, and with care; and they shall drink water by measure, and with astonishment:

17 That they may want bread and water, and be astonied one with another, and consume away for their iniquity.

CHAPTER 5

CHAPTER 5

1. et tu fili hominis sume tibi gladium acutum radentem pilos adsumes eum et duces per caput tuum et per barbam tuam et adsumes tibi stateram ponderis et divides eos

2. tertiam partem igni

AND thou, son of man, take thee a sharp knife, take thee a barber's rasor, and cause it to pass upon thine head and upon thy beard: then take thee balances to weigh, and divide the hair.

2 Thou shalt burn with fire a

conbures in medio civitatis iuxta conpletionem dierum obsidionis et adsumens tertiam partem concides gladio in circuitu eius tertiam vero aliam disperges in ventum et gladium nudabo post eos

3. et sumes inde parvum numerum et ligabis eos in summitate pallii tui

4. et ex eis rursum tolles et proicies in medio ignis et conbures eos igni ex eo egredietur ignis in omnem domum Israhel

5. haec dicit Dominus Deus ista est Hierusalem in medio gentium posui eam et in circuitu eius terras

6. et contempsit iudicia mea ut plus esset impia quam gentes et praecepta mea ultra quam terrae quae in circuitu eius sunt iudicia enim mea proiecerunt et in praeceptis meis non ambulaverunt

7. idcirco haec dicit Dominus Deus quia superastis gentes quae in circuitu vestro sunt in praeceptis meis non

third part in the midst of the city, when the days of the siege are fulfilled: and thou shalt take a third part, and smite about it with a knife: and a third part thou shalt scatter in the wind; and I will draw out a sword after them.

3 Thou shalt also take thereof a few in number, and bind them in thy skirts.

4 Then take of them again, and cast them into the midst of the fire, and burn them in the fire; for thereof shall a fire come forth into all the house of Israel.

5 Thus saith the Lord God; This is Jerusalem: I have set it in the midst of the nations and countries that are round about her.

6 And she hath changed my judgments into wickedness more than the nations, and my statutes more than the countries that are round about her: for they have refused my judgments and my statutes, they have not walked in them.

7 Therefore thus saith the Lord God; Because ye multiplied more than the nations that are round about you, and have not walked in

ambulastis et iudicia mea non fecistis et iuxta iudicia gentium quae in circuitu vestro sunt non estis operati

8. ideo haec dicit Dominus Deus ecce ego ad te et ipse ego faciam in medio tui iudicia in oculis gentium

9. et faciam in te quae non feci et quibus similia ultra non faciam propter omnes abominationes tuas

10. ideo patres comedent filios in medio tui et filii comedent patres suos et faciam in te iudicia et ventilabo universas reliquias tuas in omnem ventum

11. idcirco vivo ego dicit Dominus Deus nisi pro eo quod sanctum meum violasti in omnibus offensionibus tuis et in omnibus abominationibus tuis ego quoque confringam et non parcet oculus meus et non miserebor

12. tertia tui pars peste morietur et fame consumetur in medio tui et tertia tui pars gladio

my statutes, neither have kept my judgments, neither have done according to the judgments of the nations that are round about you;

8 Therefore thus saith the Lord God; Behold, I, even I, am against thee, and will execute judgments in the midst of thee in the sight of the nations.

9 And I will do in thee that which I have not done, and whereunto I will not do any more the like, because of all thine abominations.

10 Therefore the fathers shall eat the sons in the midst of thee, and the sons shall eat their fathers; and I will execute judgments in thee, and the whole remnant of thee will I scatter into all the winds.

11 Wherefore, as I live, saith the Lord God; Surely, because thou hast defiled my sanctuary with all thy detestable things, and with all thine abominations, therefore will I also diminish thee; neither shall mine eye spare, neither will I have any pity.

12 A third part of thee shall die with the pestilence, and

cadet in circuitu tuo tertiam vero partem tuam in omnem ventum dispergam et gladium evaginabo post eos

13. et conpleam furorem meum et requiescere faciam indignationem meam in eis et consolabor et scient quia ego Dominus locutus sum in zelo meo cum implevero indignationem meam in eis

14. et dabo te in desertum et in obprobrium in gentibus quae in circuitu tuo sunt in conspectu omnis praetereuntis

15. et eris obprobrium et blasphemia exemplum et stupor in gentibus quae in circuitu tuo sunt cum fecero in te iudicia in furore et in indignatione et in increpationibus irae

16. ego Dominus locutus sum quando misero sagittas famis pessimas in eos quae erunt mortiferae et quas mittam ut disperdam vos et famem congregabo super vos et conteram vobis baculum panis

17. et inmittam in vos

with famine shall they be consumed in the midst of thee: and a third part shall fall by the sword round about thee; and I will scatter a third part into all the winds, and I will draw out a sword after them.

13 Thus shall mine anger be accomplished, and I will cause my fury to rest upon them, and I will be comforted: and they shall know that I the Lord have spoken it in my zeal, when I have accomplished my fury in them.

14 Moreover I will make thee waste, and a reproach among the nations that are round about thee, in the sight of all that pass by.

15 So it shall be a reproach and a taunt, an instruction and an astonishment unto the nations that are round about thee, when I shall execute judgments in thee in anger and in fury and in furious rebukes. I the Lord have spoken it.

16 When I shall send upon them the evil arrows of famine, which shall be for their destruction, and which I will send to destroy you: and

famem et bestias pessimas usque ad internicionem et pestilentia et sanguis transibunt per te et gladium inducam super te ego Dominus locutus sum

I will increase the famine upon you, and will break your staff of bread:

17 So will I send upon you famine and evil beasts, and they shall bereave thee; and pestilence and blood shall pass through thee; and I will bring the sword upon thee. I the Lord have spoken it.

CHAPTER 6

1. et factus est sermo Domini ad me dicens
2. fili hominis pone faciem tuam ad montes Israhel et prophetabis ad eos
3. et dices montes Israhel audite verbum Domini Dei haec dicit Dominus Deus montibus et collibus rupibus et vallibus ecce ego inducam super vos gladium et disperdam excelsa vestra
4. et demoliar aras vestras et confringentur simulacra vestra et deiciam interfectos vestros ante idola vestra
5. et dabo cadavera filiorum Israhel ante faciem simulacrorum

CHAPTER 6

AND the word of the Lord came unto me, saying,

2 Son of man, set thy face toward the mountains of Israel, and prophesy against them,

3 And say, Ye mountains of Israel, hear the word of the Lord God; Thus saith the Lord God to the mountains, and to the hills, to the rivers, and to the valleys; Behold, I, even I, will bring a sword upon you, and I will destroy your high places.

4 And your altars shall be desolate, and your images shall be broken: and I will cast down your slain men before your idols.

5 And I will lay the dead carcases of the children of

43

vestrorum et dispergam ossa vestra circum aras vestras

6. in omnibus habitationibus vestris urbes desertae erunt et excelsa demolientur et dissipabuntur et interibunt arae vestrae et confringentur et cessabunt idola vestra et conterentur delubra vestra et delebuntur opera vestra

7. et cadet interfectus in medio vestri et scietis quoniam ego Dominus

8. et relinquam in vobis eos qui fugerint gladium in gentibus cum dispersero vos in terris

9. et recordabuntur mei liberati vestri in gentibus ad quas captivi ducti sunt quia contrivi cor eorum fornicans et recedens a me et oculos eorum fornicantes post idola sua et displicebunt sibimet super malis quae fecerunt in universis abominationibus suis

10. et scient quia ego Dominus non frustra locutus sum ut facerem eis malum hoc

11. haec dicit Dominus

Israel before their idols; and I will scatter your bones round about your altars.

6 In all your dwellingplaces the cities shall be laid waste, and the high places shall be desolate; that your altars may be laid waste and made desolate, and your idols may be broken and cease, and your images may be cut down, and your works may be abolished.

7 And the slain shall fall in the midst of you, and ye shall know that I am the Lord.

8 Yet will I leave a remnant, that ye may have some that shall escape the sword among the nations, when ye shall be scattered through the countries.

9 And they that escape of you shall remember me among the nations whither they shall be carried captives, because I am broken with their whorish heart, which hath departed from me, and with their eyes, which go a whoring after their idols: and they shall lothe themselves for the evils which they have committed in all their abominations.

10 And they shall know that I

Deus percute manu tua et adlide pedem tuum et dic eheu ad omnes abominationes malorum domus Israhel qui gladio fame peste ruituri sunt

12. qui longe est peste morietur qui autem prope gladio corruet et qui relictus fuerit et obsessus fame morietur et conpleam indignationem meam in eis

13. et scietis quia ego Dominus cum fuerint interfecti vestri in medio idolorum vestrorum in circuitu ararum vestrarum in omni colle excelso in cunctis summitatibus montium et subtus omne lignum nemorosum et subtus universam quercum frondosam locum ubi accenderunt tura redolentia universis idolis suis

14. et extendam manum meam super eos et faciam terram desolatam et destitutam a deserto Deblatha in omnibus habitationibus eorum et scient quia ego Dominus

am the Lord, and that I have not said in vain that I would do this evil unto them.

11 Thus saith the Lord God; Smite with thine hand, and stamp with thy foot, and say, Alas for all the evil abominations of the house of Israel! for they shall fall by the sword, by the famine, and by the pestilence.

12 He that is far off shall die of the pestilence; and he that is near shall fall by the sword; and he that remaineth and is besieged shall die by the famine: thus will I accomplish my fury upon them.

13 Then shall ye know that I am the Lord, when their slain men shall be among their idols round about their altars, upon every high hill, in all the tops of the mountains, and under every green tree, and under every thick oak, the place where they did offer sweet savour to all their idols.

14 So will I stretch out my hand upon them, and make the land desolate, yea, more desolate than the wilderness toward Diblath, in all their habitations: and they shall

know that I am the Lord.

CHAPTER 7

1. et factus est sermo Domini ad me dicens
2. et tu fili hominis haec dicit Dominus Deus terrae Israhel finis venit finis super quattuor plagas terrae
3. nunc finis super te et emittam furorem meum in te et iudicabo te iuxta vias tuas et ponam contra te omnes abominationes tuas
4. et non parcet oculus meus super te et non miserebor sed vias tuas ponam super te et abominationes tuae in medio tui erunt et scietis quia ego Dominus
5. haec dicit Dominus Deus adflictio una adflictio ecce venit
6. finis venit venit finis evigilavit adversum te ecce venit
7. venit contractio super te qui habitas in terra venit tempus prope est dies occisionis et non gloriae montium

CHAPTER 7

MOREOVER the word of the Lord came unto me, saying,

2 Also, thou son of man, thus saith the Lord God unto the land of Israel; An end, the end is come upon the four corners of the land.

3 Now is the end come upon thee, and I will send mine anger upon thee, and will judge thee according to thy ways, and will recompense upon thee all thine abominations.

4 And mine eye shall not spare thee, neither will I have pity: but I will recompense thy ways upon thee, and thine abominations shall be in the midst of thee: and ye shall know that I am the Lord.

5 Thus saith the Lord God; An evil, an only evil, behold, is come.

6 An end is come, the end is come: it watcheth for thee; behold, it is come.

7 The morning is come unto thee, O thou that dwellest in

8. nunc de propinquo effundam iram meam super te et conpleam furorem meum in te et iudicabo te iuxta vias tuas et inponam tibi omnia scelera tua

9. et non parcet oculus meus neque miserebor sed vias tuas inponam tibi et abominationes tuae in medio tui erunt et scietis quia ego sum Dominus percutiens

10. ecce dies ecce venit egressa est contractio floruit virga germinavit superbia

11. iniquitas surrexit in virga impietatis non ex eis et non ex populo neque ex sonitu eorum et non erit requies in eis

12. venit tempus adpropinquavit dies qui emit non laetetur et qui vendit non lugeat quia ira super omnem populum eius

13. quia qui vendit ad id quod vendidit non revertetur et adhuc in viventibus vita eorum visio enim ad omnem multitudinem eius non regredietur et vir in

the land: the time is come, the day of trouble is near, and not the sounding again of the mountains.

8 Now will I shortly pour out my fury upon thee, and accomplish mine anger upon thee: and I will judge thee according to thy ways, and will recompense thee for all thine abominations.

9 And mine eye shall not spare, neither will I have pity: I will recompense thee according to thy ways and thine abominations that are in the midst of thee; and ye shall know that I am the Lord that smiteth.

10 Behold the day, behold, it is come: the morning is gone forth; the rod hath blossomed, pride hath budded.

11 Violence is risen up into a rod of wickedness: none of them shall remain, nor of their multitude, nor of any of theirs: neither shall there be wailing for them.

12 The time is come, the day draweth near: let not the buyer rejoice, nor the seller mourn: for wrath is upon all the multitude thereof.

13 For the seller shall not

iniquitate vitae suae non confortabitur

14. canite tuba praeparentur omnes et non est qui vadat ad proelium ira enim mea super universum populum eius

15. gladius foris pestis et fames intrinsecus qui in agro est gladio morietur et qui in civitate pestilentia et fame devorabuntur

16. et salvabuntur qui fugerint ex eis et erunt in montibus quasi columbae convallium omnes trepidi unusquisque in iniquitate sua

17. omnes manus dissolventur et omnia genua fluent aquis

18. et accingent se ciliciis et operiet eos formido et in omni facie confusio et in universis capitibus eorum calvitium

19. argentum eorum foris proicietur et aurum eorum in sterquilinium erit argentum eorum et aurum eorum non valebit liberare eos in die furoris Domini animam suam non saturabunt et ventres

return to that which is sold, although they were yet alive: for the vision is touching the whole multitude thereof, which shall not return; neither shall any strengthen himself in the iniquity of his life.

14 They have blown the trumpet, even to make all ready; but none goeth to the battle: for my wrath is upon all the multitude thereof.

15 The sword is without, and the pestilence and the famine within: he that is in the field shall die with the sword; and he that is in the city, famine and pestilence shall devour him.

16 But they that escape of them shall escape, and shall be on the mountains like doves of the valleys, all of them mourning, every one for his iniquity.

17 All hands shall be feeble, and all knees shall be weak as water.

18 They shall also gird themselves with sackcloth, and horror shall cover them; and shame shall be upon all faces, and baldness upon all their heads.

19 They shall cast their silver

eorum non implebuntur quia scandalum iniquitatis eorum factum est

20. et ornamentum monilium suorum in superbiam posuerunt et imagines abominationum suarum et simulacrorum fecerunt ex eo propter hoc dedi eis illud in inmunditiam

21. et dabo illud in manus alienorum ad diripiendum et impiis terrae in praedam et contaminabunt illud

22. et avertam faciem meam ab eis et violabunt arcanum meum et introibunt in illud emissarii et contaminabunt illud

23. fac conclusionem quoniam terra plena est iudicio sanguinum et civitas plena iniquitate

24. et adducam pessimos de gentibus et possidebunt domos eorum et quiescere faciam superbiam potentium et possidebunt sanctuaria eorum

25. angustia superveniente requirent

in the streets, and their gold shall be removed: their silver and their gold shall not be able to deliver them in the day of the wrath of the Lord: they shall not satisfy their souls, neither fill their bowels: because it is the stumblingblock of their iniquity.

20 As for the beauty of his ornament, he set it in majesty: but they made the images of their abominations and of their detestable things therein: therefore have I set it far from them.

21 And I will give it into the hands of the strangers for a prey, and to the wicked of the earth for a spoil; and they shall pollute it.

22 My face will I turn also from them, and they shall pollute my secret place: for the robbers shall enter into it, and defile it.

23 Make a chain: for the land is full of bloody crimes, and the city is full of violence.

24 Wherefore I will bring the worst of the heathen, and they shall possess their houses: I will also make the pomp of the strong to cease;

pacem et non erit

26. conturbatio super conturbationem veniet et auditus super auditum et quaerent visionem de propheta et lex peribit a sacerdote et consilium a senioribus

27. rex lugebit et princeps induetur maerore et manus populi terrae conturbabuntur secundum viam eorum faciam eis et secundum iudicia eorum iudicabo eos et scient quia ego Dominus

and their holy places shall be defiled.

25 Destruction cometh; and they shall seek peace, and there shall be none.

26 Mischief shall come upon mischief, and rumour shall be upon rumour; then shall they seek a vision of the prophet; but the law shall perish from the priest, and counsel from the ancients.

27 The king shall mourn, and the prince shall be clothed with desolation, and the hands of the people of the land shall be troubled: I will do unto them after their way, and according to their deserts will I judge them; and they shall know that I am the Lord.

CHAPTER 8

CHAPTER 8

1. et factum est in anno sexto in sexto mense in quinta mensis ego sedebam in domo mea et senes Iuda sedebant coram me et cecidit super me ibi manus Domini Dei

2. et vidi et ecce similitudo quasi aspectus ignis ab aspectu

AND it came to pass in the sixth year, in the sixth month, in the fifth day of the month, as I sat in mine house, and the elders of Judah sat before me, that the hand of the Lord God fell there upon me.

2 Then I beheld, and lo a likeness as the appearance of

lumborum eius et deorsum ignis et a lumbis eius et sursum quasi aspectus splendoris ut visio electri

3. et emissa similitudo manus adprehendit me in cincinno capitis mei et elevavit me spiritus inter terram et caelum et adduxit in Hierusalem in visione Dei iuxta ostium interius quod respiciebat aquilonem ubi erat statutum idolum zeli ad provocandam aemulationem

4. et ecce ibi gloria Dei Israhel secundum visionem quam videram in campo

5. et dixit ad me fili hominis leva oculos tuos ad viam aquilonis et levavi oculos meos ad viam aquilonis et ecce ab aquilone portae altaris idolum zeli in ipso introitu

6. et dixit ad me fili hominis putasne vides tu quid isti faciant abominationes magnas quas domus Israhel facit hic ut procul recedam a sanctuario meo et adhuc

fire: from the appearance of his loins even downward, fire; and from his loins even upward, as the appearance of brightness, as the colour of amber.

3 And he put forth the form of an hand, and took me by a lock of mine head; and the spirit lifted me up between the earth and the heaven, and brought me in the visions of God to Jerusalem, to the door of the inner gate that looketh toward the north; where was the seat of the image of jealousy, which provoketh to jealousy.

4 And, behold, the glory of the God of Israel was there, according to the vision that I saw in the plain.

5 Then said he unto me, Son of man, lift up thine eyes now the way toward the north. So I lifted up mine eyes the way toward the north, and behold northward at the gate of the altar this image of jealousy in the entry.

6 He said furthermore unto me, Son of man, seest thou what they do? even the great abominations that the house of Israel committeth here,

conversus videbis abominationes maiores

7. et introduxit me ad ostium atrii et vidi et ecce foramen unum in pariete

8. et dixit ad me fili hominis fode parietem et cum perfodissem parietem apparuit ostium unum

9. et dixit ad me ingredere et vide abominationes pessimas quas isti faciunt hic

10. et ingressus vidi et ecce omnis similitudo reptilium et animalium abominatio et universa idola domus Israhel depicta erant in pariete in circuitu per totum

11. et septuaginta viri de senioribus domus Israhel et Hiezonias filius Saphan stabat in medio eorum stantium ante picturas et unusquisque habebat turibulum in manu sua et vapor nebulae de ture consurgebat

12. et dixit ad me certe vides fili hominis quae seniores domus Israhel faciunt in tenebris unusquisque in

that I should go far off from my sanctuary? but turn thee yet again, and thou shalt see greater abominations.

7 And he brought me to the door of the court; and when I looked, behold a hole in the wall.

8 Then said he unto me, Son of man, dig now in the wall: and when I had digged in the wall, behold a door.

9 And he said unto me, Go in, and behold the wicked abominations that they do here.

10 So I went in and saw; and behold every form of creeping things, and abominable beasts, and all the idols of the house of Israel, pourtrayed upon the wall round about.

11 And there stood before them seventy men of the ancients of the house of Israel, and in the midst of them stood Jaazaniah the son of Shaphan, with every man his censer in his hand; and a thick cloud of incense went up.

12 Then said he unto me, Son of man, hast thou seen what the ancients of the house of Israel do in the

abscondito cubiculi sui dicunt enim non videt Dominus nos dereliquit Dominus terram

13. et dixit ad me adhuc conversus videbis abominationes maiores quas isti faciunt

14. et introduxit me per ostium portae domus Domini quod respiciebat ad aquilonem et ecce ibi mulieres sedebant plangentes Adonidem

15. et dixit ad me certe vidisti fili hominis adhuc conversus videbis abominationes maiores his

16. et introduxit me in atrium domus Domini interius et ecce in ostio templi Domini inter vestibulum et altare quasi viginti quinque viri dorsa habentes contra templum Domini et facies ad orientem et adorabant ad ortum solis

17. et dixit ad me certe vidisti fili hominis numquid leve est hoc domui Iuda ut facerent abominationes istas quas fecerunt hic quia replentes terram

dark, every man in the chambers of his imagery? for they say, The Lord seeth us not; the Lord hath forsaken the earth.

13 He said also unto me, Turn thee yet again, and thou shalt see greater abominations that they do.

14 Then he brought me to the door of the gate of the Lord's house which was toward the north; and, behold, there sat women weeping for Tammuz.

15 Then said he unto me, Hast thou seen this, O son of man? turn thee yet again, and thou shalt see greater abominations than these.

16 And he brought me into the inner court of the Lord's house, and, behold, at the door of the temple of the Lord, between the porch and the altar, were about five and twenty men, with their backs toward the temple of the Lord, and their faces toward the east; and they worshipped the sun toward the east.

17 Then he said unto me, Hast thou seen this, O son of man? Is it a light thing to the house of Judah that they commit the abominations

iniquitate conversi sunt ad inritandum me et ecce adplicant ramum ad nares suas

18. ergo et ego faciam in furore non parcet oculus meus nec miserebor et cum clamaverint ad aures meas voce magna non exaudiam eos

which they commit here? for they have filled the land with violence, and have returned to provoke me to anger: and, lo, they put the branch to their nose.

18 Therefore will I also deal in fury: mine eye shall not spare, neither will I have pity: and though they cry in mine ears with a loud voice, yet will I not hear them.

CHAPTER 9

1. et clamavit in auribus meis voce magna dicens adpropinquaverunt visitationes urbis et unusquisque vas interfectionis habet in manu sua

2. et ecce sex viri veniebant de via portae superioris quae respicit ad aquilonem et uniuscuiusque vas interitus in manu eius vir quoque unus in medio eorum vestitus lineis et atramentarium scriptoris ad renes eius et ingressi sunt et steterunt iuxta altare aereum

3. et gloria Domini

CHAPTER 9

HE cried also in mine ears with a loud voice, saying, Cause them that have charge over the city to draw near, even every man with his destroying weapon in his hand.

2 And, behold, six men came from the way of the higher gate, which lieth toward the north, and every man a slaughter weapon in his hand; and one man among them was clothed with linen, with a writer's inkhorn by his side: and they went in, and stood beside the brasen altar.

3 And the glory of the God of Israel was gone up from the cherub, whereupon he

Israhel adsumpta est de cherub quae erat super eum ad limen domus et vocavit virum qui indutus erat lineis et atramentarium scriptoris habebat in lumbis suis

4. et dixit Dominus ad eum transi per mediam civitatem in medio Hierusalem et signa thau super frontes virorum gementium et dolentium super cunctis abominationibus quae fiunt in medio eius

5. et illis dixit audiente me transite per civitatem sequentes eum et percutite non parcat oculus vester neque misereamini

6. senem adulescentulum et virginem parvulum et mulieres interficite usque ad internicionem omnem autem super quem videritis thau ne occidatis et a sanctuario meo incipite coeperunt ergo a viris senioribus qui erant ante faciem domus

7. et dixit ad eos contaminate domum et implete atria interfectis egredimini et egressi sunt

was, to the threshold of the house. And he called to the man clothed with linen, which had the writer's inkhorn by his side;

4 And the Lord said unto him, Go through the midst of the city, through the midst of Jerusalem, and set a mark upon the foreheads of the men that sigh and that cry for all the abominations that be done in the midst thereof.

5 And to the others he said in mine hearing, Go ye after him through the city, and smite: let not your eye spare, neither have ye pity:

6 Slay utterly old and young, both maids, and little children, and women: but come not near any man upon whom is the mark; and begin at my sanctuary. Then they began at the ancient men which were before the house.

7 And he said unto them, Defile the house, and fill the courts with the slain: go ye forth. And they went forth, and slew in the city.

8 And it came to pass, while they were slaying them, and I was left, that I fell upon my face, and cried, and said, Ah Lord God! wilt thou destroy

et percutiebant eos qui erant in civitate

8. et caede conpleta remansi ego ruique super faciem meam et clamans aio heu heu heu Domine Deus ergone disperdes omnes reliquias Israhel effundens furorem tuum super Hierusalem

9. et dixit ad me iniquitas domus Israhel et Iuda magna est nimis valde et repleta est terra sanguinibus et civitas repleta est aversione dixerunt enim dereliquit Dominus terram et Dominus non videt

10. igitur et meus non parcet oculus neque miserebor viam eorum super caput eorum reddam

11. et ecce vir qui indutus erat lineis qui habebat atramentarium in dorso suo respondit verbum dicens feci sicut praecepisti mihi

all the residue of Israel in thy pouring out of thy fury upon Jerusalem?

9 Then said he unto me, The iniquity of the house of Israel and Judah is exceeding great, and the land is full of blood, and the city full of perverseness: for they say, The Lord hath forsaken the earth, and the Lord seeth not.

10 And as for me also, mine eye shall not spare, neither will I have pity, but I will recompense their way upon their head.

11 And, behold, the man clothed with linen, which had the inkhorn by his side, reported the matter, saying, I have done as thou hast commanded me.

CHAPTER 10

CHAPTER 10

1. et vidi et ecce in firmamento quod erat super caput cherubin quasi lapis sapphyrus quasi species similitudinis solii apparuit super ea

2. et dixit ad virum qui indutus erat lineis et ait ingredere in medio rotarum quae sunt subtus cherub et imple manum tuam prunis ignis quae sunt inter cherubin et effunde super civitatem ingressusque est in conspectu meo

3. cherubin autem stabant a dextris domus cum ingrederetur vir et nubes implevit atrium interius

4. et elevata est gloria Domini desuper cherub ad limen domus et repleta est domus nube et atrium repletum est splendore gloriae Domini

5. et sonitus alarum cherubin audiebatur usque ad atrium exterius quasi vox Dei omnipotentis loquentis

6. cumque praecepisset viro qui indutus erat

THEN I looked, and, behold, in the firmament that was above the head of the cherubims there appeared over them as it were a sapphire stone, as the appearance of the likeness of a throne.

2 And he spake unto the man clothed with linen, and said, Go in between the wheels, even under the cherub, and fill thine hand with coals of fire from between the cherubims, and scatter them over the city. And he went in in my sight.

3 Now the cherubims stood on the right side of the house, when the man went in; and the cloud filled the inner court.

4 Then the glory of the Lord went up from the cherub, and stood over the threshold of the house; and the house was filled with the cloud, and the court was full of the brightness of the Lord's glory.

5 And the sound of the cherubims' wings was heard even to the outer court, as the voice of the Almighty God

lineis dicens sume ignem de medio rotarum quae sunt inter cherubin ingressus ille stetit iuxta rotam

7. et extendit cherub manum de medio cherubin ad ignem qui erat inter cherubin et sumpsit et dedit in manus eius qui indutus erat lineis qui accipiens egressus est

8. et apparuit in cherubin similitudo manus hominis subtus pinnas eorum

9. et vidi et ecce quattuor rotae iuxta cherubin rota una iuxta cherub unum et rota alia iuxta cherub unum species autem erat rotarum quasi visio lapidis chrysoliti

10. et aspectus earum similitudo una quattuor quasi sit rota in medio rotae

11. cumque ambularent in quattuor partes gradiebantur non revertebantur ambulantes sed ad locum ad quem ire declinabat quae prima erat sequebantur et ceterae nec convertebantur

when he speaketh.

6 And it came to pass, that when he had commanded the man clothed with linen, saying, Take fire from between the wheels, from between the cherubims; then he went in, and stood beside the wheels.

7 And one cherub stretched forth his hand from between the cherubims unto the fire that was between the cherubims, and took thereof, and put it into the hands of him that was clothed with linen: who took it, and went out.

8 And there appeared in the cherubims the form of a man's hand under their wings.

9 And when I looked, behold the four wheels by the cherubims, one wheel by one cherub, and another wheel by another cherub: and the appearance of the wheels was as the colour of a beryl stone.

10 And as for their appearances, they four had one likeness, as if a wheel had been in the midst of a wheel.

11 When they went, they went upon their four sides;

12. et omne corpus earum et colla et manus et pinnae et circuli plena erant oculis in circuitu quattuor rotarum

13. et rotas istas vocavit volubiles audiente me

14. quattuor autem facies habebat unum facies una facies cherub et facies secunda facies hominis et in tertio facies leonis et in quarto facies aquilae

15. et elevata sunt cherubin ipsum est animal quod videram iuxta flumen Chobar

16. cumque ambularent cherubin ibant pariter et rotae iuxta ea et cum levarent cherubin alas suas ut exaltarentur de terra non residebant rotae sed et ipsae iuxta erant

17. stantibus illis stabant et cum elevatis elevabantur spiritus enim vitae erat in eis

18. et egressa est gloria Domini a limine templi et stetit super cherubin

19. et elevantia cherubin alas suas exaltata sunt a terra coram me et illis egredientibus rotae quoque subsecutae sunt et

they turned not as they went, but to the place whither the head looked they followed it; they turned not as they went.

12 And their whole body, and their backs, and their hands, and their wings, and the wheels, were full of eyes round about, even the wheels that they four had.

13 As for the wheels, it was cried unto them in my hearing, O wheel.

14 And every one had four faces: the first face was the face of a cherub, and the second face was the face of a man, and the third face of a lion, and the fourth the face of an eagle.

15 And the cherubims were lifted up. This is the living creature that I saw by the river of Chebar.

16 And when the cherubims went, the wheels went by them: and when the cherubims lifted up their wings to mount up from the earth, the same wheels also turned not from beside them.

17 When they stood, these stood; and when they were lifted up, these lifted up themselves also: for the spirit of the living creature was in

stetit in introitu portae domus Domini orientalis et gloria Dei Israhel erat super ea

20. ipsum est animal quod vidi subter Deum Israhel iuxta fluvium Chobar et intellexi quia cherubin essent

21. quattuor per quattuor vultus uni et quattuor alae uni et similitudo manus hominis sub alis eorum

22. et similitudo vultuum eorum ipsi vultus quos videram iuxta fluvium Chobar et intuitus eorum et impetus singulorum ante faciem suam ingredi

them.

18 Then the glory of the Lord departed from off the threshold of the house, and stood over the cherubims.

19 And the cherubims lifted up their wings, and mounted up from the earth in my sight: when they went out, the wheels also were beside them, and every one stood at the door of the east gate of the Lord's house; and the glory of the God of Israel was over them above.

20 This is the living creature that I saw under the God of Israel by the river of Chebar; and I knew that they were the cherubims.

21 Every one had four faces apiece, and every one four wings; and the likeness of the hands of a man was under their wings.

22 And the likeness of their faces was the same faces which I saw by the river of Chebar, their appearances and themselves: they went every one straight forward.

1. et elevavit me spiritus et introduxit me ad portam domus Domini orientalem quae respicit solis ortum et ecce in introitu portae viginti quinque viri et vidi in medio eorum Hiezoniam filium Azur et Pheltiam filium Banaiae principes populi

2. dixitque ad me fili hominis hii viri qui cogitant iniquitatem et tractant consilium pessimum in urbe ista

3. dicentes nonne dudum aedificatae sunt domus haec est lebes nos autem carnes

4. idcirco vaticinare de eis vaticinare fili hominis

5. et inruit in me spiritus Domini et dixit ad me loquere haec dicit Dominus sic locuti estis domus Israhel et cogitationes cordis vestri ego novi

6. plurimos occidistis in urbe hac et implestis vias eius interfectis

7. propterea haec dicit Dominus Deus interfecti

MOREOVER the spirit lifted me up, and brought me unto the east gate of the Lord's house, which looketh eastward: and behold at the door of the gate five and twenty men; among whom I saw Jaazaniah the son of Azur, and Pelatiah the son of Benaiah, princes of the people.

2 Then said he unto me, Son of man, these are the men that devise mischief, and give wicked counsel in this city:

3 Which say, It is not near; let us build houses: this city is the caldron, and we be the flesh.

4 Therefore prophesy against them, prophesy, O son of man.

5 And the Spirit of the Lord fell upon me, and said unto me, Speak; Thus saith the Lord; Thus have ye said, O house of Israel: for I know the things that come into your mind, every one of them.

6 Ye have multiplied your slain in this city, and ye have filled the streets thereof with

vestri quos posuistis in medio eius hii sunt carnes et haec est lebes et educam vos de medio eius

8. gladium metuistis et gladium inducam super vos ait Dominus Deus

9. et eiciam vos de medio eius daboque vos in manu hostium et faciam in vobis iudicia

10. gladio cadetis in finibus Israhel iudicabo vos et scietis quia ego Dominus

11. haec non erit vobis in lebetem et vos non eritis in medio eius in carnes in finibus Israhel iudicabo vos

12. et scietis quia ego Dominus qui in praeceptis meis non ambulastis et iudicia mea non fecistis sed iuxta iudicia gentium quae in circuitu vestro sunt estis operati

13. et factum est cum prophetarem Pheltias filius Banaiae mortuus est et cecidi in faciem meam clamans voce magna et dixi heu heu heu Domine Deus consummationem tu

the slain.

7 Therefore thus saith the Lord God; Your slain whom ye have laid in the midst of it, they are the flesh, and this city is the caldron: but I will bring you forth out of the midst of it.

8 Ye have feared the sword; and I will bring a sword upon you, saith the Lord God.

9 And I will bring you out of the midst thereof, and deliver you into the hands of strangers, and will execute judgments among you.

10 Ye shall fall by the sword; I will judge you in the border of Israel; and ye shall know that I am the Lord.

11 This city shall not be your caldron, neither shall ye be the flesh in the midst thereof; but I will judge you in the border of Israel:

12 And ye shall know that I am the Lord: for ye have not walked in my statutes, neither executed my judgments, but have done after the manners of the heathen that are round about you.

13 And it came to pass, when I prophesied, that Pelatiah the son of Benaiah

facis reliquiarum Israhel
14. et factum est verbum Domini ad me dicens
15. fili hominis fratres tui fratres tui viri propinqui tui et omnis domus Israhel universi quibus dixerunt habitatores Hierusalem longe recedite a Domino nobis data est terra in possessionem
16. propterea haec dicit Dominus Deus quia longe feci eos in gentibus et quia dispersi eos in terris ero eis in sanctificationem modicam in terris ad quas venerunt
17. propterea loquere haec dicit Dominus Deus congregabo vos de populis et adunabo de terris in quibus dispersi estis daboque vobis humum Israhel
18. et ingredientur illuc et auferent omnes offensiones cunctasque abominationes eius de illa
19. et dabo eis cor unum et spiritum novum tribuam in visceribus eorum et auferam cor lapideum de carne eorum

died. Then fell I down upon my face, and cried with a loud voice, and said, Ah Lord God! wilt thou make a full end of the remnant of Israel?

14 Again the word of the Lord came unto me, saying,

15 Son of man, thy brethren, even thy brethren, the men of thy kindred, and all the house of Israel wholly, are they unto whom the inhabitants of Jerusalem have said, Get you far from the Lord: unto us is this land given in possession.

16 Therefore say, Thus saith the Lord God; Although I have cast them far off among the heathen, and although I have scattered them among the countries, yet will I be to them as a little sanctuary in the countries where they shall come.

17 Therefore say, Thus saith the Lord God; I will even gather you from the people, and assemble you out of the countries where ye have been scattered, and I will give you the land of Israel.

18 And they shall come thither, and they shall take away all the detestable things thereof and all the

et dabo eis cor carneum

20. ut in praeceptis meis ambulent et iudicia mea custodiant faciantque ea et sint mihi in populum et ego sim eis in Deum

21. quorum cor post offendicula et abominationes suas ambulat horum viam in capite suo ponam dicit Dominus Deus

22. et elevaverunt cherubin alas suas et rotae cum eis et gloria Dei Israhel erat super ea

23. et ascendit gloria Domini de medio civitatis stetitque super montem qui est ad orientem urbis

24. et spiritus levavit me adduxitque in Chaldeam ad transmigrationem in visione in spiritu Dei et sublata est a me visio quam videram

25. et locutus sum ad transmigrationem omnia verba Domini quae ostenderat mihi

abominations thereof from thence.

19 And I will give them one heart, and I will put a new spirit within you; and I will take the stony heart out of their flesh, and will give them an heart of flesh:

20 That they may walk in my statutes, and keep mine ordinances, and do them: and they shall be my people, and I will be their God.

21 But as for them whose heart walketh after the heart of their detestable things and their abominations, I will recompense their way upon their own heads, saith the Lord God.

22 Then did the cherubims lift up their wings, and the wheels beside them; and the glory of the God of Israel was over them above.

23 And the glory of the Lord went up from the midst of the city, and stood upon the mountain which is on the east side of the city.

24 Afterwards the spirit took me up, and brought me in a vision by the Spirit of God into Chaldea, to them of the captivity. So the vision that I had seen went up from me.

25 Then I spake unto them of the captivity all the things that the Lord had shewed me.

CHAPTER 12

1. et factus est sermo Domini ad me dicens
2. fili hominis in medio domus exasperantis tu habitas qui oculos habent ad videndum et non vident et aures ad audiendum et non audiunt quia domus exasperans est
3. tu ergo fili hominis fac tibi vasa transmigrationis et transmigrabis per diem coram eis transmigrabis autem de loco tuo ad locum alterum in conspectu eorum si forte aspiciant quia domus exasperans est
4. et efferes foras vasa tua quasi vasa transmigrantis per diem in conspectu eorum tu autem egredieris vespere coram eis sicut egreditur migrans
5. ante oculos eorum perfodi tibi parietem et egredieris per eum

CHAPTER 12

THE word of the Lord also came unto me, saying,

2 Son of man, thou dwellest in the midst of a rebellious house, which have eyes to see, and see not; they have ears to hear, and hear not: for they are a rebellious house.

3 Therefore, thou son of man, prepare thee stuff for removing, and remove by day in their sight; and thou shalt remove from thy place to another place in their sight: it may be they will consider, though they be a rebellious house.

4 Then shalt thou bring forth thy stuff by day in their sight, as stuff for removing: and thou shalt go forth at even in their sight, as they that go forth into captivity.

5 Dig thou through the wall in their sight, and carry out thereby.

6 In their sight shalt thou bear it upon thy shoulders, and carry it forth in the

6. in conspectu eorum in umeris portaberis in caligine effereris faciem tuam velabis et non videbis terram quia portentum dedi te domui Israhel

7. feci ergo sicut praeceperat mihi vasa mea protuli quasi vasa transmigrantis per diem et vespere perfodi mihi parietem manu in caligine egressus sum et in umeris portatus in conspectu eorum

8. et factus est sermo Domini ad me mane dicens

9. fili hominis numquid non dixerunt ad te domus Israhel domus exasperans quid tu facis

10. dic ad eos haec dicit Dominus Deus super ducem onus istud qui est in Hierusalem et super omnem domum Israhel quae est in medio eorum

11. dic ego portentum vestrum quomodo feci sic fiet illis in transmigrationem et captivitatem ibunt

12. et dux qui est in medio eorum in umeris

twilight: thou shalt cover thy face, that thou see not the ground: for I have set thee for a sign unto the house of Israel.

7 And I did so as I was commanded: I brought forth my stuff by day, as stuff for captivity, and in the even I digged through the wall with mine hand; I brought it forth in the twilight, and I bare it upon my shoulder in their sight.

8 And in the morning came the word of the Lord unto me, saying,

9 Son of man, hath not the house of Israel, the rebellious house, said unto thee, What doest thou?

10 Say thou unto them, Thus saith the Lord God; This burden concerneth the prince in Jerusalem, and all the house of Israel that are among them.

11 Say, I am your sign: like as I have done, so shall it be done unto them: they shall remove and go into captivity.

12 And the prince that is among them shall bear upon his shoulder in the twilight, and shall go forth: they shall dig through the wall to carry

portabitur in caligine egredietur parietem perfodient ut educant eum facies eius operietur ut non videat oculo terram

13. et extendam rete meum super illum et capietur in sagena mea et adducam eum in Babylonem in terram Chaldeorum et ipsam non videbit ibique morietur

14. et omnes qui circa eum sunt praesidium eius et agmina eius dispergam in omnem ventum et gladium evaginabo post eos

15. et scient quia ego Dominus quando dispersero illos in gentibus et disseminavero eos in terris

16. et relinquam ex eis viros paucos a gladio et fame et pestilentia ut narrent omnia scelera eorum in gentibus ad quas ingredientur et scient quia ego Dominus

17. et factus est sermo Domini ad me dicens

18. fili hominis panem tuum in conturbatione comede sed et aquam

out thereby: he shall cover his face, that he see not the ground with his eyes.

13 My net also will I spread upon him, and he shall be taken in my snare: and I will bring him to Babylon to the land of the Chaldeans; yet shall he not see it, though he shall die there.

14 And I will scatter toward every wind all that are about him to help him, and all his bands; and I will draw out the sword after them.

15 And they shall know that I am the Lord, when I shall scatter them among the nations, and disperse them in the countries.

16 But I will leave a few men of them from the sword, from the famine, and from the pestilence; that they may declare all their abominations among the heathen whither they come; and they shall know that I am the Lord.

17 Moreover the word of the Lord came to me, saying,

18 Son of man, eat thy bread with quaking, and drink thy water with trembling and with carefulness;

19 And say unto the people of the land, Thus saith the

tuam in festinatione et maerore bibe

19. et dices ad populum terrae haec dicit Dominus Deus ad eos qui habitant in Hierusalem in terra Israhel panem suum in sollicitudine comedent et aquam suam in desolatione bibent ut desoletur terra a multitudine sua propter iniquitatem omnium qui habitant in ea

20. et civitates quae nunc habitantur desolatae erunt terraque deserta et scietis quia ego Dominus

21. et factus est sermo Domini ad me dicens

22. fili hominis quod est proverbium istud vobis in terra Israhel dicentium in longum differentur dies et peribit omnis visio

23. ideo dic ad eos haec dicit Dominus Deus quiescere faciam proverbium istud neque vulgo dicetur ultra in Israhel et loquere ad eos quod adpropinquaverint dies et sermo omnis visionis

24. non enim erit ultra omnis visio cassa neque

Lord God of the inhabitants of Jerusalem, and of the land of Israel; They shall eat their bread with carefulness, and drink their water with astonishment, that her land may be desolate from all that is therein, because of the violence of all them that dwell therein.

20 And the cities that are inhabited shall be laid waste, and the land shall be desolate; and ye shall know that I am the Lord.

21 And the word of the Lord came unto me, saying,

22 Son of man, what is that proverb that ye have in the land of Israel, saying, The days are prolonged, and every vision faileth?

23 Tell them therefore, Thus saith the Lord God; I will make this proverb to cease, and they shall no more use it as a proverb in Israel; but say unto them, The days are at hand, and the effect of every vision.

24 For there shall be no more any vain vision nor flattering divination within the house of Israel.

25 For I am the Lord: I will speak, and the word that I

divinatio ambigua in medio filiorum Israhel

25. quia ego Dominus loquar quodcumque locutus fuero verbum et fiet non prolongabitur amplius sed in diebus vestris domus exasperans loquar verbum et faciam illud dicit Dominus Deus

26. et factus est sermo Domini ad me dicens

27. fili hominis ecce domus Israhel dicentium visio quam hic videt in dies multos et in tempora longa iste prophetat

28. propterea dic ad eos haec dicit Dominus Deus non prolongabitur ultra omnis sermo meus verbum quod locutus fuero conplebitur dicit Dominus Deus

shall speak shall come to pass; it shall be no more prolonged: for in your days, O rebellious house, will I say the word, and will perform it, saith the Lord God.

26 Again the word of the Lord came to me, saying,

27 Son of man, behold, they of the house of Israel say, The vision that he seeth is for many days to come, and he prophesieth of the times that are far off.

28 Therefore say unto them, Thus saith the Lord God; There shall none of my words be prolonged any more, but the word which I have spoken shall be done, saith the Lord God.

CHAPTER 13

CHAPTER 13

1. et factus est sermo Domini ad me dicens

2. fili hominis vaticinare ad prophetas Israhel qui prophetant et dices prophetantibus de corde suo audite verbum Domini

AND the word of the Lord came unto me, saying,

2 Son of man, prophesy against the prophets of Israel that prophesy, and say thou unto them that prophesy out of their own hearts, Hear ye the word of the Lord;

3. haec dicit Dominus Deus vae prophetis insipientibus qui sequuntur spiritum suum et nihil vident

4. quasi vulpes in desertis prophetae tui Israhel erant

5. non ascendistis ex adverso neque opposuistis murum pro domo Israhel ut staretis in proelio in die Domini

6. vident vana et divinant mendacium dicentes ait Dominus cum Dominus non miserit eos et perseveraverunt confirmare sermonem

7. numquid non visionem cassam vidistis et divinationem mendacem locuti estis et dicitis ait Dominus cum ego non sim locutus

8. propterea haec dicit Dominus Deus quia locuti estis vana et vidistis mendacium ideo ecce ego ad vos ait Dominus Deus

9. et erit manus mea super prophetas qui vident vana et divinant mendacium in concilio populi mei non erunt et in

3 Thus saith the Lord God; Woe unto the foolish prophets, that follow their own spirit, and have seen nothing!

4 O Israel, thy prophets are like the foxes in the deserts.

5 Ye have not gone up into the gaps, neither made up the hedge for the house of Israel to stand in the battle in the day of the Lord.

6 They have seen vanity and lying divination, saying, The Lord saith: and the Lord hath not sent them: and they have made others to hope that they would confirm the word.

7 Have ye not seen a vain vision, and have ye not spoken a lying divination, whereas ye say, The Lord saith it; albeit I have not spoken?

8 Therefore thus saith the Lord God; Because ye have spoken vanity, and seen lies, therefore, behold, I am against you, saith the Lord God.

9 And mine hand shall be upon the prophets that see vanity, and that divine lies: they shall not be in the assembly of my people, neither shall they be written

scriptura domus Israhel non scribentur nec in terra Israhel ingredientur et scietis quia ego Dominus Deus

10. eo quod deceperint populum meum dicentes pax et non est pax et ipse aedificabat parietem illi autem liniebant eum luto absque paleis

11. dic ad eos qui liniunt absque temperatura quod casurus sit erit enim imber inundans et dabo lapides praegrandes desuper inruentes et ventum procellae dissipantem

12. siquidem ecce cecidit paries numquid non dicetur vobis ubi est litura quam levistis

13. propterea haec dicit Dominus Deus et erumpere faciam spiritum tempestatum in indignatione mea et imber inundans in furore meo erit et lapides grandes in ira in consummationem

14. et destruam parietem quem levistis absque temperamento et adaequabo eum terrae et

in the writing of the house of Israel, neither shall they enter into the land of Israel; and ye shall know that I am the Lord God.

10 Because, even because they have seduced my people, saying, Peace; and there was no peace; and one built up a wall, and, lo, others daubed it with untempered morter:

11 Say unto them which daub it with untempered morter, that it shall fall: there shall be an overflowing shower; and ye, O great hailstones, shall fall; and a stormy wind shall rend it.

12 Lo, when the wall is fallen, shall it not be said unto you, Where is the daubing wherewith ye have daubed it?

13 Therefore thus saith the Lord God; I will even rend it with a stormy wind in my fury; and there shall be an overflowing shower in mine anger, and great hailstones in my fury to consume it.

14 So will I break down the wall that ye have daubed with untempered morter, and bring it down to the ground, so that the foundation thereof

71

revelabitur fundamentum eius et cadet et consumetur in medio eius et scietis quia ego sum Dominus

15. et conplebo indignationem meam in parietem et in his qui linunt eum absque temperamento dicamque vobis non est paries et non sunt qui linunt eum

16. prophetae Israhel qui prophetant ad Hierusalem et vident ei visionem pacis et non est pax ait Dominus Deus

17. et tu fili hominis pone faciem tuam contra filias populi tui quae prophetant de corde suo et vaticinare super eas

18. et dic haec ait Dominus Deus vae quae consuunt pulvillos sub omni cubito manus et faciunt cervicalia sub capite universae aetatis ad capiendas animas cum caperent animas populi mei vivificabant animas eorum

19. et violabant me ad populum meum propter pugillum hordei et fragmen panis ut

shall be discovered, and it shall fall, and ye shall be consumed in the midst thereof: and ye shall know that I am the Lord.

15 Thus will I accomplish my wrath upon the wall, and upon them that have daubed it with untempered morter, and will say unto you, The wall is no more, neither they that daubed it;

16 To wit, the prophets of Israel which prophesy concerning Jerusalem, and which see visions of peace for her, and there is no peace, saith the Lord God.

17 Likewise, thou son of man, set thy face against the daughters of thy people, which prophesy out of their own heart; and prophesy thou against them,

18 And say, Thus saith the Lord God; Woe to the women that sew pillows to all armholes, and make kerchiefs upon the head of every stature to hunt souls! Will ye hunt the souls of my people, and will ye save the souls alive that come unto you?

19 And will ye pollute me among my people for

interficerent animas quae non moriuntur et vivificarent animas quae non vivunt mentientes populo meo credenti mendaciis

20. propter hoc haec dicit Dominus Deus ecce ego ad pulvillos vestros quibus vos capitis animas volantes et disrumpam eos de brachiis vestris et dimittam animas quas vos capitis animas ad volandum

21. et disrumpam cervicalia vestra et liberabo populum meum de manu vestra neque erunt ultra in manibus vestris ad praedandum et scietis quia ego Dominus

22. pro eo quod maerere fecistis cor iusti mendaciter quem ego non contristavi et confortastis manus impii ut non reverteretur a via sua mala et viveret

23. propterea vana non videbitis et divinationes non divinabitis amplius et eruam populum meum de manu vestra et scietis quoniam ego Dominus

handfuls of barley and for pieces of bread, to slay the souls that should not die, and to save the souls alive that should not live, by your lying to my people that hear your lies?

20 Wherefore thus saith the Lord God; Behold, I am against your pillows, wherewith ye there hunt the souls to make them fly, and I will tear them from your arms, and will let the souls go, even the souls that ye hunt to make them fly.

21 Your kerchiefs also will I tear, and deliver my people out of your hand, and they shall be no more in your hand to be hunted; and ye shall know that I am the Lord.

22 Because with lies ye have made the heart of the righteous sad, whom I have not made sad; and strengthened the hands of the wicked, that he should not return from his wicked way, by promising him life:

23 Therefore ye shall see no more vanity, nor divine divinations: for I will deliver my people out of your hand: and ye shall know that I am

the Lord.

CHAPTER 14

1. et venerunt ad me viri seniorum Israhel et sederunt coram me
2. et factus est sermo Domini ad me dicens
3. fili hominis viri isti posuerunt inmunditias suas in cordibus suis et scandalum iniquitatis suae statuerunt contra faciem suam numquid interrogatus respondebo eis
4. propter hoc loquere eis et dices ad eos haec dicit Dominus Deus homo homo de domo Israhel qui posuerit inmunditias suas in corde suo et scandalum iniquitatis suae statuerit contra faciem suam et venerit ad prophetam interrogans per eum me ego Dominus respondebo ei in multitudine inmunditiarum suarum
5. ut capiatur domus Israhel in corde suo quo recesserunt a me in cunctis idolis suis

CHAPTER 14

THEN came certain of the elders of Israel unto me, and sat before me.

2 And the word of the Lord came unto me, saying,

3 Son of man, these men have set up their idols in their heart, and put the stumblingblock of their iniquity before their face: should I be inquired of at all by them?

4 Therefore speak unto them, and say unto them, Thus saith the Lord God; Every man of the house of Israel that setteth up his idols in his heart, and putteth the stumblingblock of his iniquity before his face, and cometh to the prophet; I the Lord will answer him that cometh according to the multitude of his idols;

5 That I may take the house of Israel in their own heart, because they are all estranged from me through their idols.

6 Therefore say unto the house of Israel, Thus saith

6. propterea dic ad domum Israhel haec dicit Dominus Deus convertimini et recedite ab idolis vestris et ab universis contaminationibus vestris avertite facies vestras

7. quia homo homo de domo Israhel et de proselytis quicumque advena fuerit in Israhel si alienatus fuerit a me et posuerit idola sua in corde suo et scandalum iniquitatis suae statuerit contra faciem suam et venerit ad prophetam ut interroget per eum me ego Dominus respondebo ei per me

8. et ponam faciem meam super hominem illum et faciam eum in exemplum et in proverbium et disperdam eum de medio populi mei et scietis quia ego Dominus

9. et propheta cum erraverit et locutus fuerit verbum ego Dominus decepi prophetam illum et extendam manum meam super eum et delebo eum de medio populi mei Israhel

the Lord God; Repent, and turn yourselves from your idols; and turn away your faces from all your abominations.

7 For every one of the house of Israel, or of the stranger that sojourneth in Israel, which separateth himself from me, and setteth up his idols in his heart, and putteth the stumblingblock of his iniquity before his face, and cometh to a prophet to inquire of him concerning me; I the Lord will answer him by myself:

8 And I will set my face against that man, and will make him a sign and a proverb, and I will cut him off from the midst of my people; and ye shall know that I am the Lord.

9 And if the prophet be deceived when he hath spoken a thing, I the Lord have deceived that prophet, and I will stretch out my hand upon him, and will destroy him from the midst of my people Israel.

10 And they shall bear the punishment of their iniquity: the punishment of the prophet shall be even as the

10. et portabunt iniquitatem suam iuxta iniquitatem interrogantis sic iniquitas prophetae erit

11. ut non erret ultra domus Israhel a me neque polluatur in universis praevaricationibus suis sed sit mihi in populum et ego sim eis in Deum ait Dominus exercituum

12. et factus est sermo Domini ad me dicens

13. fili hominis terra cum peccaverit mihi ut praevaricetur praevaricans extendam manum meam super eam et conteram virgam panis eius et inmittam in eam famem et interficiam de ea hominem et iumentum

14. et si fuerint tres viri isti in medio eius Noe Danihel et Iob ipsi iustitia sua liberabunt animas suas ait Dominus exercituum

15. quod si et bestias pessimas induxero super terram ut vastem eam et fuerit invia eo quod non sit pertransiens propter bestias

16. tres viri isti qui

punishment of him that seeketh unto him;

11 That the house of Israel may go no more astray from me, neither be polluted any more with all their transgressions; but that they may be my people, and I may be their God, saith the Lord God.

12 The word of the Lord came again to me, saying,

13 Son of man, when the land sinneth against me by trespassing grievously, then will I stretch out mine hand upon it, and will break the staff of the bread thereof, and will send famine upon it, and will cut off man and beast from it:

14 Though these three men, Noah, Daniel, and Job, were in it, they should deliver but their own souls by their righteousness, saith the Lord God.

15 If I cause noisome beasts to pass through the land, and they spoil it, so that it be desolate, that no man may pass through because of the beasts:

16 Though these three men were in it, as I live, saith the Lord God, they shall deliver

fuerint in ea vivo ego dicit Dominus Deus quia nec filios nec filias liberabunt sed ipsi soli liberabuntur terra autem desolabitur

17. vel si gladium induxero super terram illam et dixero gladio transi per terram et interfecero de ea hominem et iumentum

18. et tres viri isti fuerint in medio eius vivo ego dicit Dominus Deus non liberabunt filios neque filias sed ipsi soli liberabuntur

19. si autem et pestilentiam inmisero super terram illam et effudero indignationem meam super eam in sanguine ut auferam ex ea hominem et iumentum

20. et Noe et Danihel et Iob fuerint in medio eius vivo ego dicit Dominus Deus quia filium et filiam non liberabunt sed ipsi iustitia sua liberabunt animas suas

21. quoniam haec dicit Dominus Deus quod si et quattuor iudicia mea pessima gladium et

neither sons nor daughters; they only shall be delivered, but the land shall be desolate. 17 Or if I bring a sword upon that land, and say, Sword, go through the land; so that I cut off man and beast from it:

18 Though these three men were in it, as I live, saith the Lord God, they shall deliver neither sons nor daughters, but they only shall be delivered themselves.

19 Or if I send a pestilence into that land, and pour out my fury upon it in blood, to cut off from it man and beast:

20 Though Noah, Daniel, and Job, were in it, as I live, saith the Lord God, they shall deliver neither son nor daughter; they shall but deliver their own souls by their righteousness.

21 For thus saith the Lord God; How much more when I send my four sore judgments upon Jerusalem, the sword, and the famine, and the noisome beast, and the pestilence, to cut off from it man and beast?

22 Yet, behold, therein shall be left a remnant that shall be brought forth, both sons and

famem et bestias malas et pestilentiam misero in Hierusalem ut interficiam de ea hominem et pecus

22. tamen relinquetur in ea salvatio educentium filios et filias ecce ipsi egredientur ad vos et videbitis viam eorum et adinventiones eorum et consolabimini super malo quod induxi in Hierusalem in omnibus quae inportavi super eam

23. et consolabuntur vos cum videritis viam eorum et adinventiones eorum et cognoscetis quod non frustra fecerim omnia quae feci in ea ait Dominus Deus

daughters: behold, they shall come forth unto you, and ye shall see their way and their doings: and ye shall be comforted concerning the evil that I have brought upon Jerusalem, even concerning all that I have brought upon it.

23 And they shall comfort you, when ye see their ways and their doings: and ye shall know that I have not done without cause all that I have done in it, saith the Lord God.

CHAPTER 15

1. et factus est sermo Domini ad me dicens

2. fili hominis quid fiet ligno vitis ex omnibus lignis nemorum quae sunt inter ligna silvarum

3. numquid tolletur de ea lignum ut fiat opus aut fabricabitur de ea paxillus ut dependeat in eo quodcumque vas

CHAPTER 15

AND the word of the Lord came unto me, saying,

2 Son of man, What is the vine tree more than any tree, or than a branch which is among the trees of the forest?

3 Shall wood be taken thereof to do any work? or will men take a pin of it to hang any vessel thereon?

4 Behold, it is cast into the

4. ecce igni datum est in escam utramque partem eius consumpsit ignis et medietas eius redacta est in favillam numquid utile erit ad opus

5. etiam cum esset integrum non erat aptum ad opus quanto magis cum ignis illud devoraverit et conbuserit nihil ex eo fiet operis

6. propterea haec dicit Dominus Deus quomodo lignum vitis inter ligna silvarum quod dedi igni ad devorandum sic tradidi habitatores Hierusalem

7. et ponam faciem meam in eos de igne egredientur et ignis consumet eos et scietis quia ego Dominus cum posuero faciem meam in eos

8. et dedero terram inviam et desolatam eo quod praevaricatores extiterint dicit Dominus Deus

fire for fuel; the fire devoureth both the ends of it, and the midst of it is burned. Is it meet for any work?

5 Behold, when it was whole, it was meet for no work: how much less shall it be meet yet for any work, when the fire hath devoured it, and it is burned?

6 Therefore thus saith the Lord God; As the vine tree among the trees of the forest, which I have given to the fire for fuel, so will I give the inhabitants of Jerusalem.

7 And I will set my face against them; they shall go out from one fire, and another fire shall devour them; and ye shall know that I am the Lord, when I set my face against them.

8 And I will make the land desolate, because they have committed a trespass, saith the Lord God.

CHAPTER 16

1. et factus est sermo Domini ad me dicens

2. fili hominis notas fac

CHAPTER 16

AGAIN the word of the Lord came unto me, saying,

2 Son of man, cause

Hierusalem abominationes suas

3. et dices haec dicit Dominus Deus Hierusalem radix tua et generatio tua de terra chananea pater tuus Amorreus et mater tua Cetthea

4. et quando nata es in die ortus tui non est praecisus umbilicus tuus et in aqua non es lota in salutem nec sale salita nec involuta pannis

5. non pepercit super te oculus ut facerem tibi unum de his miseratus tui sed proiecta es super faciem terrae in abiectione animae tuae in die qua nata es

6. transiens autem per te vidi te conculcari in sanguine tuo et dixi tibi cum esses in sanguine tuo vive dixi inquam tibi in sanguine tuo vive

7. multiplicatam quasi germen agri dedi te et multiplicata es et grandis effecta et ingressa es et pervenisti ad mundum muliebrem ubera tua intumuerunt et pilus tuus germinavit et eras nuda et

Jerusalem to know her abominations,

3 And say, Thus saith the Lord God unto Jerusalem; Thy birth and thy nativity is of the land of Canaan; thy father was an Amorite, and thy mother an Hittite.

4 And as for thy nativity, in the day thou wast born thy navel was not cut, neither wast thou washed in water to supple thee; thou wast not salted at all, nor swaddled at all.

5 None eye pitied thee, to do any of these unto thee, to have compassion upon thee; but thou wast cast out in the open field, to the lothing of thy person, in the day that thou wast born.

6 And when I passed by thee, and saw thee polluted in thine own blood, I said unto thee when thou wast in thy blood, Live; yea, I said unto thee when thou wast in thy blood, Live.

7 I have caused thee to multiply as the bud of the field, and thou hast increased and waxen great, and thou art come to excellent ornaments: thy breasts are fashioned, and thine hair is grown, whereas

confusionis plena

8. et transivi per te et vidi te et ecce tempus tuum tempus amantium et expandi amictum meum super te et operui ignominiam tuam et iuravi tibi et ingressus sum pactum tecum ait Dominus Deus et facta es mihi

9. et lavi te aqua et emundavi sanguinem tuum ex te et unxi te oleo

10. et vestivi te discoloribus et calciavi te ianthino et cinxi te bysso et indui te subtilibus

11. et ornavi te ornamento et dedi armillas in manibus tuis et torquem circa collum tuum

12. et dedi inaurem super os tuum et circulos auribus tuis et coronam decoris in capite tuo

13. et ornata es auro et argento et vestita es bysso et polymito et multicoloribus similam et mel et oleum comedisti et decora facta es vehementer nimis et profecisti in regnum

14. et egressum est

thou wast naked and bare.

8 Now when I passed by thee, and looked upon thee, behold, thy time was the time of love; and I spread my skirt over thee, and covered thy nakedness: yea, I sware unto thee, and entered into a covenant with thee, saith the Lord God, and thou becamest mine.

9 Then washed I thee with water; yea, I throughly washed away thy blood from thee, and I anointed thee with oil.

10 I clothed thee also with broidered work, and shod thee with badgers' skin, and I girded thee about with fine linen, and I covered thee with silk.

11 I decked thee also with ornaments, and I put bracelets upon thy hands, and a chain on thy neck.

12 And I put a jewel on thy forehead, and earrings in thine ears, and a beautiful crown upon thine head.

13 Thus wast thou decked with gold and silver; and thy raiment was of fine linen, and silk, and broidered work; thou didst eat fine flour, and honey, and oil: and thou wast

nomen tuum in gentes propter speciem tuam quia perfecta eras in decore meo quem posueram super te dicit Dominus Deus

15. et habens fiduciam in pulchritudine tua fornicata es in nomine tuo et exposuisti fornicationem tuam omni transeunti ut eius fieres

16. et sumens de vestimentis meis fecisti tibi excelsa hinc inde consuta et fornicata es super eis sicut non est factum neque futurum est

17. et tulisti vasa decoris tui de auro meo et argento meo quae dedi tibi et fecisti tibi imagines masculinas et fornicata es in eis

18. et sumpsisti vestimenta tua multicoloria et vestita es eis et oleum meum et thymiama meum posuisti coram eis

19. et panem meum quem dedi tibi similam et oleum et mel quibus enutrivi te posuisti in conspectu eorum in odorem suavitatis et

exceeding beautiful, and thou didst prosper into a kingdom.

14 And thy renown went forth among the heathen for thy beauty: for it was perfect through my comeliness, which I had put upon thee, saith the Lord God.

15 But thou didst trust in thine own beauty, and playedst the harlot because of thy renown, and pouredst out thy fornications on every one that passed by; his it was.

16 And of thy garments thou didst take, and deckedst thy high places with divers colours, and playedst the harlot thereupon: the like things shall not come, neither shall it be so.

17 Thou hast also taken thy fair jewels of my gold and of my silver, which I had given thee, and madest to thyself images of men, and didst commit whoredom with them,

18 And tookest thy broidered garments, and coveredst them: and thou hast set mine oil and mine incense before them.

19 My meat also which I gave thee, fine flour, and oil, and honey, wherewith I fed

factum est ait Dominus Deus

20. et tulisti filios tuos et filias tuas quas generasti mihi et immolasti eis ad devorandum numquid parva est fornicatio tua

21. immolantis filios meos et dedisti illos consecrans eis

22. et post omnes abominationes tuas et fornicationes non es recordata dierum adulescentiae tuae quando eras nuda et confusione plena conculcata in sanguine tuo

23. et accidit post omnem malitiam tuam vae vae tibi ait Dominus Deus

24. et aedificasti tibi lupanar et fecisti tibi prostibulum in cunctis plateis

25. ad omne caput viae aedificasti signum prostitutionis tuae et abominabilem fecisti decorem tuum et divisisti pedes tuos omni transeunti et multiplicasti fornicationes tuas

26. et fornicata es cum filiis Aegypti vicinis tuis

thee, thou hast even set it before them for a sweet savour: and thus it was, saith the Lord God.

20 Moreover thou hast taken thy sons and thy daughters, whom thou hast borne unto me, and these hast thou sacrificed unto them to be devoured. Is this of thy whoredoms a small matter,

21 That thou hast slain my children, and delivered them to cause them to pass through the fire for them?

22 And in all thine abominations and thy whoredoms thou hast not remembered the days of thy youth, when thou wast naked and bare, and wast polluted in thy blood.

23 And it came to pass after all thy wickedness, (woe, woe unto thee! saith the Lord God;)

24 That thou hast also built unto thee an eminent place, and hast made thee an high place in every street.

25 Thou hast built thy high place at every head of the way, and hast made thy beauty to be abhorred, and hast opened thy feet to every one that passed by, and

magnarum carnium et multiplicasti fornicationem tuam ad inritandum me

27. ecce ego extendi manum meam super te et auferam ius tuum et dabo te in animam odientium te filiarum Palestinarum quae erubescunt in via tua scelerata

28. et fornicata es in filiis Assyriorum eo quod necdum fueris expleta et postquam fornicata es nec sic es satiata

29. et multiplicasti fornicationem tuam in terra Chanaan cum Chaldeis et nec sic satiata es

30. in quo mundabo cor tuum ait Dominus Deus cum facias omnia haec opera mulieris meretricis et procacis

31. quia fabricasti lupanar tuum in capite omnis viae et excelsum tuum fecisti in omni platea nec facta es quasi meretrix fastidio augens pretium

32. sed quasi mulier adultera quae super virum suum inducit alienos

33. omnibus meretricibus multiplied thy whoredoms.

26 Thou hast also committed fornication with the Egyptians thy neighbours, great of flesh; and hast increased thy whoredoms, to provoke me to anger.

27 Behold, therefore I have stretched out my hand over thee, and have diminished thine ordinary food, and delivered thee unto the will of them that hate thee, the daughters of the Philistines, which are ashamed of thy lewd way.

28 Thou hast played the whore also with the Assyrians, because thou wast unsatiable; yea, thou hast played the harlot with them, and yet couldest not be satisfied.

29 Thou hast moreover multiplied thy fornication in the land of Canaan unto Chaldea; and yet thou wast not satisfied herewith.

30 How weak is thine heart, saith the Lord God, seeing thou doest all these things, the work of an imperious whorish woman;

31 In that thou buildest thine eminent place in the head of every way, and makest thine

dantur mercedes tu autem dedisti mercedes cunctis amatoribus tuis et donabas eis ut intrarent ad te undique ad fornicandum tecum

34. factumque in te est contra consuetudinem mulierum in fornicationibus tuis et post te non erit fornicatio in eo enim quod dedisti mercedes et mercedes non accepisti factum est in te contrarium

35. propterea meretrix audi verbum Domini

36. haec dicit Dominus Deus quia effusum est aes tuum et revelata est ignominia tua in fornicationibus tuis super amatores tuos et super idola abominationum tuarum in sanguine filiorum tuorum quos dedisti eis

37. ecce ego congregabo omnes amatores tuos quibus commixta es et omnes quos dilexisti cum universis quos oderas et congregabo eos super te undique et nudabo ignominiam tuam coram eis et videbunt omnem

high place in every street; and hast not been as an harlot, in that thou scornest hire;

32 But as a wife that committeth adultery, which taketh strangers instead of her husband!

33 They give gifts to all whores: but thou givest thy gifts to all thy lovers, and hirest them, that they may come unto thee on every side for thy whoredom.

34 And the contrary is in thee from other women in thy whoredoms, whereas none followeth thee to commit whoredoms: and in that thou givest a reward, and no reward is given unto thee, therefore thou art contrary.

35 Wherefore, O harlot, hear the word of the Lord:

36 Thus saith the Lord God; Because thy filthiness was poured out, and thy nakedness discovered through thy whoredoms with thy lovers, and with all the idols of thy abominations, and by the blood of thy children, which thou didst give unto them;

37 Behold, therefore I will gather all thy lovers, with

turpitudinem tuam

38. et iudicabo te iudiciis adulterarum et effundentium sanguinem et dabo te in sanguinem furoris et zeli

39. et dabo te in manus eorum et destruent lupanar tuum et demolientur prostibulum tuum et denudabunt te vestimentis tuis et auferent vasa decoris tui et derelinquent te nudam plenamque ignominia

40. et adducent super te multitudinem et lapidabunt te lapidibus et trucidabunt te gladiis suis

41. et conburent domos tuas igni et facient in te iudicia in oculis mulierum plurimarum et desines fornicari et mercedes ultra non dabis

42. et requiescet indignatio mea in te et auferetur zelus meus a te et quiescam nec irascar amplius

43. eo quod non fueris recordata dierum adulescentiae tuae et provocasti me in omnibus his quapropter et ego vias tuas in capite tuo dedi ait

whom thou hast taken pleasure, and all them that thou hast loved, with all them that thou hast hated; I will even gather them round about against thee, and will discover thy nakedness unto them, that they may see all thy nakedness.

38 And I will judge thee, as women that break wedlock and shed blood are judged; and I will give thee blood in fury and jealousy.

39 And I will also give thee into their hand, and they shall throw down thine eminent place, and shall break down thy high places: they shall strip thee also of thy clothes, and shall take thy fair jewels, and leave thee naked and bare.

40 They shall also bring up a company against thee, and they shall stone thee with stones, and thrust thee through with their swords.

41 And they shall burn thine houses with fire, and execute judgments upon thee in the sight of many women: and I will cause thee to cease from playing the harlot, and thou also shalt give no hire any more.

Dominus Deus et non feci iuxta scelera tua in omnibus abominationibus tuis

44. ecce omnis qui dicit vulgo proverbium in te adsumet illud dicens sicut mater ita et filia eius

45. filia matris tuae es tu quae proiecit virum suum et filios suos et soror sororum tuarum tu quae proiecerunt viros suos et filios suos mater vestra Cetthea et pater vester Amorreus

46. et soror tua maior Samaria ipsa et filiae eius quae habitat ad sinistram tuam soror autem tua minor te quae habitat a dextris tuis Sodoma et filiae eius

47. sed nec in viis earum ambulasti neque secundum scelera earum fecisti pauxillum minus paene sceleratiora fecisti illis in omnibus viis tuis

48. vivo ego dicit Dominus Deus quia non fecit Sodoma soror tua ipsa et filiae eius sicut fecisti tu et filiae tuae

49. ecce haec fuit iniquitas Sodomae sororis

42 So will I make my fury toward thee to rest, and my jealousy shall depart from thee, and I will be quiet, and will be no more angry.

43 Because thou hast not remembered the days of thy youth, but hast fretted me in all these things; behold, therefore I also will recompense thy way upon thine head, saith the Lord God: and thou shalt not commit this lewdness above all thine abominations.

44 Behold, every one that useth proverbs shall use this proverb against thee, saying, As is the mother, so is her daughter.

45 Thou art thy mother's daughter, that loatheth her husband and her children; and thou art the sister of thy sisters, which lothed their husbands and their children: your mother was an Hittite, and your father an Amorite.

46 And thine elder sister is Samaria, she and her daughters that dwell at thy left hand: and thy younger sister, that dwelleth at thy right hand, is Sodom and her daughters.

47 Yet hast thou not walked

tuae superbia saturitas panis et abundantia et otium ipsius et filiarum eius et manum egeno et pauperi non porrigebant

50. et elevatae sunt et fecerunt abominationes coram me et abstuli eas sicut vidisti

51. et Samaria dimidium peccatorum tuorum non peccavit sed vicisti eas sceleribus tuis et iustificasti sorores tuas in omnibus abominationibus tuis quas operata es

52. ergo et tu porta confusionem tuam quae vicisti sorores tuas peccatis tuis sceleratius agens ab eis iustificatae sunt enim a te ergo et tu confundere et porta ignominiam tuam quae iustificasti sorores tuas

53. et convertam restituens eas conversione Sodomorum cum filiabus suis et conversione Samariae et filiarum eius et convertam reversionem tuam in medio earum

54. ut portes ignominiam tuam et confundaris in omnibus quae fecisti consolans eas

after their ways, nor done after their abominations: but, as if that were a very little thing, thou wast corrupted more than they in all thy ways.

48 As I live, saith the Lord God, Sodom thy sister hath not done, she nor her daughters, as thou hast done, thou and thy daughters.

49 Behold, this was the iniquity of thy sister Sodom, pride, fulness of bread, and abundance of idleness was in her and in her daughters, neither did she strengthen the hand of the poor and needy.

50 And they were haughty, and committed abomination before me: therefore I took them away as I saw good.

51 Neither hath Samaria committed half of thy sins; but thou hast multiplied thine abominations more than they, and hast justified thy sisters in all thine abominations which thou hast done.

52 Thou also, which hast judged thy sisters, bear thine own shame for thy sins that thou hast committed more abominable than they: they are more righteous than thou: yea, be thou confounded

55. et soror tua Sodoma et filiae eius revertentur ad antiquitatem suam et Samaria et filiae eius revertentur ad antiquitatem suam et tu et filiae tuae revertimini ad antiquitatem vestram

56. non fuit autem Sodoma soror tua audita in ore tuo in die superbiae tuae

57. antequam revelaretur malitia tua sicut hoc tempore in obprobrium filiarum Syriae et cunctarum in circuitu tuo filiarum Palestinarum quae ambiunt te per gyrum

58. scelus tuum et ignominiam tuam tu portasti ait Dominus Deus

59. quia haec dicit Dominus Deus et faciam tibi sicut dispexisti iuramentum ut irritum faceres pactum

60. et recordabor ego pacti mei tecum in diebus adulescentiae tuae et suscitabo tibi pactum sempiternum

61. et recordaberis viarum tuarum et

also, and bear thy shame, in that thou hast justified thy sisters.

53 When I shall bring again their captivity, the captivity of Sodom and her daughters, and the captivity of Samaria and her daughters, then will I bring again the captivity of thy captives in the midst of them:

54 That thou mayest bear thine own shame, and mayest be confounded in all that thou hast done, in that thou art a comfort unto them.

55 When thy sisters, Sodom and her daughters, shall return to their former estate, and Samaria and her daughters shall return to their former estate, then thou and thy daughters shall return to your former estate.

56 For thy sister Sodom was not mentioned by thy mouth in the day of thy pride,

57 Before thy wickedness was discovered, as at the time of thy reproach of the daughters of Syria, and all that are round about her, the daughters of the Philistines, which despise thee round about.

58 Thou hast borne thy

confunderis cum receperis sorores tuas te maiores cum minoribus tuis et dabo eas tibi in filias sed non ex pacto tuo

62. et suscitabo ego pactum meum tecum et scies quia ego Dominus

63. ut recorderis et confundaris et non sit tibi ultra aperire os prae confusione tua cum placatus fuero tibi in omnibus quae fecisti ait Dominus Deus

lewdness and thine abominations, saith the Lord.

59 For thus saith the Lord God; I will even deal with thee as thou hast done, which hast despised the oath in breaking the covenant.

60 Nevertheless I will remember my covenant with thee in the days of thy youth, and I will establish unto thee an everlasting covenant.

61 Then thou shalt remember thy ways, and be ashamed, when thou shalt receive thy sisters, thine elder and thy younger: and I will give them unto thee for daughters, but not by thy covenant.

62 And I will establish my covenant with thee; and thou shalt know that I am the Lord:

63 That thou mayest remember, and be confounded, and never open thy mouth any more because of thy shame, when I am pacified toward thee for all that thou hast done, saith the Lord God.

CHAPTER 17

1. et factum est verbum Domini ad me dicens

2. fili hominis propone enigma et narra parabolam ad domum Israhel

3. et dices haec dicit Dominus Deus aquila grandis magnarum alarum longo membrorum ductu plena plumis et varietate venit ad Libanum et tulit medullam cedri

4. summitatem frondium eius avellit et transportavit eam in terram Chanaan in urbem negotiatorum posuit illam

5. et tulit de semente terrae et posuit illud in terra pro semine ut firmaret radicem super aquas multas in superficie posuit illud

6. cumque germinasset crevit in vineam latiorem humili statura respicientibus ramis eius ad eam et radices eius sub illa erunt facta est ergo vinea et fructificavit in palmites et emisit propagines

AND the word of the Lord came unto me, saying,

2 Son of man, put forth a riddle, and speak a parable unto the house of Israel;

3 And say, Thus saith the Lord God; A great eagle with great wings, longwinged, full of feathers, which had divers colours, came unto Lebanon, and took the highest branch of the cedar:

4 He cropped off the top of his young twigs, and carried it into a land of traffick; he set it in a city of merchants.

5 He took also of the seed of the land, and planted it in a fruitful field; he placed it by great waters, and set it as a willow tree.

6 And it grew, and became a spreading vine of low stature, whose branches turned toward him, and the roots thereof were under him: so it became a vine, and brought forth branches, and shot forth sprigs.

7 There was also another great eagle with great wings and many feathers: and, behold, this vine did bend her roots toward him, and shot

7. et facta est aquila altera grandis magnis alis multisque plumis et ecce vinea ista quasi mittens radices suas ad eam palmites suos extendit ad illam ut inrigaret eam de areolis germinis sui

8. in terra bona super aquas multas plantata est ut faciat frondes et portet fructum et sit in vineam grandem

9. dic haec dicit Dominus Deus ergone prosperabitur nonne radices eius evellet et fructum eius distringet et siccabit omnes palmites germinis eius et arescet et non in brachio grandi neque in populo multo ut evelleret eam radicitus

10. ecce plantata est ergone prosperabitur nonne cum tetigerit eam ventus urens siccabitur et in areis germinis sui arescet

11. et factum est verbum Domini ad me dicens

12. dic ad domum exasperantem nescitis quid ista significent dic ecce venit rex Babylonis Hierusalem et adsumet

forth her branches toward him, that he might water it by the furrows of her plantation.

8 It was planted in a good soil by great waters, that it might bring forth branches, and that it might bear fruit, that it might be a goodly vine.

9 Say thou, Thus saith the Lord God; Shall it prosper? shall he not pull up the roots thereof, and cut off the fruit thereof, that it wither? it shall wither in all the leaves of her spring, even without great power or many people to pluck it up by the roots thereof.

10 Yea, behold, being planted, shall it prosper? shall it not utterly wither, when the east wind toucheth it? it shall wither in the furrows where it grew.

11 Moreover the word of the Lord came unto me, saying,

12 Say now to the rebellious house, Know ye not what these things mean? tell them, Behold, the king of Babylon is come to Jerusalem, and hath taken the king thereof, and the princes thereof, and led them with him to Babylon;

regem et principes eius et adducet eos ad semet ipsum in Babylonem

13. et tollet de semine regni ferietque cum eo foedus et accipiet ab eo iusiurandum sed et fortes terrae tollet

14. ut sit regnum humile et non elevetur sed custodiat pactum eius et servet illud

15. qui recedens ab eo misit nuntios ad Aegyptum ut daret sibi equos et populum multum numquid prosperabitur vel consequetur salutem qui fecit haec et qui dissolvit pactum numquid effugiet

16. vivo ego dicit Dominus Deus quoniam in loco regis qui constituit eum regem cuius fecit irritum iuramentum et solvit pactum quod habebat cum eo in medio Babylonis morietur

17. et non in exercitu grandi neque in populo multo faciet contra eum Pharao proelium in iactu aggeris et in extructione vallorum ut interficiat animas multas

13 And hath taken of the king's seed, and made a covenant with him, and hath taken an oath of him: he hath also taken the mighty of the land:

14 That the kingdom might be base, that it might not lift itself up, but that by keeping of his covenant it might stand.

15 But he rebelled against him in sending his ambassadors into Egypt, that they might give him horses and much people. Shall he prosper? shall he escape that doeth such things? or shall he break the covenant, and be delivered?

16 As I live, saith the Lord God, surely in the place where the king dwelleth that made him king, whose oath he despised, and whose covenant he brake, even with him in the midst of Babylon he shall die.

17 Neither shall Pharaoh with his mighty army and great company make for him in the war, by casting up mounts, and building forts, to cut off many persons:

18 Seeing he despised the oath by breaking the

18. spreverat enim iuramentum ut solveret foedus et ecce dedit manum suam et cum omnia haec fecerit non effugiet

19. propterea haec dicit Dominus Deus vivo ego quoniam iuramentum quod sprevit et foedus quod praevaricatus est ponam in caput eius

20. et expandam super eum rete meum et conprehendetur sagena mea et adducam eum in Babylonem et iudicabo illum ibi in praevaricatione qua despexit me

21. et omnes profugi eius cum universo agmine gladio cadent residui autem in omnem ventum dispergentur et scietis quia ego Dominus locutus sum

22. haec dicit Dominus Deus et sumam ego de medulla cedri sublimis et ponam de vertice ramorum eius tenerum distringam et plantabo super montem excelsum et eminentem

23. in monte sublimi

covenant, when, lo, he had given his hand, and hath done all these things, he shall not escape.

19 Therefore thus saith the Lord God; As I live, surely mine oath that he hath despised, and my covenant that he hath broken, even it will I recompense upon his own head.

20 And I will spread my net upon him, and he shall be taken in my snare, and I will bring him to Babylon, and will plead with him there for his trespass that he hath trespassed against me.

21 And all his fugitives with all his bands shall fall by the sword, and they that remain shall be scattered toward all winds: and ye shall know that I the Lord have spoken it.

22 Thus saith the Lord God; I will also take of the highest branch of the high cedar, and will set it; I will crop off from the top of his young twigs a tender one, and will plant it upon an high mountain and eminent:

23 In the mountain of the height of Israel will I plant it: and it shall bring forth

Israhel plantabo illud et erumpet in germen et faciet fructum et erit in cedrum magnam et habitabunt sub eo omnes volucres universum volatile sub umbra frondium eius nidificabit

24. et scient omnia ligna regionis quia ego Dominus humiliavi lignum sublime et exaltavi lignum humile et siccavi lignum viride et frondere feci lignum aridum ego Dominus locutus sum et feci

boughs, and bear fruit, and be a goodly cedar: and under it shall dwell all fowl of every wing; in the shadow of the branches thereof shall they dwell.

24 And all the trees of the field shall know that I the Lord have brought down the high tree, have exalted the low tree, have dried up the green tree, and have made the dry tree to flourish: I the Lord have spoken and have done it.

CHAPTER 18

1. et factus est sermo Domini ad me dicens
2. quid est quod inter vos parabolam vertitis in proverbium istud in terra Israhel dicentes patres comederunt uvam acerbam et dentes filiorum obstupescunt
3. vivo ego dicit Dominus Deus si erit vobis ultra parabola haec in proverbium in Israhel
4. ecce omnes animae meae sunt ut anima patris

CHAPTER 18

THE word of the Lord came unto me again, saying,

2 What mean ye, that ye use this proverb concerning the land of Israel, saying, The fathers have eaten sour grapes, and the children's teeth are set on edge?

3 As I live, saith the Lord God, ye shall not have occasion any more to use this proverb in Israel.

4 Behold, all souls are mine; as the soul of the father, so also the soul of the son is

ita et anima filii mea est anima quae peccaverit ipsa morietur

5. et vir si fuerit iustus et fecerit iudicium et iustitiam

6. in montibus non comederit et oculos suos non levaverit ad idola domus Israhel et uxorem proximi sui non violaverit et ad mulierem menstruatam non accesserit

7. et hominem non contristaverit pignus debitori reddiderit per vim nihil rapuerit panem suum esurienti dederit et nudum operuerit vestimento

8. ad usuram non commodaverit et amplius non acceperit ab iniquitate averterit manum suam iudicium verum fecerit inter virum et virum

9. in praeceptis meis ambulaverit et iudicia mea custodierit ut faciat veritatem hic iustus est vita vivet ait Dominus Deus

10. quod si genuerit filium latronem

mine: the soul that sinneth, it shall die.

5 But if a man be just, and do that which is lawful and right,

6 And hath not eaten upon the mountains, neither hath lifted up his eyes to the idols of the house of Israel, neither hath defiled his neighbour's wife, neither hath come near to a menstruous woman,

7 And hath not oppressed any, but hath restored to the debtor his pledge, hath spoiled none by violence, hath given his bread to the hungry, and hath covered the naked with a garment;

8 He that hath not given forth upon usury, neither hath taken any increase, that hath withdrawn his hand from iniquity, hath executed true judgment between man and man,

9 Hath walked in my statutes, and hath kept my judgments, to deal truly; he is just, he shall surely live, saith the Lord God.

10 If he beget a son that is a robber, a shedder of blood, and that doeth the like to any one of these things,

11 And that doeth not any of

effundentem sanguinem et fecerit unum de istis

11. et haec quidem omnia non facientem sed in montibus comedentem et uxorem proximi sui polluentem

12. egenum et pauperem contristantem rapientem rapinas pignus non reddentem et ad idola levantem oculos suos abominationem facientem

13. ad usuram dantem et amplius accipientem numquid vivet non vivet cum universa detestanda haec fecerit morte morietur sanguis eius in ipso erit

14. quod si genuerit filium qui videns omnia peccata patris sui quae fecit timuerit et non fecerit simile eis

15. super montes non comederit et oculos suos non levaverit ad idola domus Israhel et uxorem proximi sui non violaverit

16. et virum non contristaverit pignus non retinuerit et rapinam non rapuerit panem suum esurienti dederit et nudum operuerit

those duties, but even hath eaten upon the mountains, and defiled his neighbour's wife,

12 Hath oppressed the poor and needy, hath spoiled by violence, hath not restored the pledge, and hath lifted up his eyes to the idols, hath committed abomination,

13 Hath given forth upon usury, and hath taken increase: shall he then live? he shall not live: he hath done all these abominations; he shall surely die; his blood shall be upon him.

14 Now, lo, if he beget a son, that seeth all his father's sins which he hath done, and considereth, and doeth not such like,

15 That hath not eaten upon the mountains, neither hath lifted up his eyes to the idols of the house of Israel, hath not defiled his neighbour's wife,

16 Neither hath oppressed any, hath not withholden the pledge, neither hath spoiled by violence, but hath given his bread to the hungry, and hath covered the naked with a garment,

17 That hath taken off his

vestimento

17. a pauperis iniuria averterit manum suam usuram et superabundantiam non acceperit iudicia mea fecerit in praeceptis meis ambulaverit hic non morietur in iniquitate patris sui sed vita vivet

18. pater eius quia calumniatus est et vim fecit fratri et malum operatus est in medio populi sui ecce mortuus est in iniquitate sua

19. et dicitis quare non portavit filius iniquitatem patris videlicet quia filius iudicium et iustitiam operatus est omnia praecepta mea custodivit et fecit illa vita vivet

20. anima quae peccaverit ipsa morietur filius non portabit iniquitatem patris et pater non portabit iniquitatem filii iustitia iusti super eum erit et impietas impii erit super eum

21. si autem impius egerit paenitentiam ab omnibus peccatis suis quae operatus est et custodierit universa praecepta mea et

hand from the poor, that hath not received usury nor increase, hath executed my judgments, hath walked in my statutes; he shall not die for the iniquity of his father, he shall surely live.

18 As for his father, because he cruelly oppressed, spoiled his brother by violence, and did that which is not good among his people, lo, even he shall die in his iniquity.

19 Yet say ye, Why? doth not the son bear the iniquity of the father? When the son hath done that which is lawful and right, and hath kept all my statutes, and hath done them, he shall surely live.

20 The soul that sinneth, it shall die. The son shall not bear the iniquity of the father, neither shall the father bear the iniquity of the son: the righteousness of the righteous shall be upon him, and the wickedness of the wicked shall be upon him.

21 But if the wicked will turn from all his sins that he hath committed, and keep all my statutes, and do that which is lawful and right, he shall surely live, he shall not die.

fecerit iudicium et iustitiam vita vivet non morietur

22. omnium iniquitatum eius quas operatus est non recordabor in iustitia sua quam operatus est vivet

23. numquid voluntatis meae est mors impii dicit Dominus Deus et non ut convertatur a viis suis et vivat

24. si autem averterit se iustus a iustitia sua et fecerit iniquitatem secundum omnes abominationes quas operari solet impius numquid vivet omnes iustitiae eius quas fecerat non recordabuntur in praevaricatione qua praevaricatus est et in peccato suo quod peccavit in ipsis morietur

25. et dixistis non est aequa via Domini audite domus Israhel numquid via mea non est aequa et non magis viae vestrae pravae sunt

26. cum enim averterit se iustus a iustitia sua et fecerit iniquitatem morietur in eis in iniustitia quam operatus

22 All his transgressions that he hath committed, they shall not be mentioned unto him: in his righteousness that he hath done he shall live.

23 Have I any pleasure at all that the wicked should die? saith the Lord God: and not that he should return from his ways, and live?

24 But when the righteous turneth away from his righteousness, and committeth iniquity, and doeth according to all the abominations that the wicked man doeth, shall he live? All his righteousness that he hath done shall not be mentioned: in his trespass that he hath trespassed, and in his sin that he hath sinned, in them shall he die.

25 Yet ye say, The way of the Lord is not equal. Hear now, O house of Israel; Is not my way equal? are not your ways unequal?

26 When a righteous man turneth away from his righteousness, and committeth iniquity, and dieth in them; for his iniquity that he hath done shall he die.

27 Again, when the wicked

est morietur

27. et cum averterit se impius ab impietate sua quam operatus est et fecerit iudicium et iustitiam ipse animam suam vivificabit

28. considerans enim et avertens se ab omnibus iniquitatibus suis quas operatus est vita vivet et non morietur

29. et dicunt filii Israhel non est aequa via Domini numquid viae meae non sunt aequae domus Israhel et non magis viae vestrae pravae

30. idcirco unumquemque iuxta vias suas iudicabo domus Israhel ait Dominus Deus convertimini et agite paenitentiam ab omnibus iniquitatibus vestris et non erit vobis in ruinam iniquitas

31. proicite a vobis omnes praevaricationes vestras in quibus praevaricati estis et facite vobis cor novum et spiritum novum et quare moriemini domus Israhel

32. quia nolo mortem morientis dicit Dominus

man turneth away from his wickedness that he hath committed, and doeth that which is lawful and right, he shall save his soul alive.

28 Because he considereth, and turneth away from all his transgressions that he hath committed, he shall surely live, he shall not die.

29 Yet saith the house of Israel, The way of the Lord is not equal. O house of Israel, are not my ways equal? are not your ways unequal?

30 Therefore I will judge you, O house of Israel, every one according to his ways, saith the Lord God. Repent, and turn yourselves from all your transgressions; so iniquity shall not be your ruin.

31 Cast away from you all your transgressions, whereby ye have transgressed; and make you a new heart and a new spirit: for why will ye die, O house of Israel?

32 For I have no pleasure in the death of him that dieth, saith the Lord God: wherefore turn yourselves, and live ye.

Deus revertimini et vivite

CHAPTER 19

1. et tu adsume planctum super principes Israhel
2. et dices quare mater tua leaena inter leones cubavit in medio leunculorum enutrivit catulos suos
3. et eduxit unum de leunculis suis leo factus est et didicit capere praedam hominemque comedere
4. et audierunt de eo gentes et non absque vulneribus suis ceperunt eum et adduxerunt eum in catenis in terram Aegypti
5. quae cum vidisset quoniam infirmata est et periit expectatio eius tulit unum de leunculis suis leonem constituit eum
6. qui incedebat inter leones et factus est leo didicit praedam capere et homines devorare
7. didicit viduas facere et civitates eorum in desertum adducere et desolata est terra et plenitudo eius a voce

CHAPTER 19

MOREOVER take thou up a lamentation for the princes of Israel,
2 And say, What is thy mother? A lioness: she lay down among lions, she nourished her whelps among young lions.
3 And she brought up one of her whelps: it became a young lion, and it learned to catch the prey; it devoured men.
4 The nations also heard of him; he was taken in their pit, and they brought him with chains unto the land of Egypt.
5 Now when she saw that she had waited, and her hope was lost, then she took another of her whelps, and made him a young lion.
6 And he went up and down among the lions, he became a young lion, and learned to catch the prey, and devoured men.
7 And he knew their desolate palaces, and he laid waste their cities; and the land was

rugitus illius

8. et convenerunt adversum eum gentes undique de provinciis et expanderunt super eum rete suum in vulneribus earum captus est

9. et miserunt eum in caveam in catenis adduxerunt eum ad regem Babylonis miseruntque eum in carcerem ne audiretur vox eius ultra super montes Israhel

10. mater tua quasi vinea in sanguine tuo super aquam plantata fructus eius et frondes eius creverunt ex aquis multis

11. et factae sunt ei virgae solidae in sceptra dominantium et exaltata est statura eius inter frondes et vidit altitudinem suam in multitudine palmitum suorum

12. et evulsa est in ira in terramque proiecta et ventus urens siccavit fructum eius marcuerunt et arefactae sunt virgae roboris eius ignis comedit eam

13. et nunc transplantata est in desertum in terra

desolate, and the fulness thereof, by the noise of his roaring.

8 Then the nations set against him on every side from the provinces, and spread their net over him: he was taken in their pit.

9 And they put him in ward in chains, and brought him to the king of Babylon: they brought him into holds, that his voice should no more be heard upon the mountains of Israel.

10 Thy mother is like a vine in thy blood, planted by the waters: she was fruitful and full of branches by reason of many waters.

11 And she had strong rods for the sceptres of them that bare rule, and her stature was exalted among the thick branches, and she appeared in her height with the multitude of her branches.

12 But she was plucked up in fury, she was cast down to the ground, and the east wind dried up her fruit: her strong rods were broken and withered; the fire consumed them.

13 And now she is planted in the wilderness, in a dry and

invia et sitienti

14. et egressus est ignis de virga ramorum eius qui fructum eius comedit et non fuit in ea virga fortis sceptrum dominantium planctus est et erit in planctum

thirsty ground.

14 And fire is gone out of a rod of her branches, which hath devoured her fruit, so that she hath no strong rod to be a sceptre to rule. This is a lamentation, and shall be for a lamentation.

CHAPTER 20

CHAPTER 20

1. et factum est in anno septimo in quinto mense in decima mensis venerunt viri de senioribus Israhel ut interrogarent Dominum et sederunt coram me

2. et factus est sermo Domini ad me dicens

3. fili hominis loquere senioribus Israhel et dices ad eos haec dicit Dominus Deus num ad interrogandum me vos venistis vivo ego quia non respondebo vobis ait Dominus Deus

4. si iudicas eos si iudicas fili hominis abominationes patrum eorum ostende eis

5. et dices ad eos haec dicit Dominus Deus in die qua elegi Israhel et

AND it came to pass in the seventh year, in the fifth month, the tenth day of the month, that certain of the elders of Israel came to inquire of the Lord, and sat before me.

2 Then came the word of the Lord unto me, saying,

3 Son of man, speak unto the elders of Israel, and say unto them, Thus saith the Lord God; Are ye come to inquire of me? As I live, saith the Lord God, I will not be inquired of by you.

4 Wilt thou judge them, son of man, wilt thou judge them? cause them to know the abominations of their fathers:

5 And say unto them, Thus saith the Lord God; In the day when I chose Israel, and

levavi manum meam pro stirpe domus Iacob et apparui eis in terra Aegypti et levavi manum meam pro eis dicens ego Dominus Deus vester

6. in die illa levavi manum meam pro eis ut educerem eos de terra Aegypti in terram quam provideram eis fluentem lacte et melle quae est egregia inter omnes terras

7. et dixi ad eos unusquisque offensiones oculorum suorum abiciat et in idolis Aegypti nolite pollui ego Dominus Deus vester

8. et inritaverunt me nolueruntque audire unusquisque abominationes oculorum suorum non proiecit nec idola Aegypti reliquerunt et dixi ut effunderem indignationem meam super eos et implerem iram meam in eis in medio terrae Aegypti

9. et feci propter nomen meum ut non violaretur coram gentibus in quarum medio erant et inter quas apparui eis ut educerem eos de terra

lifted up mine hand unto the seed of the house of Jacob, and made myself known unto them in the land of Egypt, when I lifted up mine hand unto them, saying, I am the Lord your God;

6 In the day that I lifted up mine hand unto them, to bring them forth of the land of Egypt into a land that I had espied for them, flowing with milk and honey, which is the glory of all lands:

7 Then said I unto them, Cast ye away every man the abominations of his eyes, and defile not yourselves with the idols of Egypt: I am the Lord your God.

8 But they rebelled against me, and would not hearken unto me: they did not every man cast away the abominations of their eyes, neither did they forsake the idols of Egypt: then I said, I will pour out my fury upon them, to accomplish my anger against them in the midst of the land of Egypt.

9 But I wrought for my name's sake, that it should not be polluted before the heathen, among whom they were, in whose sight I made

Aegypti

10. eieci ergo eos de terra Aegypti et eduxi in desertum

11. et dedi eis praecepta mea et iudicia mea ostendi eis quae faciat homo et vivat in eis

12. insuper et sabbata mea dedi eis ut esset signum inter me et eos et scirent quia ego Dominus sanctificans eos

13. et inritaverunt me domus Israhel in deserto in praeceptis meis non ambulaverunt et iudicia mea proiecerunt quae faciens homo vivet in eis et sabbata mea violaverunt vehementer dixi ergo ut effunderem furorem meum super eos in deserto et consumerem eos

14. et feci propter nomen meum ne violaretur coram gentibus de quibus eieci eos in conspectu earum

15. ego igitur levavi manum meam super eos in deserto ne inducerem eos in terram quam dedi eis fluentem lacte et melle praecipuam

myself known unto them, in bringing them forth out of the land of Egypt.

10 Wherefore I caused them to go forth out of the land of Egypt, and brought them into the wilderness.

11 And I gave them my statutes, and shewed them my judgments, which if a man do, he shall even live in them.

12 Moreover also I gave them my sabbaths, to be a sign between me and them, that they might know that I am the Lord that sanctify them.

13 But the house of Israel rebelled against me in the wilderness: they walked not in my statutes, and they despised my judgments, which if a man do, he shall even live in them; and my sabbaths they greatly polluted: then I said, I would pour out my fury upon them in the wilderness, to consume them.

14 But I wrought for my name's sake, that it should not be polluted before the heathen, in whose sight I brought them out.

15 Yet also I lifted up my

terrarum omnium

16. quia iudicia mea proiecerunt et in praeceptis meis non ambulaverunt et sabbata mea violaverunt post idola enim cor eorum gradiebatur

17. et pepercit oculus meus super eos ut non interficerem eos nec consumpsi eos in deserto

18. dixi autem ad filios eorum in solitudine in praeceptis patrum vestrorum nolite incedere nec iudicia eorum custodiatis nec in idolis eorum polluamini

19. ego Dominus Deus vester in praeceptis meis ambulate et iudicia mea custodite et facite ea

20. et sabbata mea sanctificate ut sit signum inter me et vos et sciatur quia ego Dominus Deus vester

21. et exacerbaverunt me filii in praeceptis meis non ambulaverunt et iudicia mea non custodierunt ut facerent ea quae cum fecerit homo vivet in eis et sabbata mea violaverunt et

hand unto them in the wilderness, that I would not bring them into the land which I had given them, flowing with milk and honey, which is the glory of all lands;

16 Because they despised my judgments, and walked not in my statutes, but polluted my sabbaths: for their heart went after their idols.

17 Nevertheless mine eye spared them from destroying them, neither did I make an end of them in the wilderness.

18 But I said unto their children in the wilderness, Walk ye not in the statutes of your fathers, neither observe their judgments, nor defile yourselves with their idols:

19 I am the Lord your God; walk in my statutes, and keep my judgments, and do them;

20 And hallow my sabbaths; and they shall be a sign between me and you, that ye may know that I am the Lord your God.

21 Notwithstanding the children rebelled against me: they walked not in my statutes, neither kept my judgments to do them, which

comminatus sum ut effunderem furorem meum super eos et implerem iram meam in eis in deserto

22. averti autem manum meam et feci propter nomen meum ut non violaretur coram gentibus de quibus eieci eos in oculis earum

23. iterum levavi manum meam in eos in solitudine ut dispergerem illos in nationes et ventilarem in terras

24. eo quod iudicia mea non fecissent et praecepta mea reprobassent et sabbata mea violassent et post idola patrum suorum fuissent oculi eorum

25. ergo et ego dedi eis praecepta non bona et iudicia in quibus non vivent

26. et pollui eos in muneribus suis cum offerrent omne quod aperit vulvam propter delicta sua et scient quia ego Dominus

27. quam ob rem loquere ad domum Israhel fili hominis et dices ad eos haec dicit Dominus Deus

if a man do, he shall even live in them; they polluted my sabbaths: then I said, I would pour out my fury upon them, to accomplish my anger against them in the wilderness.

22 Nevertheless I withdrew mine hand, and wrought for my name's sake, that it should not be polluted in the sight of the heathen, in whose sight I brought them forth.

23 I lifted up mine hand unto them also in the wilderness, that I would scatter them among the heathen, and disperse them through the countries;

24 Because they had not executed my judgments, but had despised my statutes, and had polluted my sabbaths, and their eyes were after their fathers' idols.

25 Wherefore I gave them also statutes that were not good, and judgments whereby they should not live;

26 And I polluted them in their own gifts, in that they caused to pass through the fire all that openeth the womb, that I might make them desolate, to the end that

adhuc et in hoc blasphemaverunt me patres vestri cum sprevissent me contemnentes

28. et induxissem eos in terram super quam levavi manum meam ut darem eis viderunt omnem collem excelsum et omne lignum nemorosum et immolaverunt ibi victimas suas et dederunt ibi inritationem oblationis suae et posuerunt ibi odorem suavitatis suae et libaverunt libationes suas

29. et dixi ad eos quid est excelsum ad quod vos ingredimini et vocatum est nomen eius Excelsum usque ad hanc diem

30. propterea dic ad domum Israhel haec dicit Dominus Deus certe in via patrum vestrorum vos polluimini et post offendicula eorum vos fornicamini

31. et in oblatione donorum vestrorum cum transducitis filios vestros per ignem vos polluimini in omnibus idolis vestris usque hodie et ego respondebo vobis domus

they might know that I am the Lord.

27 Therefore, son of man, speak unto the house of Israel, and say unto them, Thus saith the Lord God; Yet in this your fathers have blasphemed me, in that they have committed a trespass against me.

28 For when I had brought them into the land, for the which I lifted up mine hand to give it to them, then they saw every high hill, and all the thick trees, and they offered there their sacrifices, and there they presented the provocation of their offering: there also they made their sweet savour, and poured out there their drink offerings.

29 Then I said unto them, What is the high place whereunto ye go? And the name thereof is called Bamah unto this day.

30 Wherefore say unto the house of Israel, Thus saith the Lord God; Are ye polluted after the manner of your fathers? and commit ye whoredom after their abominations?

31 For when ye offer your gifts, when ye make your

Israhel vivo ego dicit Dominus Deus quia non respondebo vobis

32. neque cogitatio mentis vestrae fiet dicentium erimus sicut gentes et sicut cognationes terrae ut colamus ligna et lapides

33. vivo ego dicit Dominus Deus quoniam in manu forti et brachio extento et in furore effuso regnabo super vos

34. et educam vos de populis et congregabo vos de terris in quibus dispersi estis in manu valida et brachio extento et in furore effuso regnabo super vos

35. et adducam vos in desertum populorum et iudicabor vobiscum ibi facie ad faciem

36. sicut iudicio contendi adversum patres vestros in deserto terrae Aegypti sic iudicabo vos dicit Dominus Deus

37. et subiciam vos sceptro meo et inducam vos in vinculis foederis

38. et eligam de vobis transgressores et impios et de terra incolatus

sons to pass through the fire, ye pollute yourselves with all your idols, even unto this day: and shall I be inquired of by you, O house of Israel? As I live, saith the Lord God, I will not be inquired of by you.

32 And that which cometh into your mind shall not be at all, that ye say, We will be as the heathen, as the families of the countries, to serve wood and stone.

33 As I live, saith the Lord God, surely with a mighty hand, and with a stretched out arm, and with fury poured out, will I rule over you:

34 And I will bring you out from the people, and will gather you out of the countries wherein ye are scattered, with a mighty hand, and with a stretched out arm, and with fury poured out.

35 And I will bring you into the wilderness of the people, and there will I plead with you face to face.

36 Like as I pleaded with your fathers in the wilderness of the land of Egypt, so will I plead with you, saith the

eorum educam eos et terram Israhel non ingredientur et scietis quia ego Dominus

39. et vos domus Israhel haec dicit Dominus Deus singuli post idola vestra ambulate et servite eis quod si et in hoc non audieritis me et nomen meum sanctum pollueritis ultra in muneribus vestris et in idolis vestris

40. in monte sancto meo in monte excelso Israhel ait Dominus Deus ibi serviet mihi omnis domus Israhel omnes inquam in terra in qua placebunt mihi et ibi quaeram primitias vestras et initium decimarum vestrarum in omnibus sanctificationibus vestris

41. in odorem suavitatis suscipiam vos cum eduxero vos de populis et congregavero vos de terris in quas dispersi estis et sanctificabor in vobis in oculis nationum

42. et scietis quia ego Dominus cum induxero vos ad terram Israhel in terram pro qua levavi manum meam ut darem

Lord God.

37 And I will cause you to pass under the rod, and I will bring you into the bond of the covenant:

38 And I will purge out from among you the rebels, and them that transgress against me: I will bring them forth out of the country where they sojourn, and they shall not enter into the land of Israel: and ye shall know that I am the Lord.

39 As for you, O house of Israel, thus saith the Lord God; Go ye, serve ye every one his idols, and hereafter also, if ye will not hearken unto me: but pollute ye my holy name no more with your gifts, and with your idols.

40 For in mine holy mountain, in the mountain of the height of Israel, saith the Lord God, there shall all the house of Israel, all of them in the land, serve me: there will I accept them, and there will I require your offerings, and the firstfruits of your oblations, with all your holy things.

41 I will accept you with your sweet savour, when I bring you out from the

eam patribus vestris

43. et recordabimini ibi viarum vestrarum et omnium scelerum vestrorum quibus polluti estis in eis et displicebitis vobis in conspectu vestro in omnibus malitiis vestris quas fecistis

44. et scietis quia ego Dominus cum benefecero vobis propter nomen meum non secundum vias vestras malas neque secundum scelera vestra pessima domus Israhel ait Dominus Deus

45. et factus est sermo Domini ad me dicens

46. fili hominis pone faciem tuam contra viam austri et stilla ad africum et propheta ad saltum agri meridiani

47. et dices saltui meridiano audi verbum Domini haec dicit Dominus Deus ecce ego succendam in te ignem et conburam in te omne lignum viride et omne lignum aridum non extinguetur flamma succensionis et conburetur in ea omnis facies ab austro usque ad

people, and gather you out of the countries wherein ye have been scattered; and I will be sanctified in you before the heathen.

42 And ye shall know that I am the Lord, when I shall bring you into the land of Israel, into the country for the which I lifted up mine hand to give it to your fathers.

43 And there shall ye remember your ways, and all your doings, wherein ye have been defiled; and ye shall lothe yourselves in your own sight for all your evils that ye have committed.

44 And ye shall know that I am the Lord, when I have wrought with you for my name's sake, not according to your wicked ways, nor according to your corrupt doings, O ye house of Israel, saith the Lord God.

45 Moreover the word of the Lord came unto me, saying,

46 Son of man, set thy face toward the south, and drop thy word toward the south, and prophesy against the forest of the south field;

47 And say to the forest of the south, Hear the word of

aquilonem

48. et videbit universa caro quia ego Dominus succendi eam nec extinguetur

49. et dixi ha ha ha Domine Deus ipsi dicunt de me numquid non per parabolas loquitur iste

the Lord; Thus saith the Lord God; Behold, I will kindle a fire in thee, and it shall devour every green tree in thee, and every dry tree: the flaming flame shall not be quenched, and all faces from the south to the north shall be burned therein.

48 And all flesh shall see that I the Lord have kindled it: it shall not be quenched.

49 Then said I, Ah Lord God! they say of me, Doth he not speak parables?

CHAPTER 21

1. et factus est sermo Domini ad me dicens

2. fili hominis pone faciem tuam ad Hierusalem et stilla ad sanctuaria et propheta contra humum Israhel

3. et dices terrae Israhel haec dicit Dominus Deus ecce ego ad te et eiciam gladium meum de vagina sua et occidam in te iustum et impium

4. pro eo autem quod occidi in te iustum et impium idcirco egredietur gladius meus de vagina

CHAPTER 21

AND the word of the Lord came unto me, saying,

2 Son of man, set thy face toward Jerusalem, and drop thy word toward the holy places, and prophesy against the land of Israel,

3 And say to the land of Israel, Thus saith the Lord; Behold, I am against thee, and will draw forth my sword out of his sheath, and will cut off from thee the righteous and the wicked.

4 Seeing then that I will cut off from thee the righteous and the wicked, therefore

112

sua ad omnem carnem ab austro ad aquilonem

5. ut sciat omnis caro quia ego Dominus eduxi gladium meum de vagina sua inrevocabilem

6. et tu fili hominis ingemesce in contritione lumborum et in amaritudinibus

ingemesce coram eis

7. cumque dixerint ad te quare tu gemis dices pro auditu quia venit et tabescet omne cor et dissolventur universae manus et infirmabitur omnis spiritus et per cuncta genua fluent aquae ecce venit et fiet ait Dominus Deus

8. et factus est sermo Domini ad me dicens

9. fili hominis propheta et dices haec dicit Dominus Deus loquere gladius gladius exacutus est et limatus

10. ut caedat victimas exacutus est ut splendeat limatus est qui moves sceptrum filii mei succidisti omne lignum

11. et dedi eum ad levigandum ut teneatur manu iste exacutus est

shall my sword go forth out of his sheath against all flesh from the south to the north:

5 That all flesh may know that I the Lord have drawn forth my sword out of his sheath: it shall not return any more.

6 Sigh therefore, thou son of man, with the breaking of thy loins; and with bitterness sigh before their eyes.

7 And it shall be, when they say unto thee, Wherefore sighest thou? that thou shalt answer, For the tidings; because it cometh: and every heart shall melt, and all hands shall be feeble, and every spirit shall faint, and all knees shall be weak as water: behold, it cometh, and shall be brought to pass, saith the Lord God.

8 Again the word of the Lord came unto me, saying,

9 Son of man, prophesy, and say, Thus saith the Lord; Say, A sword, a sword is sharpened, and also furbished:

10 It is sharpened to make a sore slaughter; it is furbished that it may glitter: should we then make mirth? it contemneth the rod of my

gladius et iste limatus ut sit in manu interficientis

12. clama et ulula fili hominis quia hic factus est in populo meo hic in cunctis ducibus Israhel qui fugerant gladio traditi sunt cum populo meo idcirco plaude super femur

13. quia probatus est et hoc cum sceptrum subverterit et non erit dicit Dominus Deus

14. tu ergo fili hominis propheta et percute manu ad manum et duplicetur gladius ac triplicetur gladius interfectorum hic est gladius occisionis magnae qui obstupescere eos facit

15. et corde tabescere et multiplicat ruinas in omnibus portis eorum dedi conturbationem gladii acuti et limati ad fulgendum amicti ad caedem

16. exacuere vade ad dextram sive ad sinistram quocumque faciei tuae est appetitus

17. quin et ego plaudam manu ad manum et implebo indignationem

son, as every tree.

11 And he hath given it to be furbished, that it may be handled: this sword is sharpened, and it is furbished, to give it into the hand of the slayer.

12 Cry and howl, son of man: for it shall be upon my people, it shall be upon all the princes of Israel: terrors by reason of the sword shall be upon my people: smite therefore upon thy thigh.

13 Because it is a trial, and what if the sword contemn even the rod? it shall be no more, saith the Lord God.

14 Thou therefore, son of man, prophesy, and smite thine hands together, and let the sword be doubled the third time, the sword of the slain: it is the sword of the great men that are slain, which entereth into their privy chambers.

15 I have set the point of the sword against all their gates, that their heart may faint, and their ruins be multiplied: ah! it is made bright, it is wrapped up for the slaughter.

16 Go thee one way or other, either on the right hand, or on the left, whithersoever thy

meam ego Dominus locutus sum

18. et factus est sermo Domini ad me dicens

19. et tu fili hominis pone tibi duas vias ut veniat gladius regis Babylonis de terra una egredientur ambo et manu capiet coniecturam in capite viae civitatis coniciet

20. viam pones ut veniat gladius ad Rabbath filiorum Ammon et ad Iudam in Hierusalem munitissimam

21. stetit enim rex Babylonis in bivio in capite duarum viarum divinationem quaerens commiscens sagittas interrogavit idola exta consuluit

22. ad dextram eius facta est divinatio super Hierusalem ut ponat arietes ut aperiat os in caede ut elevet vocem in ululatu ut ponat arietes contra portas ut conportet aggerem ut aedificet munitiones

23. eritque quasi consulens frustra oraculum in oculis eorum et sabbatorum otium

face is set.

17 I will also smite mine hands together, and I will cause my fury to rest: I the Lord have said it.

18 The word of the Lord came unto me again, saying,

19 Also, thou son of man, appoint thee two ways, that the sword of the king of Babylon may come: both twain shall come forth out of one land: and choose thou a place, choose it at the head of the way to the city.

20 Appoint a way, that the sword may come to Rabbath of the Ammonites, and to Judah in Jerusalem the defenced.

21 For the king of Babylon stood at the parting of the way, at the head of the two ways, to use divination: he made his arrows bright, he consulted with images, he looked in the liver.

22 At his right hand was the divination for Jerusalem, to appoint captains, to open the mouth in the slaughter, to lift up the voice with shouting, to appoint battering rams against the gates, to cast a mount, and to build a fort.

23 And it shall be unto them

imitans ipse autem recordabitur iniquitatis ad capiendum

24. idcirco haec dicit Dominus Deus pro eo quod recordati estis iniquitatis vestrae et revelastis praevaricationes vestras et apparuerunt peccata vestra in omnibus cogitationibus vestris pro eo inquam quod recordati estis manu capiemini

25. tu autem profane impie dux Israhel cuius venit dies in tempore iniquitatis praefinita

26. haec dicit Dominus Deus aufer cidarim tolle coronam nonne haec est quae humilem sublevavit et sublimem humiliavit

27. iniquitatem iniquitatem iniquitatem ponam eam et hoc nunc factum est donec veniret cuius est iudicium et tradam ei

28. et tu fili hominis propheta et dic haec dicit Dominus Deus ad filios Ammon et ad obprobrium eorum et dices mucro mucro evaginate ad occidendum limate ut

as a false divination in their sight, to them that have sworn oaths: but he will call to remembrance the iniquity, that they may be taken.

24 Therefore thus saith the Lord God; Because ye have made your iniquity to be remembered, in that your transgressions are discovered, so that in all your doings your sins do appear; because, I say, that ye are come to remembrance, ye shall be taken with the hand.

25 And thou, profane wicked prince of Israel, whose day is come, when iniquity shall have an end,

26 Thus saith the Lord God; Remove the diadem, and take off the crown: this shall not be the same: exalt him that is low, and abase him that is high.

27 I will overturn, overturn, overturn, it: and it shall be no more, until he come whose right it is; and I will give it him.

28 And thou, son of man, prophesy and say, Thus saith the Lord God concerning the Ammonites, and concerning their reproach; even say thou, The sword, the sword is

interficias et fulgeas

29. cum tibi viderentur vana et divinarentur mendacia ut dareris super colla vulneratorum impiorum quorum venit dies in tempore iniquitatis praefinita

30. revertere ad vaginam tuam in loco in quo creatus es in terra nativitatis tuae iudicabo te

31. et effundam super te indignationem meam in igne furoris mei sufflabo in te daboque te in manus hominum insipientium et fabricantium interitum

32. igni eris cibus sanguis tuus erit in medio terrae oblivioni traderis quia ego Dominus locutus sum

drawn: for the slaughter it is furbished, to consume because of the glittering:

29 Whiles they see vanity unto thee, whiles they divine a lie unto thee, to bring thee upon the necks of them that are slain, of the wicked, whose day is come, when their iniquity shall have an end.

30 Shall I cause it to return into his sheath? I will judge thee in the place where thou wast created, in the land of thy nativity.

31 And I will pour out mine indignation upon thee, I will blow against thee in the fire of my wrath, and deliver thee into the hand of brutish men, and skilful to destroy.

32 Thou shalt be for fuel to the fire; thy blood shall be in the midst of the land; thou shalt be no more remembered: for I the Lord have spoken it.

CHAPTER 22

CHAPTER 22

1. et factum est verbum Domini ad me dicens

2. et tu fili hominis num iudicas num iudicas

MOREOVER the word of the Lord came unto me, saying,

2 Now, thou son of man, wilt

117

civitatem sanguinum

3. et ostendes ei omnes abominationes suas et dices haec dicit Dominus Deus civitas effundens sanguinem in medio sui ut veniat tempus eius et quae fecit idola contra semet ipsam ut pollueretur

4. in sanguine tuo qui a te effusus est deliquisti et in idolis tuis quae fecisti polluta es et adpropinquare fecisti dies tuos et adduxisti tempus annorum tuorum propterea dedi te obprobrium gentibus et inrisionem universis terris

5. quae iuxta sunt et quae procul a te triumphabunt de te sordida nobilis grandis interitu

6. ecce principes Israhel singuli in brachio suo fuerunt in te ad effundendum sanguinem

7. patrem et matrem contumeliis adfecerunt in te advenam calumniati sunt in medio tui pupillum et viduam contristaverunt apud te

8. sanctuaria mea sprevistis et sabbata mea

thou judge, wilt thou judge the bloody city? yea, thou shalt shew her all her abominations.

3 Then say thou, Thus saith the Lord God, The city sheddeth blood in the midst of it, that her time may come, and maketh idols against herself to defile herself.

4 Thou art become guilty in thy blood that thou hast shed; and hast defiled thyself in thine idols which thou hast made; and thou hast caused thy days to draw near, and art come even unto thy years: therefore have I made thee a reproach unto the heathen, and a mocking to all countries.

5 Those that be near, and those that be far from thee, shall mock thee, which art infamous and much vexed.

6 Behold, the princes of Israel, every one were in thee to their power to shed blood.

7 In thee have they set light by father and mother: in the midst of thee have they dealt by oppression with the stranger: in thee have they vexed the fatherless and the widow.

8 Thou hast despised mine

polluistis

9. viri detractores fuerunt in te ad effundendum sanguinem et super montes comederunt in te scelus operati sunt in medio tui

10. verecundiora patris discoperuerunt in te inmunditiam menstruatae humiliaverunt in te

11. et unusquisque in uxorem proximi sui operatus est abominationem et socer nurum suam polluit nefarie frater sororem suam filiam patris sui oppressit in te

12. munera acceperunt apud te ad effundendum sanguinem usuram et superabundantiam accepisti et avare proximos tuos calumniabaris meique oblita es ait Dominus Deus

13. ecce conplosi manus meas super avaritiam tuam quam fecisti et super sanguinem qui effusus est in medio tui

14. numquid sustinebit cor tuum aut praevalebunt manus tuae

holy things, and hast profaned my sabbaths.

9 In thee are men that carry tales to shed blood: and in thee they eat upon the mountains: in the midst of thee they commit lewdness.

10 In thee have they discovered their fathers' nakedness: in thee have they humbled her that was set apart for pollution.

11 And one hath committed abomination with his neighbour's wife; and another hath lewdly defiled his daughter in law; and another in thee hath humbled his sister, his father's daughter.

12 In thee have they taken gifts to shed blood; thou hast taken usury and increase, and thou hast greedily gained of thy neighbours by extortion, and hast forgotten me, saith the Lord God.

13 Behold, therefore I have smitten mine hand at thy dishonest gain which thou hast made, and at thy blood which hath been in the midst of thee.

14 Can thine heart endure, or can thine hands be strong, in the days that I shall deal with

in diebus quos ego faciam tibi ego Dominus locutus sum et faciam

15. et dispergam te in nationes et ventilabo te in terras et deficere faciam inmunditiam tuam a te

16. et possidebo te in conspectu gentium et scies quia ego Dominus

17. et factum est verbum Domini ad me dicens

18. fili hominis versa est mihi domus Israhel in scoriam omnes isti aes et stagnum et ferrum et plumbum in medio fornacis scoria argenti facti sunt

19. propterea haec dicit Dominus Deus eo quod versi estis omnes in scoriam propterea ecce ego congregabo vos in medium Hierusalem

20. congregatione argenti et aeris et ferri et stagni et plumbi in medium fornacis ut succendam in eam ignem ad conflandum sic congregabo in furore meo et in ira mea et requiescam et conflabo vos

21. et congregabo vos et

thee? I the Lord have spoken it, and will do it.

15 And I will scatter thee among the heathen, and disperse thee in the countries, and will consume thy filthiness out of thee.

16 And thou shalt take thine inheritance in thyself in the sight of the heathen, and thou shalt know that I am the Lord.

17 And the word of the Lord came unto me, saying,

18 Son of man, the house of Israel is to me become dross: all they are brass, and tin, and iron, and lead, in the midst of the furnace; they are even the dross of silver.

19 Therefore thus saith the Lord God; Because ye are all become dross, behold, therefore I will gather you into the midst of Jerusalem.

20 As they gather silver, and brass, and iron, and lead, and tin, into the midst of the furnace, to blow the fire upon it, to melt it; so will I gather you in mine anger and in my fury, and I will leave you there, and melt you.

21 Yea, I will gather you, and blow upon you in the fire of my wrath, and ye shall be

succendam vos in igne furoris mei et conflabimini in medio eius

22. ut conflatur argentum in medio fornacis sic eritis in medio eius et scietis quia ego Dominus effuderim indignationem meam super vos

23. et factum est verbum Domini ad me dicens

24. fili hominis dic ei tu es terra inmunda et non conpluta in die furoris

25. coniuratio prophetarum in medio eius sicut leo rugiens capiensque praedam animam devoraverunt opes et pretium acceperunt viduas eius multiplicaverunt in medio illius

26. sacerdotes eius contempserunt legem meam et polluerunt sanctuaria mea inter sanctum et profanum non habuere distantiam et inter pollutum et mundum non intellexerunt et a sabbatis meis averterunt oculos suos et coinquinabar in medio eorum

melted in the midst thereof.

22 As silver is melted in the midst of the furnace, so shall ye be melted in the midst thereof; and ye shall know that I the Lord have poured out my fury upon you.

23 And the word of the Lord came unto me, saying,

24 Son of man, say unto her, Thou art the land that is not cleansed, nor rained upon in the day of indignation.

25 There is a conspiracy of her prophets in the midst thereof, like a roaring lion ravening the prey; they have devoured souls; they have taken the treasure and precious things; they have made her many widows in the midst thereof.

26 Her priests have violated my law, and have profaned mine holy things: they have put no difference between the holy and profane, neither have they shewed difference between the unclean and the clean, and have hid their eyes from my sabbaths, and I am profaned among them.

27 Her princes in the midst thereof are like wolves ravening the prey, to shed blood, and to destroy souls,

27. principes eius in medio illius quasi lupi rapientes praedam ad effundendum sanguinem et perdendas animas et avare sectanda lucra

28. prophetae autem eius liniebant eos absque temperamento videntes vana et divinantes eis mendacium dicentes haec dicit Dominus Deus cum Dominus non sit locutus

29. populi terrae calumniabantur calumniam et rapiebant violenter egenum et pauperem adfligebant et advenam opprimebant calumnia absque iudicio

30. et quaesivi de eis virum qui interponeret sepem et staret oppositus contra me pro terra ne dissiparem eam et non inveni

31. et effudi super eos indignationem meam in igne irae meae consumpsi eos viam eorum in caput eorum reddidi ait Dominus Deus

to get dishonest gain.

28 And her prophets have daubed them with untempered morter, seeing vanity, and divining lies unto them, saying, Thus saith the Lord God, when the Lord hath not spoken.

29 The people of the land have used oppression, and exercised robbery, and have vexed the poor and needy: yea, they have oppressed the stranger wrongfully.

30 And I sought for a man among them, that should make up the hedge, and stand in the gap before me for the land, that I should not destroy it: but I found none.

31 Therefore have I poured out mine indignation upon them; I have consumed them with the fire of my wrath: their own way have I recompensed upon their heads, saith the Lord God.

1. et factus est sermo Domini ad me dicens

2. fili hominis duae mulieres filiae matris unius fuerunt

3. et fornicatae sunt in Aegypto in adulescentia sua fornicatae sunt ibi subacta sunt ubera earum et fractae sunt mammae pubertatis earum

4. nomina autem earum Oolla maior et Ooliba soror eius et habui eas et pepererunt filios et filias porro earum nomina Samaria Oolla et Hierusalem Ooliba

5. fornicata est igitur Oolla super me et insanivit in amatores suos in Assyrios propinquantes

6. vestitos hyacintho principes et magistratus iuvenes cupidinis universos equites ascensores equorum

7. et dedit fornicationes suas super eos electos filios Assyriorum universos et in omnibus in quos insanivit in inmunditiis eorum polluta est

THE word of the Lord came again unto me, saying,

2 Son of man, there were two women, the daughters of one mother:

3 And they committed whoredoms in Egypt; they committed whoredoms in their youth: there were their breasts pressed, and there they bruised the teats of their virginity.

4 And the names of them were Aholah the elder, and Aholibah her sister: and they were mine, and they bare sons and daughters. Thus were their names; Samaria is Aholah, and Jerusalem Aholibah.

5 And Aholah played the harlot when she was mine; and she doted on her lovers, on the Assyrians her neighbours,

6 Which were clothed with blue, captains and rulers, all of them desirable young men, horsemen riding upon horses.

7 Thus she committed her whoredoms with them, with all them that were the chosen men of Assyria, and with all

8. insuper et fornicationes suas quas habuerat in Aegypto non reliquit nam et illi dormierant cum ea in adulescentia eius et illi confregerant ubera pubertatis eius et effuderant fornicationem suam super eam

9. propterea tradidi eam in manu amatorum suorum in manus filiorum Assur super quorum insanivit libidinem

10. ipsi discoperuerunt ignominiam eius filios et filias illius tulerunt et ipsam occiderunt gladio et factae sunt famosae mulieres et iudicia perpetrarunt in ea

11. quod cum vidisset soror eius Ooliba plus quam illa insanivit libidine et fornicationem suam super fornicationem sororis suae

12. ad filios Assyriorum praebuit inpudenter ducibus et magistratibus ad se venientibus indutis veste varia equitibus qui vectabantur equis et adulescentibus forma cunctis egregia

13. et vidi quod polluta

on whom she doted: with all their idols she defiled herself. 8 Neither left she her whoredoms brought from Egypt: for in her youth they lay with her, and they bruised the breasts of her virginity, and poured their whoredom upon her.

9 Wherefore I have delivered her into the hand of her lovers, into the hand of the Assyrians, upon whom she doted.

10 These discovered her nakedness: they took her sons and her daughters, and slew her with the sword: and she became famous among women; for they had executed judgment upon her.

11 And when her sister Aholibah saw this, she was more corrupt in her inordinate love than she, and in her whoredoms more than her sister in her whoredoms.

12 She doted upon the Assyrians her neighbours, captains and rulers clothed most gorgeously, horsemen riding upon horses, all of them desirable young men.

13 Then I saw that she was defiled, that they took both one way,

esset via una ambarum

14. et auxit fornicationes suas cumque vidisset viros depictos in pariete imagines Chaldeorum expressas coloribus

15. et accinctos balteis renes et tiaras tinctas in capitibus eorum formam ducum omnium similitudinem filiorum Babylonis terraeque Chaldeorum in qua orti sunt

16. et insanivit super eos concupiscentia oculorum suorum et misit nuntios ad eos in Chaldeam

17. cumque venissent ad eam filii Babylonis ad cubile mammarum polluerunt eam stupris suis et polluta est ab eis et saturata est anima eius ab illis

18. denudavit quoque fornicationes suas et discoperuit ignominiam suam et recessit anima mea ab ea sicut recesserat anima mea a sorore eius

19. multiplicavit enim fornicationes suas recordans dies adulescentiae suae quibus fornicata est in terra

14 And that she increased her whoredoms: for when she saw men pourtrayed upon the wall, the images of the Chaldeans pourtrayed with vermilion,

15 Girded with girdles upon their loins, exceeding in dyed attire upon their heads, all of them princes to look to, after the manner of the Babylonians of Chaldea, the land of their nativity:

16 And as soon as she saw them with her eyes, she doted upon them, and sent messengers unto them into Chaldea.

17 And the Babylonians came to her into the bed of love, and they defiled her with their whoredom, and she was polluted with them, and her mind was alienated from them.

18 So she discovered her whoredoms, and discovered her nakedness: then my mind was alienated from her, like as my mind was alienated from her sister.

19 Yet she multiplied her whoredoms, in calling to remembrance the days of her youth, wherein she had played the harlot in the land

Aegypti

20. et insanivit libidine super concubitu eorum quorum carnes sunt ut carnes asinorum et sicut fluxus equorum fluxus eorum

21. et visitasti scelus adulescentiae tuae quando subacta sunt in Aegypto ubera tua et confractae mammae pubertatis tuae

22. propterea Ooliba haec dicit Dominus Deus ecce ego suscitabo omnes amatores tuos contra te de quibus satiata est anima tua et congregabo eos adversum te in circuitu

23. filios Babylonis et universos Chaldeos nobiles tyrannosque et principes omnes filios Assyriorum iuvenes forma egregia duces et magistratus universos principes principum et nominatos ascensores equorum

24. et venient super te instructi curru et rota multitudo populorum lorica et clypeo et galea armabuntur contra te undique et dabo coram

of Egypt.

20 For she doted upon their paramours, whose flesh is as the flesh of asses, and whose issue is like the issue of horses.

21 Thus thou calledst to remembrance the lewdness of thy youth, in bruising thy teats by the Egyptians for the paps of thy youth.

22 Therefore, O Aholibah, thus saith the Lord God; Behold, I will raise up thy lovers against thee, from whom thy mind is alienated, and I will bring them against thee on every side;

23 The Babylonians, and all the Chaldeans, Pekod, and Shoa, and Koa, and all the Assyrians with them: all of them desirable young men, captains and rulers, great lords and renowned, all of them riding upon horses.

24 And they shall come against thee with chariots, wagons, and wheels, and with an assembly of people, which shall set against thee buckler and shield and helmet round about: and I will set judgment before them, and they shall judge thee according to their

eis iudicium et iudicabunt te iudiciis suis

25. et ponam zelum meum in te quem exercent tecum in furore nasum tuum et aures tuas praecident et quae remanserint gladio concident ipsi filios tuos et filias tuas capient et novissimum tuum devorabitur igni

26. et denudabunt te vestimentis tuis et tollent vasa gloriae tuae

27. et requiescere faciam scelus tuum de te et fornicationem tuam de terra Aegypti nec levabis oculos tuos ad eos et Aegypti non recordaberis amplius

28. quia haec dicit Dominus Deus ecce ego tradam te in manu eorum quos odisti in manu de quibus satiata est anima tua

29. et agent tecum in odio et tollent omnes labores tuos et dimittent te nudam et ignominia plenam revelabitur ignominia fornicationum tuarum scelus tuum et fornicationes tuae

judgments.

25 And I will set my jealousy against thee, and they shall deal furiously with thee: they shall take away thy nose and thine ears; and thy remnant shall fall by the sword: they shall take thy sons and thy daughters; and thy residue shall be devoured by the fire.

26 They shall also strip thee out of thy clothes, and take away thy fair jewels.

27 Thus will I make thy lewdness to cease from thee, and thy whoredom brought from the land of Egypt: so that thou shalt not lift up thine eyes unto them, nor remember Egypt any more.

28 For thus saith the Lord God; Behold, I will deliver thee into the hand of them whom thou hatest, into the hand of them from whom thy mind is alienated:

29 And they shall deal with thee hatefully, and shall take away all thy labour, and shall leave thee naked and bare: and the nakedness of thy whoredoms shall be discovered, both thy lewdness and thy whoredoms.

30 I will do these things unto

30. fecerunt haec tibi quia fornicata es post gentes inter quas polluta es in idolis eorum

31. in via sororis tuae ambulasti et dabo calicem eius in manu tua

32. haec dicit Dominus Deus calicem sororis tuae bibes profundum et latum eris in derisum et in subsannationem quae es capacissima

33. ebrietate et dolore repleberis calice maeroris et tristitiae calice sororis tuae Samariae

34. et bibes illum et epotabis usque ad feces et fragmenta eius devorabis et ubera tua lacerabis quia ego locutus sum ait Dominus Deus

35. propterea haec dicit Dominus Deus quia oblita es mei et proiecisti me post corpus tuum tu quoque porta scelus tuum et fornicationes tuas

36. et ait Dominus ad me dicens fili hominis numquid iudicas Oollam et Oolibam et adnuntias eis scelera earum

37. quia adulterae sunt et sanguis in manibus earum

thee, because thou hast gone a whoring after the heathen, and because thou art polluted with their idols.

31 Thou hast walked in the way of thy sister; therefore will I give her cup into thine hand.

32 Thus saith the Lord God; Thou shalt drink of thy sister's cup deep and large: thou shalt be laughed to scorn and had in derision; it containeth much.

33 Thou shalt be filled with drunkenness and sorrow, with the cup of astonishment and desolation, with the cup of thy sister Samaria.

34 Thou shalt even drink it and suck it out, and thou shalt break the sherds thereof, and pluck off thine own breasts: for I have spoken it, saith the Lord God.

35 Therefore thus saith the Lord God; Because thou hast forgotten me, and cast me behind thy back, therefore bear thou also thy lewdness and thy whoredoms.

36 The Lord said moreover unto me; Son of man, wilt thou judge Aholah and Aholibah? yea, declare unto

et cum idolis suis fornicatae sunt insuper et filios suos quos genuerunt mihi obtulerunt eis ad devorandum

38. sed et hoc fecerunt mihi polluerunt sanctuarium meum in die illa et sabbata mea profanaverunt

39. cumque immolarent filios suos idolis suis et ingrederentur sanctuarium meum in die illa ut polluerent illud etiam haec fecerunt in medio domus meae

40. miserunt ad viros venientes de longe ad quos nuntium miserant itaque ecce venerunt quibus te lavisti et circumlevisti stibio oculos tuos et ornata es mundo muliebri

41. sedisti in lecto pulcherrimo et mensa ordinata est ante te thymiama meum et unguentum meum posuisti super eam

42. et vox multitudinis exultantis erat in ea et in viris qui de multitudine hominum adducebantur et veniebant de deserto

them their abominations;

37 That they have committed adultery, and blood is in their hands, and with their idols have they committed adultery, and have also caused their sons, whom they bare unto me, to pass for them through the fire, to devour them.

38 Moreover this they have done unto me: they have defiled my sanctuary in the same day, and have profaned my sabbaths.

39 For when they had slain their children to their idols, then they came the same day into my sanctuary to profane it; and, lo, thus have they done in the midst of mine house.

40 And furthermore, that ye have sent for men to come from far, unto whom a messenger was sent; and, lo, they came: for whom thou didst wash thyself, paintedst thy eyes, and deckedst thyself with ornaments,

41 And satest upon a stately bed, and a table prepared before it, whereupon thou hast set mine incense and mine oil.

42 And a voice of a

posuerunt armillas in manibus eorum et coronas speciosas in capitibus eorum

43. et dixi ei quae adtrita est in adulteriis nunc fornicabitur in fornicatione sua etiam haec

44. et ingressi sunt ad eam quasi ad mulierem meretricem sic ingrediebantur ad Oollam et ad Oolibam mulieres nefarias

45. viri ergo iusti sunt hii iudicabunt eas iudicio adulterarum et iudicio effundentium sanguinem quia adulterae sunt et sanguis in manibus earum

46. haec enim dicit Dominus Deus adduc ad eas multitudinem et trade eas in tumultum et in rapinam

47. et lapidentur lapidibus populorum et confodiantur gladiis eorum filios et filias earum interficient et domos earum igne succendent

48. et auferam scelus de terra et discent omnes mulieres ne faciant

multitude being at ease was with her: and with the men of the common sort were brought Sabeans from the wilderness, which put bracelets upon their hands, and beautiful crowns upon their heads.

43 Then said I unto her that was old in adulteries, Will they now commit whoredoms with her, and she with them?

44 Yet they went in unto her, as they go in unto a woman that playeth the harlot: so went they in unto Aholah and unto Aholibah, the lewd women.

45 And the righteous men, they shall judge them after the manner of adulteresses, and after the manner of women that shed blood; because they are adulteresses, and blood is in their hands.

46 For thus saith the Lord God; I will bring up a company upon them, and will give them to be removed and spoiled.

47 And the company shall stone them with stones, and dispatch them with their swords; they shall slay their

secundum scelus earum

49. et dabunt scelus vestrum super vos et peccata idolorum vestrorum portabitis et scietis quia ego Dominus Deus

sons and their daughters, and burn up their houses with fire.

48 Thus will I cause lewdness to cease out of the land, that all women may be taught not to do after your lewdness.

49 And they shall recompense your lewdness upon you, and ye shall bear the sins of your idols: and ye shall know that I am the Lord God.

CHAPTER 24

CHAPTER 24

1. et factum est verbum Domini ad me in anno nono in mense decimo decima mensis dicens

2. fili hominis scribe tibi nomen diei huius in qua confirmatus est rex Babylonis adversum Hierusalem hodie

3. et dices per proverbium ad domum inritatricem parabolam et loqueris ad eos haec dicit Dominus Deus pone ollam pone inquam et mitte in ea aquam

4. congere frusta eius in ea omnem partem bonam

AGAIN in the ninth year, in the tenth month, in the tenth day of the month, the word of the Lord came unto me, saying,

2 Son of man, write thee the name of the day, even of this same day: the king of Babylon set himself against Jerusalem this same day.

3 And utter a parable unto the rebellious house, and say unto them, Thus saith the Lord God; Set on a pot, set it on, and also pour water into it:

4 Gather the pieces thereof into it, even every good

femur et armum electa et ossibus plena

5. pinguissimum pecus adsume conpone quoque struices ossuum sub ea efferbuit coctio eius et discocta sunt ossa illius in medio eius

6. propterea haec dicit Dominus Deus vae civitati sanguinum ollae cuius rubigo in ea est et rubigo eius non exivit de ea per partes et per partes suas eice eam non cecidit super eam sors

7. sanguis enim eius in medio eius est super limpidissimam petram effudit illum non effudit illum super terram ut possit operiri pulvere

8. ut superducerem indignationem meam et vindicta ulciscerer dedi sanguinem eius super petram limpidissimam ne operiretur

9. propterea haec dicit Dominus Deus vae civitati sanguinum cuius ego grandem faciam pyram

10. congere ossa quae igne succendam consumentur carnes et

piece, the thigh, and the shoulder; fill it with the choice bones.

5 Take the choice of the flock, and burn also the bones under it, and make it boil well, and let them seethe the bones of it therein.

6 Wherefore thus saith the Lord God; Woe to the bloody city, to the pot whose scum is therein, and whose scum is not gone out of it! bring it out piece by piece; let no lot fall upon it.

7 For her blood is in the midst of her; she set it upon the top of a rock; she poured it not upon the ground, to cover it with dust;

8 That it might cause fury to come up to take vengeance; I have set her blood upon the top of a rock, that it should not be covered.

9 Therefore thus saith the Lord God; Woe to the bloody city! I will even make the pile for fire great.

10 Heap on wood, kindle the fire, consume the flesh, and spice it well, and let the bones be burned.

11 Then set it empty upon the coals thereof, that the brass of it may be hot, and

concoquetur universa conpositio et ossa tabescent

11. pone quoque eam super prunas vacuam ut incalescat et liquefiat aes eius et confletur in medio eius inquinamentum eius et consumatur rubigo eius

12. multo labore sudatum est et non exibit de ea nimia rubigo eius neque per ignem

13. inmunditia tua execrabilis quia mundare te volui et non es mundata a sordibus tuis sed nec mundaberis prius donec quiescere faciam indignationem meam in te

14. ego Dominus locutus sum venit et faciam non transeam nec parcam nec placabor iuxta vias tuas et iuxta adinventiones tuas iudicavi te dicit Dominus

15. et factum est verbum Domini ad me dicens

16. fili hominis ecce ego tollo a te desiderabile oculorum tuorum in plaga et non planges neque plorabis neque fluent lacrimae tuae

17. ingemesce tacens

may burn, and that the filthiness of it may be molten in it, that the scum of it may be consumed.

12 She hath wearied herself with lies, and her great scum went not forth out of her: her scum shall be in the fire.

13 In thy filthiness is lewdness: because I have purged thee, and thou wast not purged, thou shalt not be purged from thy filthiness any more, till I have caused my fury to rest upon thee.

14 I the Lord have spoken it: it shall come to pass, and I will do it; I will not go back, neither will I spare, neither will I repent; according to thy ways, and according to thy doings, shall they judge thee, saith the Lord God.

15 Also the word of the Lord came unto me, saying,

16 Son of man, behold, I take away from thee the desire of thine eyes with a stroke: yet neither shalt thou mourn nor weep, neither shall thy tears run down.

17 Forbear to cry, make no mourning for the dead, bind the tire of thine head upon thee, and put on thy shoes upon thy feet, and cover not

133

mortuorum luctum non facies corona tua circumligata sit tibi et calciamenta tua erunt in pedibus tuis nec amictu ora velabis nec cibos lugentium comedes

18. locutus sum ergo ad populum mane et mortua est uxor mea vesperi fecique mane sicut praeceperat mihi

19. et dixit ad me populus quare non indicas nobis quid ista significent quae tu facis

20. et dixi ad eos sermo Domini factus est ad me dicens

21. loquere domui Israhel haec dicit Dominus Deus ecce ego polluam sanctuarium meum superbiam imperii vestri et desiderabile oculorum vestrorum et super quo pavet anima vestra et filii vestri et filiae quas reliquistis gladio cadent

22. et facietis sicut feci ora amictu non velabitis et cibos lugentium non comedetis

23. coronas habebitis in capitibus vestris et calciamenta in pedibus

thy lips, and eat not the bread of men.

18 So I spake unto the people in the morning: and at even my wife died; and I did in the morning as I was commanded.

19 And the people said unto me, Wilt thou not tell us what these things are to us, that thou doest so?

20 Then I answered them, The word of the Lord came unto me, saying,

21 Speak unto the house of Israel, Thus saith the Lord God; Behold, I will profane my sanctuary, the excellency of your strength, the desire of your eyes, and that which your soul pitieth; and your sons and your daughters whom ye have left shall fall by the sword.

22 And ye shall do as I have done: ye shall not cover your lips, nor eat the bread of men.

23 And your tires shall be upon your heads, and your shoes upon your feet: ye shall not mourn nor weep; but ye shall pine away for your iniquities, and mourn one toward another.

24 Thus Ezekiel is unto you a

non plangetis neque flebitis sed tabescetis in iniquitatibus vestris et unusquisque gemet ad fratrem suum

24. eritque Hiezecihel vobis in portentum iuxta omnia quae fecit facietis cum venerit istud et scietis quia ego Dominus Deus

25. et tu fili hominis ecce in die quo tollam ab eis fortitudinem eorum et gaudium dignitatis et desiderium oculorum eorum super quo requiescunt animae eorum filios et filias eorum

26. in die illa cum venerit fugiens ad te ut adnuntiet tibi

27. in die inquam illa aperietur os tuum cum eo qui fugit et loqueris et non silebis ultra erisque eis in portentum et scietis quia ego Dominus

sign: according to all that he hath done shall ye do: and when this cometh, ye shall know that I am the Lord God.

25 Also, thou son of man, shall it not be in the day when I take from them their strength, the joy of their glory, the desire of their eyes, and that whereupon they set their minds, their sons and their daughters,

26 That he that escapeth in that day shall come unto thee, to cause thee to hear it with thine ears?

27 In that day shall thy mouth be opened to him which is escaped, and thou shalt speak, and be no more dumb: and thou shalt be a sign unto them; and they shall know that I am the Lord.

CHAPTER 25

CHAPTER 25

1. et factus est sermo Domini ad me dicens

2. fili hominis pone

THE word of the Lord came again unto me, saying,

2 Son of man, set thy face

faciem tuam contra filios Ammon et prophetabis de eis

3. et dices filiis Ammon audite verbum Domini Dei haec dicit Dominus Deus pro eo quod dixisti euge euge super sanctuarium meum quia pollutum est et super terram Israhel quoniam desolata est et super domum Iuda quoniam ducti sunt in captivitatem

4. idcirco ego tradam te filiis orientalibus in hereditatem et conlocabunt caulas suas in te et ponent in te tentoria sua ipsi comedent fruges tuas et ipsi bibent lac tuum

5. daboque Rabbath in habitaculum camelorum et filios Ammon in cubile pecorum et scietis quia ego Dominus

6. quia haec dicit Dominus Deus pro eo quod plausisti manu et percussisti pede et gavisa es ex toto affectu super terram Israhel

7. idcirco ecce ego extendam manum meam super te et tradam te in

against the Ammonites, and prophesy against them;

3 And say unto the Ammonites, Hear the word of the Lord God; Thus saith the Lord God; Because thou saidst, Aha, against my sanctuary, when it was profaned; and against the land of Israel, when it was desolate; and against the house of Judah, when they went into captivity;

4 Behold, therefore I will deliver thee to the men of the east for a possession, and they shall set their palaces in thee, and make their dwellings in thee: they shall eat thy fruit, and they shall drink thy milk.

5 And I will make Rabbah a stable for camels, and the Ammonites a couchingplace for flocks: and ye shall know that I am the Lord.

6 For thus saith the Lord God; Because thou hast clapped thine hands, and stamped with the feet, and rejoiced in heart with all thy despite against the land of Israel;

7 Behold, therefore I will stretch out mine hand upon thee, and will deliver thee for

136

direptionem gentium et interficiam te de populis et perdam de terris et conteram et scies quia ego Dominus

8. haec dicit Dominus Deus pro eo quod dixerunt Moab et Seir ecce sicut omnes gentes domus Iuda

9. idcirco ecce ego aperiam umerum Moab de civitatibus de civitatibus inquam eius et de finibus eius inclitas terrae Bethiesimoth et Beelmeon et Cariathaim

10. filiis orientis cum filiis Ammon et dabo eam in hereditatem ut non sit memoria ultra filiorum Ammon in gentibus

11. et in Moab faciam iudicia et scient quia ego Dominus

12. haec dicit Dominus Deus pro eo quod fecit Idumea ultionem ut se vindicaret de filiis Iuda peccavitque delinquens et vindictam expetivit de eis

13. idcirco haec dicit Dominus Deus extendam manum meam super Idumeam et auferam de ea hominem et iumentum

a spoil to the heathen; and I will cut thee off from the people, and I will cause thee to perish out of the countries: I will destroy thee; and thou shalt know that I am the Lord.

8 Thus saith the Lord God; Because that Moab and Seir do say, Behold, the house of Judah is like unto all the heathen;

9 Therefore, behold, I will open the side of Moab from the cities, from his cities which are on his frontiers, the glory of the country, Beth-jeshimoth, Baal-meon, and Kiriathaim,

10 Unto the men of the east with the Ammonites, and will give them in possession, that the Ammonites may not be remembered among the nations.

11 And I will execute judgments upon Moab; and they shall know that I am the Lord.

12 Thus saith the Lord God; Because that Edom hath dealt against the house of Judah by taking vengeance, and hath greatly offended, and revenged himself upon them;

13 Therefore thus saith the

et faciam eam desertum ab austro et qui sunt in Daedan gladio cadent

14. et dabo ultionem meam super Idumeam per manum populi mei Israhel et facient in Edom iuxta iram meam et furorem meum et scient vindictam meam dicit Dominus Deus

15. haec dicit Dominus Deus pro eo quod fecerunt Palestini in vindictam et ulti se sunt toto animo interficientes et implentes inimicitias veteres

16. propterea haec dicit Dominus Deus ecce ego extendam manum meam super Palestinos et interficiam interfectores et perdam reliquias maritimae regionis

17. faciamque in eis ultiones magnas arguens in furore et scient quia ego Dominus cum dedero vindictam meam super eos

Lord God; I will also stretch out mine hand upon Edom, and will cut off man and beast from it; and I will make it desolate from Teman; and they of Dedan shall fall by the sword.

14 And I will lay my vengeance upon Edom by the hand of my people Israel: and they shall do in Edom according to mine anger and according to my fury; and they shall know my vengeance, saith the Lord God.

15 Thus saith the Lord God; Because the Philistines have dealt by revenge, and have taken vengeance with a despiteful heart, to destroy it for the old hatred;

16 Therefore thus saith the Lord God; Behold, I will stretch out mine hand upon the Philistines, and I will cut off the Cherethims, and destroy the remnant of the sea coast.

17 And I will execute great vengeance upon them with furious rebukes; and they shall know that I am the Lord, when I shall lay my vengeance upon them.

1. et factum est in undecimo anno prima mensis factus est sermo Domini ad me dicens

2. fili hominis pro eo quod dixit Tyrus de Hierusalem euge confractae sunt portae populorum conversa est ad me implebor deserta est

3. propterea haec dicit Dominus Deus ecce ego super te Tyre et ascendere faciam ad te gentes multas sicut ascendit mare fluctuans

4. et dissipabunt muros Tyri et destruent turres eius et radam pulverem eius de ea et dabo eam in limpidissimam petram

5. siccatio sagenarum erit in medio maris quia ego locutus sum ait Dominus Deus et erit in direptionem gentibus

6. filiae quoque eius quae sunt in agro gladio interficientur et scient quia ego Dominus

7. quia haec dicit Dominus Deus ecce ego adducam ad Tyrum

AND it came to pass in the eleventh year, in the first day of the month, that the word of the Lord came unto me, saying,

2 Son of man, because that Tyrus hath said against Jerusalem, Aha, she is broken that was the gates of the people: she is turned unto me: I shall be replenished, now she is laid waste:

3 Therefore thus saith the Lord God; Behold, I am against thee, O Tyrus, and will cause many nations to come up against thee, as the sea causeth his waves to come up.

4 And they shall destroy the walls of Tyrus, and break down her towers: I will also scrape her dust from her, and make her like the top of a rock.

5 It shall be a place for the spreading of nets in the midst of the sea: for I have spoken it, saith the Lord God: and it shall become a spoil to the nations.

6 And her daughters which are in the field shall be slain by the sword; and they shall

Nabuchodonosor regem Babylonis ab aquilone regem regum cum equis et curribus et equitibus et coetu populoque magno

8. filias tuas quae sunt in agro gladio interficiet et circumdabit te munitionibus et conportabit aggerem in gyro et levabit contra te clypeum

9. et vineas et arietes temperabit in muros tuos et turres tuas destruet in armatura sua

10. inundatione equorum eius operiet te pulvis eorum a sonitu equitum et rotarum et curruum movebuntur muri tui dum ingressus fuerit portas tuas quasi per introitus urbis dissipatae

11. ungulis equorum suorum conculcabit omnes plateas tuas populum tuum gladio caedet et statuae tuae nobiles in terram corruent

12. vastabunt opes tuas diripient negotiationes tuas et destruent muros tuos et domos tuas praeclaras subvertent et lapides tuos et ligna tua et

know that I am the Lord.

7 For thus saith the Lord God; Behold, I will bring upon Tyrus Nebuchadrezzar king of Babylon, a king of kings, from the north, with horses, and with chariots, and with horsemen, and companies, and much people.

8 He shall slay with the sword thy daughters in the field: and he shall make a fort against thee, and cast a mount against thee, and lift up the buckler against thee.

9 And he shall set engines of war against thy walls, and with his axes he shall break down thy towers.

10 By reason of the abundance of his horses their dust shall cover thee: thy walls shall shake at the noise of the horsemen, and of the wheels, and of the chariots, when he shall enter into thy gates, as men enter into a city wherein is made a breach.

11 With the hoofs of his horses shall he tread down all thy streets: he shall slay thy people by the sword, and thy strong garrisons shall go down to the ground.

12 And they shall make a spoil of thy riches, and make

pulverem tuum in medio aquarum ponent

13. et quiescere faciam multitudinem canticorum tuorum et sonitus cithararam tuarum non audietur amplius

14. et dabo te in limpidissimam petram siccatio sagenarum eris nec aedificaberis ultra quia ego locutus sum dicit Dominus Deus

15. haec dicit Dominus Deus Tyro numquid non a sonitu ruinae tuae et gemitu interfectorum tuorum cum occisi fuerint in medio tui commovebuntur insulae

16. et descendent de sedibus suis omnes principes maris et auferent exuvias suas et vestimenta sua varia abicient et induentur stupore in terra sedebunt et adtoniti super repentino casu tuo admirabuntur

17. et adsumentes super te lamentum dicent tibi quomodo peristi quae habitas in mari urbs inclita quae fuisti fortis in mari cum habitatoribus

a prey of thy merchandise: and they shall break down thy walls, and destroy thy pleasant houses: and they shall lay thy stones and thy timber and thy dust in the midst of the water.

13 And I will cause the noise of thy songs to cease; and the sound of thy harps shall be no more heard.

14 And I will make thee like the top of a rock: thou shalt be a place to spread nets upon; thou shalt be built no more: for I the Lord have spoken it, saith the Lord God.

15 Thus saith the Lord God to Tyrus; Shall not the isles shake at the sound of thy fall, when the wounded cry, when the slaughter is made in the midst of thee?

16 Then all the princes of the sea shall come down from their thrones, and lay away their robes, and put off their broidered garments: they shall clothe themselves with trembling; they shall sit upon the ground, and shall tremble at every moment, and be astonished at thee.

17 And they shall take up a lamentation for thee, and say

tuis quos formidabant universi

18. nunc stupebunt naves in die pavoris tui et turbabuntur insulae in mari eo quod nullus egrediatur ex te

19. quia haec dicit Dominus Deus cum dedero te urbem desolatam sicut civitates quae non habitantur et adduxero super te abyssum et operuerint te aquae multae

20. et detraxero te cum his qui descendunt in lacum ad populum sempiternum et conlocavero te in terra novissima sicut solitudines veteres cum his qui deducuntur in lacum ut non habiteris porro dedero gloriam in terra viventium

21. in nihilum redigam te et non eris et requisita non invenieris ultra in sempiternum dicit Dominus Deus

to thee, How art thou destroyed, that wast inhabited of seafaring men, the renowned city, which wast strong in the sea, she and her inhabitants, which cause their terror to be on all that haunt it!

18 Now shall the isles tremble in the day of thy fall; yea, the isles that are in the sea shall be troubled at thy departure.

19 For thus saith the Lord God; When I shall make thee a desolate city, like the cities that are not inhabited; when I shall bring up the deep upon thee, and great waters shall cover thee;

20 When I shall bring thee down with them that descend into the pit, with the people of old time, and shall set thee in the low parts of the earth, in places desolate of old, with them that go down to the pit, that thou be not inhabited; and I shall set glory in the land of the living;

21 I will make thee a terror, and thou shalt be no more: though thou be sought for, yet shalt thou never be found again, saith the Lord God.

CHAPTER 27

1. et factum est verbum Domini ad me dicens
2. tu ergo fili hominis adsume super Tyrum lamentum
3. et dices Tyro quae habitat in introitu maris negotiationi populorum ad insulas multas haec dicit Dominus Deus o Tyre tu dixisti perfecti decoris ego sum
4. et in corde maris sita finitimi tui qui te aedificaverunt impleverunt decorem tuum
5. abietibus de Sanir extruxerunt te cum omnibus tabulatis maris cedrum de Libano tulerunt ut facerent tibi malum
6. quercus de Basan dolaverunt in remos tuos transtra tua fecerunt tibi ex ebore indico et praetoriola de insulis Italiae
7. byssus varia de Aegypto texta est tibi in velum ut poneretur in

CHAPTER 27

THE word of the Lord came again unto me, saying,

2 Now, thou son of man, take up a lamentation for Tyrus;

3 And say unto Tyrus, O thou that art situate at the entry of the sea, which art a merchant of the people for many isles, Thus saith the Lord God; O Tyrus, thou hast said, I am of perfect beauty.

4 Thy borders are in the midst of the seas, thy builders have perfected thy beauty.

5 They have made all thy ship boards of fir trees of Senir: they have taken cedars from Lebanon to make masts for thee.

6 Of the oaks of Bashan have they made thine oars; the company of the Ashurites have made thy benches of ivory, brought out of the isles of Chittim.

7 Fine linen with broidered work from Egypt was that which thou spreadest forth to be thy sail; blue and purple from the isles of Elishah was that which covered thee.

malo hyacinthus et purpura de insulis Elisa facta sunt operimentum tuum

8. habitatores Sidonis et Aradii fuerunt remiges tui sapientes tui Tyre facti sunt gubernatores tui

9. senes Bibli et prudentes eius habuerunt nautas ad ministerium variae supellectilis tuae omnes naves maris et nautae earum fuerunt in populo negotiationis tuae

10. Persae et Lydi et Lybies erant in exercitu tuo viri bellatores tui clypeum et galeam suspenderunt in te pro ornatu tuo

11. filii Aradii cum exercitu tuo erant super muros tuos in circuitu sed et Pigmei qui erant in turribus tuis faretras suas suspenderunt in muris tuis per gyrum ipsi conpleverunt pulchritudinem tuam

12. Carthaginienses negotiatores tui a multitudine cunctarum divitiarum argento ferro stagno plumboque repleverunt nundinas tuas

8 The inhabitants of Zidon and Arvad were thy mariners: thy wise men, O Tyrus, that were in thee, were thy pilots.

9 The ancients of Gebal and the wise men thereof were in thee thy calkers: all the ships of the sea with their mariners were in thee to occupy thy merchandise.

10 They of Persia and of Lud and of Phut were in thine army, thy men of war: they hanged the shield and helmet in thee; they set forth thy comeliness.

11 The men of Arvad with thine army were upon thy walls round about, and the Gammadims were in thy towers: they hanged their shields upon thy walls round about; they have made thy beauty perfect.

12 Tarshish was thy merchant by reason of the multitude of all kind of riches; with silver, iron, tin, and lead, they traded in thy fairs.

13 Javan, Tubal, and Meshech, they were thy merchants: they traded the persons of men and vessels of brass in thy market.

13. Graecia Thubal et Mosoch ipsi institores tui mancipia et vasa aerea adduxerunt populo tuo

14. de domo Thogorma equos et equites et mulos adduxerunt ad forum tuum

15. filii Dadan negotiatores tui insulae multae negotiatio manus tuae dentes eburneos et hebeninos

commutaverunt in pretio tuo

16. Syrus negotiator tuus propter multitudinem operum tuorum gemmam purpuram et scutulata et byssum et sericum et chodchod proposuerunt in mercatu tuo

17. Iuda et terra Israhel ipsi institores tui in frumento primo balsamum et mel et oleum et resinam proposuerunt in nundinis tuis

18. Damascenus negotiator tuus in multitudine operum tuorum in multitudine diversarum opum in vino pingui in lanis coloris optimi

14 They of the house of Togarmah traded in thy fairs with horses and horsemen and mules.

15 The men of Dedan were thy merchants; many isles were the merchandise of thine hand: they brought thee for a present horns of ivory and ebony.

16 Syria was thy merchant by reason of the multitude of the wares of thy making: they occupied in thy fairs with emeralds, purple, and broidered work, and fine linen, and coral, and agate.

17 Judah, and the land of Israel, they were thy merchants: they traded in thy market wheat of Minnith, and Pannag, and honey, and oil, and balm.

18 Damascus was thy merchant in the multitude of the wares of thy making, for the multitude of all riches; in the wine of Helbon, and white wool.

19 Dan also and Javan going to and fro occupied in thy fairs: bright iron, cassia, and calamus, were in thy market.

20 Dedan was thy merchant in precious clothes for chariots.

19. Dan et Graecia et Mozel in nundinis tuis proposuerunt ferrum fabrefactum stacte et calamus in negotiatione tua

20. Dadan institores tui in tapetibus ad sedendum

21. Arabia et universi principes Cedar ipsi negotiatores manus tuae cum agnis et arietibus et hedis venerunt ad te negotiatores tui

22. venditores Saba et Reema ipsi negotiatores tui cum universis primis aromatibus et lapide pretioso et auro quod proposuerunt in mercatu tuo

23. Aran et Chenne et Eden negotiatores Saba Assur Chelmad venditores tui

24. ipsi negotiatores tui multifariam involucris hyacinthi et polymitorum gazarumque pretiosarum quae obvolutae et adstrictae erant funibus cedros quoque habebant in negotiationibus tuis

25. naves maris principes tuae in negotiatione tua et repleta es et glorificata

21 Arabia, and all the princes of Kedar, they occupied with thee in lambs, and rams, and goats: in these were they thy merchants.

22 The merchants of Sheba and Raamah, they were thy merchants: they occupied in thy fairs with chief of all spices, and with all precious stones, and gold.

23 Haran, and Canneh, and Eden, the merchants of Sheba, Asshur, and Chilmad, were thy merchants.

24 These were thy merchants in all sorts of things, in blue clothes, and broidered work, and in chests of rich apparel, bound with cords, and made of cedar, among thy merchandise.

25 The ships of Tarshish did sing of thee in thy market: and thou wast replenished, and made very glorious in the midst of the seas.

26 Thy rowers have brought thee into great waters: the east wind hath broken thee in the midst of the seas.

27 Thy riches, and thy fairs, thy merchandise, thy mariners, and thy pilots, thy calkers, and the occupiers of thy merchandise, and all thy

nimis in corde maris

26. in aquis multis adduxerunt te remiges tui ventus auster contrivit te in corde maris

27. divitiae tuae et thesauri tui et multiplex instrumentum tuum nautae tui et gubernatores tui qui tenebant supellectilem tuam et populo tuo praeerant viri quoque bellatores tui qui erant in te cum universa multitudine tua quae est in medio tui cadent in corde maris in die ruinae tuae

28. a sonitu clamoris gubernatorum tuorum conturbabuntur classes

29. et descendent de navibus suis omnes qui tenebant remum nautae et universi gubernatores maris in terra stabunt

30. et heiulabunt super te voce magna et clamabunt amare et superiacient pulverem capitibus suis et cinere conspergentur

31. et radent super te calvitium et accingentur ciliciis et plorabunt te in amaritudine animae ploratu amarissimo

men of war, that are in thee, and in all thy company which is in the midst of thee, shall fall into the midst of the seas in the day of thy ruin.

28 The suburbs shall shake at the sound of the cry of thy pilots.

29 And all that handle the oar, the mariners, and all the pilots of the sea, shall come down from their ships, they shall stand upon the land;

30 And shall cause their voice to be heard against thee, and shall cry bitterly, and shall cast up dust upon their heads, they shall wallow themselves in the ashes:

31 And they shall make themselves utterly bald for thee, and gird them with sackcloth, and they shall weep for thee with bitterness of heart and bitter wailing.

32 And in their wailing they shall take up a lamentation for thee, and lament over thee, saying, What city is like Tyrus, like the destroyed in the midst of the sea?

33 When thy wares went forth out of the seas, thou filledst many people; thou didst enrich the kings of the

32. et adsument super te carmen lugubre et plangent te quae est ut Tyrus quae obmutuit in medio maris

33. quae in exitu negotiationum tuarum de mari implesti populos multos in multitudine divitiarum tuarum et populorum tuorum ditasti reges terrae

34. nunc contrita es a mari in profundis aquarum opes tuae et omnis multitudo tua quae erat in medio tui ceciderunt

35. universi habitatores insularum obstipuerunt super te et reges earum omnes tempestate perculsi mutaverunt vultus

36. negotiatores populorum sibilaverunt super te ad nihilum deducta es et non eris usque in perpetuum

earth with the multitude of thy riches and of thy merchandise.

34 In the time when thou shalt be broken by the seas in the depths of the waters thy merchandise and all thy company in the midst of thee shall fall.

35 All the inhabitants of the isles shall be astonished at thee, and their kings shall be sore afraid, they shall be troubled in their countenance.

36 The merchants among the people shall hiss at thee; thou shalt be a terror, and never shalt be any more.

CHAPTER 28

CHAPTER 28

1. et factus est sermo Domini ad me dicens

2. fili hominis dic

THE word of the Lord came again unto me, saying,

2 Son of man, say unto the

principi Tyri haec dicit Dominus Deus eo quod elevatum est cor tuum et dixisti Deus ego sum et in cathedra Dei sedi in corde maris cum sis homo et non Deus et dedisti cor tuum quasi cor Dei

3. ecce sapientior es tu Danihele omne secretum non est absconditum a te

4. in sapientia et prudentia tua fecisti tibi fortitudinem et adquisisti aurum et argentum in thesauris tuis

5. in multitudine sapientiae tuae et in negotiatione tua multiplicasti tibi fortitudinem et elevatum est cor tuum in robore tuo

6. propterea haec dicit Dominus Deus eo quod elevatum est cor tuum quasi cor Dei

7. idcirco ecce ego adducam super te alienos robustissimos gentium et nudabunt gladios suos super pulchritudinem sapientiae tuae et polluent decorem tuum

8. interficient et detrahent te et morieris interitu occisorum in corde maris

prince of Tyrus, Thus saith the Lord God; Because thine heart is lifted up, and thou hast said, I am a God, I sit in the seat of God, in the midst of the seas; yet thou art a man, and not God, though thou set thine heart as the heart of God:

3 Behold, thou art wiser than Daniel; there is no secret that they can hide from thee:

4 With thy wisdom and with thine understanding thou hast gotten thee riches, and hast gotten gold and silver into thy treasures:

5 By thy great wisdom and by thy traffick hast thou increased thy riches, and thine heart is lifted up because of thy riches:

6 Therefore thus saith the Lord God; Because thou hast set thine heart as the heart of God;

7 Behold, therefore I will bring strangers upon thee, the terrible of the nations: and they shall draw their swords against the beauty of thy wisdom, and they shall defile thy brightness.

8 They shall bring thee down to the pit, and thou shalt die the deaths of them that are

9. numquid dicens loqueris Deus ego sum coram interficientibus te cum sis homo et non Deus in manu occidentium te

10. morte incircumcisorum morieris in manu alienorum quia ego locutus sum ait Dominus Deus

11. et factus est sermo Domini ad me dicens fili hominis leva planctum super regem Tyri

12. et dices ei haec dicit Dominus Deus tu signaculum similitudinis plenus sapientia et perfectus decore

13. in deliciis paradisi Dei fuisti omnis lapis pretiosus operimentum tuum sardius topazius et iaspis chrysolitus et onyx et berillus sapphyrus et carbunculus et zmaragdus aurum opus decoris tui et foramina tua in die qua conditus es praeparata sunt

14. tu cherub extentus et protegens et posui te in monte sancto Dei in medio lapidum ignitorum ambulasti

slain in the midst of the seas.

9 Wilt thou yet say before him that slayeth thee, I am God? but thou shalt be a man, and no God, in the hand of him that slayeth thee.

10 Thou shalt die the deaths of the uncircumcised by the hand of strangers: for I have spoken it, saith the Lord God.

11 Moreover the word of the Lord came unto me, saying,

12 Son of man, take up a lamentation upon the king of Tyrus, and say unto him, Thus saith the Lord God; Thou sealest up the sum, full of wisdom, and perfect in beauty.

13 Thou hast been in Eden the garden of God; every precious stone was thy covering, the sardius, topaz, and the diamond, the beryl, the onyx, and the jasper, the sapphire, the emerald, and the carbuncle, and gold: the workmanship of thy tabrets and of thy pipes was prepared in thee in the day that thou wast created.

14 Thou art the anointed cherub that covereth; and I have set thee so: thou wast upon the holy mountain of

15. perfectus in viis tuis a die conditionis tuae donec inventa est iniquitas in te

16. in multitudine negotiationis tuae repleta sunt interiora tua iniquitate et peccasti et eieci te de monte Dei et perdidi te o cherub protegens de medio lapidum ignitorum

17. elevatum est cor tuum in decore tuo perdidisti sapientiam tuam in decore tuo in terram proieci te ante faciem regum dedi te ut cernerent te

18. in multitudine iniquitatum tuarum et iniquitate negotiationis tuae polluisti sanctificationem tuam producam ergo ignem de medio tui qui comedat te et dabo te in cinerem super terram in conspectu omnium videntium te

19. omnes qui viderint te in gentibus obstupescent super te nihili factus es et non eris in perpetuum

20. et factus est sermo Domini ad me dicens

21. fili hominis pone

God; thou hast walked up and down in the midst of the stones of fire.

15 Thou wast perfect in thy ways from the day that thou wast created, till iniquity was found in thee.

16 By the multitude of thy merchandise they have filled the midst of thee with violence, and thou hast sinned: therefore I will cast thee as profane out of the mountain of God: and I will destroy thee, O covering cherub, from the midst of the stones of fire.

17 Thine heart was lifted up because of thy beauty, thou hast corrupted thy wisdom by reason of thy brightness: I will cast thee to the ground, I will lay thee before kings, that they may behold thee.

18 Thou hast defiled thy sanctuaries by the multitude of thine iniquities, by the iniquity of thy traffick; therefore will I bring forth a fire from the midst of thee, it shall devour thee, and I will bring thee to ashes upon the earth in the sight of all them that behold thee.

19 All they that know thee among the people shall be

faciem tuam contra Sidonem et prophetabis de ea

22. et dices haec dicit Dominus Deus ecce ego ad te Sidon et glorificabor in medio tui et scient quia ego Dominus cum fecero in ea iudicia et sanctificatus fuero in ea

23. et inmittam ei pestilentiam et sanguinem in plateis eius et corruent interfecti in medio eius gladio per circuitum et scient quia ego Dominus

24. et non erit ultra domui Israhel offendiculum amaritudinis et spina dolorem inferens undique per circuitum eorum qui adversantur eis et scient quia ego Dominus Deus

25. haec dicit Dominus Deus quando congregavero domum Israhel de populis in quibus dispersi sunt sanctificabor in eis coram gentibus et habitabunt in terra sua quam dedi servo meo Iacob

26. et habitabunt in ea securi et aedificabunt domos plantabuntque vineas et habitabunt

astonished at thee: thou shalt be a terror, and never shalt thou be any more.

20 Again the word of the Lord came unto me, saying,

21 Son of man, set thy face against Zidon, and prophesy against it,

22 And say, Thus saith the Lord God; Behold, I am against thee, O Zidon; and I will be glorified in the midst of thee: and they shall know that I am the Lord, when I shall have executed judgments in her, and shall be sanctified in her.

23 For I will send into her pestilence, and blood into her streets; and the wounded shall be judged in the midst of her by the sword upon her on every side; and they shall know that I am the Lord.

24 And there shall be no more a pricking brier unto the house of Israel, nor any grieving thorn of all that are round about them, that despised them; and they shall know that I am the Lord God.

25 Thus saith the Lord God; When I shall have gathered the house of Israel from the people among whom they are

confidenter cum fecero iudicia in omnibus qui adversantur eis per circuitum et scient quia ego Dominus Deus eorum

scattered, and shall be sanctified in them in the sight of the heathen, then shall they dwell in their land that I have given to my servant Jacob.

26 And they shall dwell safely therein, and shall build houses, and plant vineyards; yea, they shall dwell with confidence, when I have executed judgments upon all those that despise them round about them; and they shall know that I am the Lord their God.

CHAPTER 29

1. in anno decimo in decimo mense undecima mensis factum est verbum Domini ad me dicens
2. fili hominis pone faciem tuam contra Pharaonem regem Aegypti et prophetabis de eo et de Aegypto universa
3. loquere et dices haec dicit Dominus Deus ecce ego ad te Pharao rex Aegypti draco magne qui cubas in medio fluminum tuorum et dicis meus est

CHAPTER 29

IN the tenth year, in the tenth month, in the twelfth day of the month, the word of the Lord came unto me, saying,

2 Son of man, set thy face against Pharaoh king of Egypt, and prophesy against him, and against all Egypt:

3 Speak, and say, Thus saith the Lord God; Behold, I am against thee, Pharaoh king of Egypt, the great dragon that lieth in the midst of his rivers, which hath said, My river is mine own, and I have made it for myself.

fluvius et ego feci memet ipsum

4. et ponam frenum in maxillis tuis et adglutinabo pisces fluminum tuorum squamis tuis et extraham te de medio fluminum tuorum et universi pisces tui squamis tuis adherebunt

5. et proiciam te in desertum et omnes pisces fluminis tui super faciem terrae cades non colligeris neque congregaberis bestiis terrae et volatilibus caeli dedi te ad devorandum

6. et scient omnes habitatores Aegypti quia ego Dominus pro eo quod fuisti baculus harundineus domui Israhel

7. quando adprehenderunt te manu et confractus es et lacerasti omnem umerum eorum et innitentibus eis super te comminutus es et dissolvisti omnes renes eorum

8. propterea haec dicit Dominus Deus ecce ego adducam super te

4 But I will put hooks in thy jaws, and I will cause the fish of thy rivers to stick unto thy scales, and I will bring thee up out of the midst of thy rivers, and all the fish of thy rivers shall stick unto thy scales.

5 And I will leave thee thrown into the wilderness, thee and all the fish of thy rivers: thou shalt fall upon the open fields; thou shalt not be brought together, nor gathered: I have given thee for meat to the beasts of the field and to the fowls of the heaven.

6 And all the inhabitants of Egypt shall know that I am the Lord, because they have been a staff of reed to the house of Israel.

7 When they took hold of thee by thy hand, thou didst break, and rend all their shoulder: and when they leaned upon thee, thou brakest, and madest all their loins to be at a stand.

8 Therefore thus saith the Lord God; Behold, I will bring a sword upon thee, and cut off man and beast out of thee.

9 And the land of Egypt shall

gladium et interficiam de te hominem et iumentum

9. et erit terra Aegypti in desertum et solitudinem et scient quia ego Dominus eo quod dixerit fluvius meus est et ego feci

10. idcirco ecce ego ad te et ad flumina tua daboque terram Aegypti in solitudines gladio dissipatam a turre Syenes usque ad terminos Aethiopiae

11. non pertransibit eam pes hominis neque pes iumenti gradietur in ea et non habitabitur quadraginta annis

12. daboque terram Aegypti desertam in medio terrarum desertarum et civitates eius in medio urbium subversarum erunt desolatae quadraginta annis et dispergam Aegyptios in nationes et ventilabo eos in terras

13. quia haec dicit Dominus Deus post finem quadraginta annorum congregabo Aegyptum de populis in quibus dispersi fuerunt

be desolate and waste; and they shall know that I am the Lord: because he hath said, The river is mine, and I have made it.

10 Behold, therefore I am against thee, and against thy rivers, and I will make the land of Egypt utterly waste and desolate, from the tower of Syene even unto the border of Ethiopia.

11 No foot of man shall pass through it, nor foot of beast shall pass through it, neither shall it be inhabited forty years.

12 And I will make the land of Egypt desolate in the midst of the countries that are desolate, and her cities among the cities that are laid waste shall be desolate forty years: and I will scatter the Egyptians among the nations, and will disperse them through the countries.

13 Yet thus saith the Lord God; At the end of forty years will I gather the Egyptians from the people whither they were scattered:

14 And I will bring again the captivity of Egypt, and will cause them to return into the land of Pathros, into the land

14.   et   reducam captivitatem Aegypti et conlocabo eos in terra Fatures in terra nativitatis suae et erunt ibi in regnum humile

15. inter regna cetera erit humillima   et   non elevabitur   ultra   super nationes et inminuam eos ne imperent gentibus

16. neque   erunt   ultra domui   Israhel   in confidentia   docentes iniquitatem ut fugiant et sequantur eos et scient quia ego Dominus Deus

17. et   factum   est   in vicesimo et septimo anno in primo in una mensis factum   est   verbum Domini ad me dicens

18.   fili   hominis Nabuchodonosor   rex Babylonis servire fecit exercitum suum servitute magna adversum Tyrum omne caput decalvatum et   omnis   umerus depilatus est et merces non est reddita ei neque exercitui eius de Tyro pro servitute   qua   servivit mihi adversum eam

19. propterea haec dicit Dominus Deus ecce ego

of their habitation; and they shall   be   there   a   base kingdom.

15 It shall be the basest of the kingdoms; neither shall it exalt itself any more above the   nations: for   I   will diminish them, that they shall no   more   rule   over   the nations.

16 And it shall be no more the confidence of the house of   Israel,   which   bringeth their   iniquity   to remembrance,   when   they shall look after them: but they shall know that I am the Lord God.

17 And it came to pass in the seven and twentieth year, in the first month, in the first day of the month, the word of the Lord came unto me, saying,

18   Son   of   man, Nebuchadrezzar   king   of Babylon caused his army to serve a great service against Tyrus: every head was made bald, and every shoulder was peeled: yet had he no wages, nor his army, for Tyrus, for the service that he had served against it:

19 Therefore thus saith the Lord   God;   Behold,   I   will

dabo Nabuchodonosor regem Babylonis in terra Aegypti et accipiet multitudinem eius et depraedabitur manubias eius et diripiet spolia eius et erit merces exercitui illius

20. et operi pro quo servivit adversum eam dedi ei terram Aegypti pro eo quod laboraverunt mihi ait Dominus Deus

21. in die illo pullulabit cornu domui Israhel et tibi dabo apertum os in medio eorum et scient quoniam ego Dominus

give the land of Egypt unto Nebuchadrezzar king of Babylon; and he shall take her multitude, and take her spoil, and take her prey; and it shall be the wages for his army.

20 I have given him the land of Egypt for his labour wherewith he served against it, because they wrought for me, saith the Lord God.

21 In that day will I cause the horn of the house of Israel to bud forth, and I will give thee the opening of the mouth in the midst of them; and they shall know that I am the Lord.

CHAPTER 30

1. et factum est verbum Domini ad me dicens

2. fili hominis propheta et dic haec dicit Dominus Deus ululate vae vae diei

3. quia iuxta est dies et adpropinquavit dies Domini dies nubis tempus gentium erit

4. et veniet gladius in Aegyptum et erit pavor in Aethiopia cum ceciderint vulnerati in Aegypto et

CHAPTER 30

THE word of the Lord came again unto me, saying,

2 Son of man, prophesy and say, Thus saith the Lord God; Howl ye, Woe worth the day!

3 For the day is near, even the day of the Lord is near, a cloudy day; it shall be the time of the heathen.

4 And the sword shall come upon Egypt, and great pain shall be in Ethiopia, when the slain shall fall in Egypt, and

ablata fuerit multitudo illius et destructa fundamenta eius

5. Aethiopia et Lybia et Lydii et omne reliquum vulgus et Chub et filii terrae foederis cum eis gladio cadent

6. haec dicit Dominus Deus et corruent fulcientes Aegyptum et destruetur superbia imperii eius a turre Syenes gladio cadent in ea ait Dominus exercituum

7. et dissipabuntur in medio terrarum desolatarum et urbes eius in medio civitatum desertarum erunt

8. et scient quoniam ego Dominus cum dedero ignem in Aegyptum et adtriti fuerint omnes auxiliatores eius

9. in die illa egredientur nuntii a facie mea in trieribus ad conterendam Aethiopiae confidentiam et erit pavor in eis in die Aegypti quia absque dubio veniet

10. haec dicit Dominus Deus et cessare faciam multitudinem Aegypti in

they shall take away her multitude, and her foundations shall be broken down.

5 Ethiopia, and Libya, and Lydia, and all the mingled people, and Chub, and the men of the land that is in league, shall fall with them by the sword.

6 Thus saith the Lord; They also that uphold Egypt shall fall; and the pride of her power shall come down: from the tower of Syene shall they fall in it by the sword, saith the Lord God.

7 And they shall be desolate in the midst of the countries that are desolate, and her cities shall be in the midst of the cities that are wasted.

8 And they shall know that I am the Lord, when I have set a fire in Egypt, and when all her helpers shall be destroyed.

9 In that day shall messengers go forth from me in ships to make the careless Ethiopians afraid, and great pain shall come upon them, as in the day of Egypt: for, lo, it cometh.

10 Thus saith the Lord God; I will also make the multitude

manu Nabuchodonosor regis Babylonis

11. ipse et populus eius cum eo fortissimi gentium adducentur ad disperdendam terram et evaginabunt gladios suos super Aegyptum et implebunt terram interfectis

12. et faciam alveos fluminum aridos et tradam terram in manu pessimorum et dissipabo terram et plenitudinem eius in manu alienorum ego Dominus locutus sum

13. haec dicit Dominus Deus et disperdam simulacra et cessare faciam idola de Memphis et dux de terra Aegypti non erit amplius et dabo terrorem in terra Aegypti

14. et disperdam terram Fatures et dabo ignem in Tafnis et faciam iudicia in Alexandriam

15. et effundam indignationem meam super Pelusium robur Aegypti et interficiam multitudinem Alexandriae

16. et dabo ignem in Aegypto quasi parturiens

of Egypt to cease by the hand of Nebuchadrezzar king of Babylon.

11 He and his people with him, the terrible of the nations, shall be brought to destroy the land: and they shall draw their swords against Egypt, and fill the land with the slain.

12 And I will make the rivers dry, and sell the land into the hand of the wicked: and I will make the land waste, and all that is therein, by the hand of strangers: I the Lord have spoken it.

13 Thus saith the Lord God; I will also destroy the idols, and I will cause their images to cease out of Noph; and there shall be no more a prince of the land of Egypt: and I will put a fear in the land of Egypt.

14 And I will make Pathros desolate, and will set fire in Zoan, and will execute judgments in No.

15 And I will pour my fury upon Sin, the strength of Egypt; and I will cut off the multitude of No.

16 And I will set fire in Egypt: Sin shall have great pain, and No shall be rent

dolebit Pelusium et Alexandria erit dissipata et in Memphis angustiae cotidianae

17. iuvenes Eliupoleos et Bubasti gladio cadent et ipsae captivae ducentur

18. et in Tafnis nigrescet dies cum contrivero ibi sceptra Aegypti et defecerit in ea superbia potentiae eius ipsam nubes operiet filiae autem eius in captivitatem ducentur

19. et faciam iudicia in Aegypto et scient quia ego Dominus

20. et factum est in undecimo anno in primo in septima mensis factum est verbum Domini ad me dicens

21. fili hominis brachium Pharao regis Aegypti confregi et ecce non est obvolutum ut restitueretur ei sanitas ut ligaretur pannis et farciretur linteolis et recepto robore posset tenere gladium

22. propterea haec dicit Dominus Deus ecce ego ad Pharao regem Aegypti et comminuam brachium eius forte sed confractum

asunder, and Noph shall have distresses daily.

17 The young men of Aven and of Pi-beseth shall fall by the sword: and these cities shall go into captivity.

18 At Tehaphnehes also the day shall be darkened, when I shall break there the yokes of Egypt: and the pomp of her strength shall cease in her: as for her, a cloud shall cover her, and her daughters shall go into captivity.

19 Thus will I execute judgments in Egypt: and they shall know that I am the Lord.

20 And it came to pass in the eleventh year, in the first month, in the seventh day of the month, that the word of the Lord came unto me, saying,

21 Son of man, I have broken the arm of Pharaoh king of Egypt; and, lo, it shall not be bound up to be healed, to put a roller to bind it, to make it strong to hold the sword.

22 Therefore thus saith the Lord God; Behold, I am against Pharaoh king of Egypt, and will break his arms, the strong, and that which was broken; and I will

et deiciam gladium de manu eius

23. et dispergam Aegyptum in gentibus et ventilabo eos in terris

24. et confortabo brachia regis Babylonis daboque gladium meum in manu eius et confringam brachia Pharaonis et gement gemitibus interfecti coram facie eius

25. et confortabo brachia regis Babylonis et brachia Pharaonis concident et scient quia ego Dominus cum dedero gladium meum in manu regis Babylonis et extenderit eum super terram Aegypti

26. et dispergam Aegyptum in nationes et ventilabo eos in terris et scient quia ego Dominus

cause the sword to fall out of his hand.

23 And I will scatter the Egyptians among the nations, and will disperse them through the countries.

24 And I will strengthen the arms of the king of Babylon, and put my sword in his hand: but I will break Pharaoh's arms, and he shall groan before him with the groanings of a deadly wounded man.

25 But I will strengthen the arms of the king of Babylon, and the arms of Pharaoh shall fall down; and they shall know that I am the Lord, when I shall put my sword into the hand of the king of Babylon, and he shall stretch it out upon the land of Egypt.

26 And I will scatter the Egyptians among the nations, and disperse them among the countries; and they shall know that I am the Lord.

CHAPTER 31

1. et factum est in undecimo anno tertio una mensis factum est verbum Domini ad me

CHAPTER 31

AND it came to pass in the eleventh year, in the third month, in the first day of the month, that the word of the

dicens

2. fili hominis dic Pharaoni regi Aegypti et populo eius cui similis factus es in magnitudine tua

3. ecce Assur quasi cedrus in Libano pulcher ramis et frondibus nemorosus excelsusque altitudine et inter condensas frondes elevatum est cacumen eius

4. aquae nutrierunt illum abyssus exaltavit eum flumina eius manabant in circuitu radicum eius et rivos suos emisit ad universa ligna regionis

5. propterea elevata est altitudo eius super omnia ligna regionis et multiplicata sunt arbusta eius et elevati sunt rami eius prae aquis multis

6. cumque extendisset umbram suam in ramis eius fecerunt nidos omnia volatilia caeli et sub frondibus eius genuerunt omnes bestiae saltuum et sub umbraculo illius habitabat coetus gentium plurimarum

7. eratque pulcherrimus

Lord came unto me, saying,

2 Son of man, speak unto Pharaoh king of Egypt, and to his multitude; Whom art thou like in thy greatness?

3 Behold, the Assyrian was a cedar in Lebanon with fair branches, and with a shadowing shroud, and of an high stature; and his top was among the thick boughs.

4 The waters made him great, the deep set him up on high with her rivers running round about his plants, and sent out her little rivers unto all the trees of the field.

5 Therefore his height was exalted above all the trees of the field, and his boughs were multiplied, and his branches became long because of the multitude of waters, when he shot forth.

6 All the fowls of heaven made their nests in his boughs, and under his branches did all the beasts of the field bring forth their young, and under his shadow dwelt all great nations.

7 Thus was he fair in his greatness, in the length of his branches: for his root was by great waters.

8 The cedars in the garden of

in magnitudine sua et in dilatatione arbustorum suorum erat enim radix illius iuxta aquas multas

8. cedri non fuerunt altiores illo in paradiso Dei abietes non adaequaverunt summitatem eius et platani non fuerunt aequae frondibus illius omne lignum paradisi Dei non est adsimilatum illi et pulchritudini eius

9. quoniam speciosum feci eum et multis condensisque frondibus et aemulata sunt eum omnia ligna voluptatis quae erant in paradiso Dei

10. propterea haec dicit Dominus Deus pro eo quod sublimatus est in altitudine et dedit summitatem suam virentem atque condensam et elevatum est cor eius in altitudine sua

11. tradidi eum in manu fortissimi gentium faciens faciet ei iuxta impietatem eius eieci eum

12. et succident illum alieni et crudelissimi nationum et proicient

God could not hide him: the fir trees were not like his boughs, and the chesnut trees were not like his branches; nor any tree in the garden of God was like unto him in his beauty.

9 I have made him fair by the multitude of his branches: so that all the trees of Eden, that were in the garden of God, envied him.

10 Therefore thus saith the Lord God; Because thou hast lifted up thyself in height, and he hath shot up his top among the thick boughs, and his heart is lifted up in his height;

11 I have therefore delivered him into the hand of the mighty one of the heathen; he shall surely deal with him: I have driven him out for his wickedness.

12 And strangers, the terrible of the nations, have cut him off, and have left him: upon the mountains and in all the valleys his branches are fallen, and his boughs are broken by all the rivers of the land; and all the people of the earth are gone down from his shadow, and have left him.

13 Upon his ruin shall all the

eum super montes et in cunctis convallibus corruent rami eius et confringentur arbusta eius in universis rupibus terrae et recedent de umbraculo eius omnes populi terrae et relinquent eum

13. in ruina eius habitaverunt omnia volatilia caeli et in ramis eius fuerunt universae bestiae regionis

14. quam ob rem non elevabuntur in altitudine sua omnia ligna aquarum neque ponent sublimitatem suam inter nemorosa atque frondosa nec stabunt in sublimitate eorum omnia quae inrigantur aquis quia omnes traditi sunt in mortem ad terram ultimam in medio filiorum hominum ad eos qui descendunt in lacum

15. haec dicit Dominus Deus in die quando descendit ad inferos indixi luctum operui eum abysso et prohibui flumina eius et coercui aquas multas contristatus est super eum Libanus et omnia ligna agri concussa

fowls of the heaven remain, and all the beasts of the field shall be upon his branches:

14 To the end that none of all the trees by the waters exalt themselves for their height, neither shoot up their top among the thick boughs, neither their trees stand up in their height, all that drink water: for they are all delivered unto death, to the nether parts of the earth, in the midst of the children of men, with them that go down to the pit.

15 Thus saith the Lord God; In the day when he went down to the grave I caused a mourning: I covered the deep for him, and I restrained the floods thereof, and the great waters were stayed: and I caused Lebanon to mourn for him, and all the trees of the field fainted for him.

16 I made the nations to shake at the sound of his fall, when I cast him down to hell with them that descend into the pit: and all the trees of Eden, the choice and best of Lebanon, all that drink water, shall be comforted in the nether parts of the earth.

17 They also went down into

sunt

16. a sonitu ruinae eius commovi gentes cum deducerem eum ad infernum cum his qui descendebant in lacum et consolata sunt in terra infima omnia ligna voluptatis egregia atque praeclara in Libano universa quae inrigabantur aquis

17. nam et ipsi cum ea descendent ad infernum ad interfectos gladio et brachium uniuscuiusque sedebit sub umbraculo eius in medio nationum

18. cui adsimilatus es o inclite atque sublimis inter ligna voluptatis ecce deductus es cum lignis voluptatis ad terram ultimam in medio incircumcisorum dormies cum his qui interfecti sunt gladio ipse est Pharao et omnis multitudo eius dicit Dominus Deus

hell with him unto them that be slain with the sword; and they that were his arm, that dwelt under his shadow in the midst of the heathen.

18 To whom art thou thus like in glory and in greatness among the trees of Eden? yet shalt thou be brought down with the trees of Eden unto the nether parts of the earth: thou shalt lie in the midst of the uncircumcised with them that be slain by the sword. This is Pharaoh and all his multitude, saith the Lord God.

CHAPTER 32

CHAPTER 32

1. et factum est duodecimo anno in mense duodecimo in una

AND it came to pass in the twelfth year, in the twelfth month, in the first day of the

mensis factum est verbum Domini ad me dicens

2. fili hominis adsume lamentum super Pharao regem Aegypti et dices ad eum leoni gentium adsimilatus es et draconi qui est in mari et ventilabas cornu in fluminibus tuis et conturbabas aquas pedibus tuis et conculcabas flumina eorum

3. propterea haec dicit Dominus Deus expandam super te rete meum in multitudine populorum multorum et extrahent te in sagena mea

4. et proiciam te in terram super faciem agri abiciam te et habitare faciam super te omnia volatilia caeli et saturabo de te bestias universae terrae

5. et dabo carnes tuas super montes et implebo colles tuos sanie tua

6. et inrigabo terram pedore sanguinis tui super montes et valles implebuntur ex te

7. et operiam cum extinctus fueris caelos et

month, that the word of the Lord came unto me, saying,

2 Son of man, take up a lamentation for Pharaoh king of Egypt, and say unto him, Thou art like a young lion of the nations, and thou art as a whale in the seas: and thou camest forth with thy rivers, and troubledst the waters with thy feet, and fouledst their rivers.

3 Thus saith the Lord God; I will therefore spread out my net over thee with a company of many people; and they shall bring thee up in my net.

4 Then will I leave thee upon the land, I will cast thee forth upon the open field, and will cause all the fowls of the heaven to remain upon thee, and I will fill the beasts of the whole earth with thee.

5 And I will lay thy flesh upon the mountains, and fill the valleys with thy height.

6 I will also water with thy blood the land wherein thou swimmest, even to the mountains; and the rivers shall be full of thee.

7 And when I shall put thee out, I will cover the heaven, and make the stars thereof dark; I will cover the sun

nigrescere faciam stellas eius solem nube tegam et luna non dabit lumen suum

8. omnia luminaria caeli maerere faciam super te et dabo tenebras super terram tuam dicit Dominus Deus

9. et inritabo cor populorum multorum cum induxero contritionem tuam in gentibus super terras quas nescis

10. et stupescere faciam super te populos multos et reges eorum horrore nimio formidabunt super te cum volare coeperit gladius meus super facies eorum et obstupescent repente singuli pro anima sua in die ruinae suae

11. quia haec dicit Dominus Deus gladius regis Babylonis veniet tibi

12. in gladiis fortium deiciam multitudinem tuam inexpugnabiles gentes omnes heae et vastabunt superbiam Aegypti et dissipabitur multitudo eius

13. et perdam omnia

with a cloud, and the moon shall not give her light.

8 All the bright lights of heaven will I make dark over thee, and set darkness upon thy land, saith the Lord God.

9 I will also vex the hearts of many people, when I shall bring thy destruction among the nations, into the countries which thou hast not known.

10 Yea, I will make many people amazed at thee, and their kings shall be horribly afraid for thee, when I shall brandish my sword before them; and they shall tremble at every moment, every man for his own life, in the day of thy fall.

11 For thus saith the Lord God; The sword of the king of Babylon shall come upon thee.

12 By the swords of the mighty will I cause thy multitude to fall, the terrible of the nations, all of them: and they shall spoil the pomp of Egypt, and all the multitude thereof shall be destroyed.

13 I will destroy also all the beasts thereof from beside the great waters; neither shall the foot of man trouble them

iumenta eius quae erant super aquas plurimas et non conturbabit eas pes hominis ultra neque ungula iumentorum turbabit eas

14. tunc purissimas reddam aquas eorum et flumina eorum quasi oleum adducam ait Dominus Deus

15. cum dedero terram Aegypti desolatam deseretur autem terra a plenitudine sua quando percussero omnes habitatores eius et scient quia ego Dominus

16. planctus est et plangent eum filiae gentium plangent eum super Aegypto et super multitudine eius plangent eum ait Dominus Deus

17. et factum est in duodecimo anno in quintadecima mensis factum est verbum Domini ad me dicens

18. fili hominis cane lugubre super multitudine Aegypti et detrahe eam ipsam et filias gentium robustarum ad terram ultimam cum his qui descendunt in lacum

any more, nor the hoofs of beasts trouble them.

14 Then will I make their waters deep, and cause their rivers to run like oil, saith the Lord God.

15 When I shall make the land of Egypt desolate, and the country shall be destitute of that whereof it was full, when I shall smite all them that dwell therein, then shall they know that I am the Lord.

16 This is the lamentation wherewith they shall lament her: the daughters of the nations shall lament her: they shall lament for her, even for Egypt, and for all her multitude, saith the Lord God.

17 It came to pass also in the twelfth year, in the fifteenth day of the month, that the word of the Lord came unto me, saying,

18 Son of man, wail for the multitude of Egypt, and cast them down, even her, and the daughters of the famous nations, unto the nether parts of the earth, with them that go down into the pit.

19 Whom dost thou pass in beauty? go down, and be

19. quo pulchrior es descende et dormi cum incircumcisis

20. in medio interfectorum gladio cadent gladius datus est adtraxerunt eam et omnes populos eius

21. loquentur ei potentissimi robustorum de medio inferni qui cum auxiliatoribus eius descenderunt et dormierunt incircumcisi interfecti gladio

22. ibi Assur et omnis multitudo eius in circuitu illius sepulchra eius omnes interfecti et qui ceciderunt gladio

23. quorum data sunt sepulchra in novissimis laci et facta est multitudo eius per gyrum sepulchri eius universi interfecti cadentesque gladio qui dederant quondam formidinem in terra viventium

24. ibi Aelam et omnis multitudo eius per gyrum sepulchri sui omnes hii interfecti ruentesque gladio qui descenderunt incircumcisi ad terram ultimam qui posuerunt thou laid with the uncircumcised.

20 They shall fall in the midst of them that are slain by the sword: she is delivered to the sword: draw her and all her multitudes.

21 The strong among the mighty shall speak to him out of the midst of hell with them that help him: they are gone down, they lie uncircumcised, slain by the sword.

22 Asshur is there and all her company: his graves are about him: all of them slain, fallen by the sword:

23 Whose graves are set in the sides of the pit, and her company is round about her grave: all of them slain, fallen by the sword, which caused terror in the land of the living.

24 There is Elam and all her multitude round about her grave, all of them slain, fallen by the sword, which are gone down uncircumcised into the nether parts of the earth, which caused their terror in the land of the living; yet have they borne their shame with them that go down to the pit.

terrorem suum in terra viventium et portaverunt ignominiam suam cum his qui descendunt in lacum

25. in medio interfectorum posuerunt cubile eius in universis populis eius in circuitu eius sepulchrum illius omnes hii incircumcisi interfectique gladio dederant enim terrorem in terra viventium et portaverunt ignominiam suam cum his qui descendunt in lacum in medio interfectorum positi sunt

26. ibi Mosoch et Thubal et omnis multitudo eius in circuitu illius sepulchra eius omnes hii incircumcisi interfectique et cadentes gladio quia dederunt formidinem suam in terra viventium

27. et non dormient cum fortibus cadentibusque et incircumcisis qui descenderunt ad infernum cum armis suis et posuerunt gladios suos sub capitibus suis et fuerunt iniquitates eorum in ossibus eorum quia

25 They have set her a bed in the midst of the slain with all her multitude: her graves are round about him: all of them uncircumcised, slain by the sword: though their terror was caused in the land of the living, yet have they borne their shame with them that go down to the pit: he is put in the midst of them that be slain.

26 There is Meshech, Tubal, and all her multitude: her graves are round about him: all of them uncircumcised, slain by the sword, though they caused their terror in the land of the living.

27 And they shall not lie with the mighty that are fallen of the uncircumcised, which are gone down to hell with their weapons of war: and they have laid their swords under their heads, but their iniquities shall be upon their bones, though they were the terror of the mighty in the land of the living.

28 Yea, thou shalt be broken in the midst of the uncircumcised, and shalt lie with them that are slain with the sword.

29 There is Edom, her kings,

terror fortium facti sunt in terra viventium

28. et tu ergo in medio incircumcisorum contereris et dormies cum interfectis gladio

29. ibi Idumea et reges eius omnes duces eius qui dati sunt cum exercitu suo cum interfectis gladio et qui cum incircumcisis dormierunt et cum his qui descenderunt in lacum

30. ibi principes aquilonis omnes et universi venatores qui deducti sunt cum interfectis paventes et in sua fortitudine confusi qui dormierunt incircumcisi cum interfectis gladio et portaverunt confusionem suam cum his qui descendunt in lacum

31. vidit eos Pharao et consolatus est super universa multitudine sua quae interfecta est gladio Pharao et omnis exercitus eius ait Dominus Deus

32. quia dedi terrorem meum in terra viventium et dormivit in medio incircumcisorum cum interfectis gladio Pharao et omnis multitudo eius

and all her princes, which with their might are laid by them that were slain by the sword: they shall lie with the uncircumcised, and with them that go down to the pit.

30 There be the princes of the north, all of them, and all the Zidonians, which are gone down with the slain; with their terror they are ashamed of their might; and they lie uncircumcised with them that be slain by the sword, and bear their shame with them that go down to the pit.

31 Pharaoh shall see them, and shall be comforted over all his multitude, even Pharaoh and all his army slain by the sword, saith the Lord God.

32 For I have caused my terror in the land of the living: and he shall be laid in the midst of the uncircumcised with them that are slain with the sword, even Pharaoh and all his multitude, saith the Lord God.

171

ait Dominus Deus

CHAPTER 33

1. et factum est verbum Domini ad me dicens
2. fili hominis loquere ad filios populi tui et dices ad eos terra cum induxero super eam gladium et tulerit populus terrae virum unum de novissimis suis et constituerit eum super se speculatorem
3. et ille viderit gladium venientem super terram et cecinerit bucina et adnuntiaverit populo
4. audiens autem quisquis ille est sonum bucinae non se observaverit veneritque gladius et tulerit eum sanguis ipsius super caput eius erit
5. sonum bucinae audivit et non se observavit sanguis eius in ipso erit si autem custodierit animam suam salvavit
6. quod si speculator viderit gladium venientem et non insonuerit bucina et populus non se

AGAIN the word of the Lord came unto me, saying,
2 Son of man, speak to the children of thy people, and say unto them, When I bring the sword upon a land, if the people of the land take a man of their coasts, and set him for their watchman:
3 If when he seeth the sword come upon the land, he blow the trumpet, and warn the people;
4 Then whosoever heareth the sound of the trumpet, and taketh not warning; if the sword come, and take him away, his blood shall be upon his own head.
5 He heard the sound of the trumpet, and took not warning; his blood shall be upon him. But he that taketh warning shall deliver his soul.
6 But if the watchman see the sword come, and blow not the trumpet, and the people be not warned; if the sword come, and take any person from among them, he is

custodierit veneritque gladius et tulerit de eis animam ille quidem in iniquitate sua captus est sanguinem autem eius de manu speculatoris requiram

7. et tu fili hominis speculatorem dedi te domui Israhel audiens ergo ex ore meo sermonem adnuntiabis eis ex me

8. si me dicente ad impium impie morte morieris non fueris locutus ut se custodiat impius a via sua ipse impius in iniquitate sua morietur sanguinem autem eius de manu tua requiram

9. si autem adnuntiante te ad impium ut a viis suis convertatur non fuerit conversus a via sua ipse in iniquitate sua morietur porro tu animam tuam liberasti

10. tu ergo fili hominis dic ad domum Israhel sic locuti estis dicentes iniquitates nostrae et peccata nostra super nos sunt et in ipsis nos tabescimus quomodo

taken away in his iniquity; but his blood will I require at the watchman's hand.

7 So thou, O son of man, I have set thee a watchman unto the house of Israel; therefore thou shalt hear the word at my mouth, and warn them from me.

8 When I say unto the wicked, O wicked man, thou shalt surely die; if thou dost not speak to warn the wicked from his way, that wicked man shall die in his iniquity; but his blood will I require at thine hand.

9 Nevertheless, if thou warn the wicked of his way to turn from it; if he do not turn from his way, he shall die in his iniquity; but thou hast delivered thy soul.

10 Therefore, O thou son of man, speak unto the house of Israel; Thus ye speak, saying, If our transgressions and our sins be upon us, and we pine away in them, how should we then live?

11 Say unto them, As I live, saith the Lord God, I have no pleasure in the death of the wicked; but that the wicked turn from his way and live: turn ye, turn ye from your

ergo vivere poterimus

11. dic ad eos vivo ego dicit Dominus Deus nolo mortem impii sed ut revertatur impius a via sua et vivat convertimini a viis vestris pessimis et quare moriemini domus Israhel

12. tu itaque fili hominis dic ad filios populi tui iustitia iusti non liberabit eum in quacumque die peccaverit et impietas impii non nocebit ei in quacumque die conversus fuerit ab impietate sua et iustus non poterit vivere in iustitia sua in quacumque die peccaverit

13. etiam si dixero iusto quod vita vivat et confisus in iustitia sua fecerit iniquitatem omnes iustitiae eius oblivioni tradentur et in iniquitate sua quam operatus est in ipsa morietur

14. sin autem dixero impio morte morieris et egerit paenitentiam a peccato suo feceritque iudicium et iustitiam

15. pignus restituerit ille impius rapinamque reddiderit in mandatis

evil ways; for why will ye die, O house of Israel?

12 Therefore, thou son of man, say unto the children of thy people, The righteousness of the righteous shall not deliver him in the day of his transgression: as for the wickedness of the wicked, he shall not fall thereby in the day that he turneth from his wickedness; neither shall the righteous be able to live for his righteousness in the day that he sinneth.

13 When I shall say to the righteous, that he shall surely live; if he trust to his own righteousness, and commit iniquity, all his righteousnesses shall not be remembered; but for his iniquity that he hath committed, he shall die for it.

14 Again, when I say unto the wicked, Thou shalt surely die; if he turn from his sin, and do that which is lawful and right;

15 If the wicked restore the pledge, give again that he had robbed, walk in the statutes of life, without committing iniquity; he shall surely live, he shall not die.

vitae ambulaverit nec fecerit quicquam iniustum vita vivet et non morietur

16. omnia peccata eius quae peccavit non inputabuntur ei iudicium et iustitiam fecit vita vivet

17. et dixerunt filii populi tui non est aequi ponderis via Domini et ipsorum via iniusta est

18. cum enim recesserit iustus a iustitia sua feceritque iniquitatem morietur in eis

19. et cum recesserit impius ab impietate sua feceritque iudicium et iustitiam vivet in eis

20. et dicitis non est recta via Domini unumquemque iuxta vias suas iudicabo de vobis domus Israhel

21. et factum est in duodecimo anno in duodecimo mense in quinta mensis transmigrationis nostrae venit ad me qui fugerat de Hierusalem dicens vastata est civitas

22. manus autem Domini facta fuerat ad me

16 None of his sins that he hath committed shall be mentioned unto him: he hath done that which is lawful and right; he shall surely live.

17 Yet the children of thy people say, The way of the Lord is not equal: but as for them, their way is not equal.

18 When the righteous turneth from his righteousness, and committeth iniquity, he shall even die thereby.

19 But if the wicked turn from his wickedness, and do that which is lawful and right, he shall live thereby.

20 Yet ye say, The way of the Lord is not equal. O ye house of Israel, I will judge you every one after his ways.

21 And it came to pass in the twelfth year of our captivity, in the tenth month, in the fifth day of the month, that one that had escaped out of Jerusalem came unto me, saying, The city is smitten.

22 Now the hand of the Lord was upon me in the evening, afore he that was escaped came; and had opened my mouth, until he came to me in the morning; and my mouth was opened, and I was

vespere antequam veniret qui fugerat aperuitque os meum donec veniret ad me mane et aperto ore meo non silui amplius

23. et factum est verbum Domini ad me dicens

24. fili hominis qui habitant in ruinosis his super humum Israhel loquentes aiunt unus erat Abraham et hereditate possedit terram nos autem multi nobis data est terra in possessionem

25. idcirco dices ad eos haec dicit Dominus Deus qui in sanguine comeditis et oculos vestros levatis ad inmunditias vestras et sanguinem funditis numquid terram hereditate possidebitis

26. stetistis in gladiis vestris fecistis abominationes et unusquisque uxorem proximi sui polluit et terram hereditate possidebitis

27. haec dices ad eos sic dicit Dominus Deus vivo ego quia qui in ruinosis habitant gladio cadent et qui in agro est bestiis tradetur ad devorandum

no more dumb.

23 Then the word of the Lord came unto me, saying,

24 Son of man, they that inhabit those wastes of the land of Israel speak, saying, Abraham was one, and he inherited the land: but we are many; the land is given us for inheritance.

25 Wherefore say unto them, Thus saith the Lord God; Ye eat with the blood, and lift up your eyes toward your idols, and shed blood: and shall ye possess the land?

26 Ye stand upon your sword, ye work abomination, and ye defile every one his neighbour's wife: and shall ye possess the land?

27 Say thou thus unto them, Thus saith the Lord God; As I live, surely they that are in the wastes shall fall by the sword, and him that is in the open field will I give to the beasts to be devoured, and they that be in the forts and in the caves shall die of the pestilence.

28 For I will lay the land most desolate, and the pomp of her strength shall cease; and the mountains of Israel shall be desolate, that none

qui autem in praesidiis et in speluncis sunt peste morientur

28. et dabo terram in solitudinem et desertum et deficiet superba fortitudo eius et desolabuntur montes Israhel eo quod nullus sit qui per eos transeat

29. et scient quia ego Dominus cum dedero terram desolatam et desertam propter universas abominationes suas quas operati sunt

30. et tu fili hominis filii populi tui qui loquuntur de te iuxta muros et in ostiis domorum et dicunt unus ad alterum vir ad proximum suum loquentes venite et audiamus qui sit sermo egrediens a Domino

31. et veniunt ad te quasi si ingrediatur populus et sedent coram te populus meus et audiunt sermones tuos et non faciunt eos quia in canticum oris sui vertunt illos et avaritiam suam sequitur cor eorum

32. et es eis quasi carmen musicum quod suavi dulcique sono canitur et

shall pass through.

29 Then shall they know that I am the Lord, when I have laid the land most desolate because of all their abominations which they have committed.

30 Also, thou son of man, the children of thy people still are talking against thee by the walls and in the doors of the houses, and speak one to another, every one to his brother, saying, Come, I pray you, and hear what is the word that cometh forth from the Lord.

31 And they come unto thee as the people cometh, and they sit before thee as my people, and they hear thy words, but they will not do them: for with their mouth they shew much love, but their heart goeth after their covetousness.

32 And, lo, thou art unto them as a very lovely song of one that hath a pleasant voice, and can play well on an instrument: for they hear thy words, but they do them not.

33 And when this cometh to pass, (lo, it will come,) then shall they know that a

audient verba tua et non facient ea

33. et cum venerit quod praedictum est ecce enim venit tunc scient quod prophetes fuerit inter eos

prophet hath been among them.

CHAPTER 34

1. et factum est verbum Domini ad me dicens

2. fili hominis propheta de pastoribus Israhel propheta et dices pastoribus haec dicit Dominus Deus vae pastoribus Israhel qui pascebant semet ipsos nonne greges pascuntur a pastoribus

3. lac comedebatis et lanis operiebamini et quod crassum erat occidebatis gregem autem meum non pascebatis

4. quod infirmum fuit non consolidastis et quod aegrotum non sanastis quod fractum est non alligastis et quod abiectum est non reduxistis quod perierat non quaesistis sed cum austeritate imperabatis eis et cum potentia

CHAPTER 34

AND the word of the Lord came unto me, saying,

2 Son of man, prophesy against the shepherds of Israel, prophesy, and say unto them, Thus saith the Lord God unto the shepherds; Woe be to the shepherds of Israel that do feed themselves! should not the shepherds feed the flocks?

3 Ye eat the fat, and ye clothe you with the wool, ye kill them that are fed: but ye feed not the flock.

4 The diseased have ye not strengthened, neither have ye healed that which was sick, neither have ye bound up that which was broken, neither have ye brought again that which was driven away, neither have ye sought that which was lost; but with force and with cruelty have

5. et dispersae sunt oves meae eo quod non esset pastor et factae sunt in devorationem omnium bestiarum agri et dispersae sunt

6. erraverunt greges mei in cunctis montibus et in universo colle excelso et super omnem faciem terrae dispersi sunt greges mei et non erat qui requireret non erat inquam qui requireret

7. propterea pastores audite verbum Domini

8. vivo ego dicit Dominus Deus quia pro eo quod facti sunt greges mei in rapinam et oves meae in devorationem omnium bestiarum agri eo quod non esset pastor neque enim quaesierunt pastores gregem meum sed pascebant pastores semet ipsos et greges meos non pascebant

9. propterea pastores audite verbum Domini

10. haec dicit Dominus Deus ecce ego ipse super pastores requiram gregem meum de manu eorum et cessare eos faciam ut ultra non pascant gregem

ye ruled them.

5 And they were scattered, because there is no shepherd: and they became meat to all the beasts of the field, when they were scattered.

6 My sheep wandered through all the mountains, and upon every high hill: yea, my flock was scattered upon all the face of the earth, and none did search or seek after them.

7 Therefore, ye shepherds, hear the word of the Lord;

8 As I live, saith the Lord God, surely because my flock became a prey, and my flock became meat to every beast of the field, because there was no shepherd, neither did my shepherds search for my flock, but the shepherds fed themselves, and fed not my flock;

9 Therefore, O ye shepherds, hear the word of the Lord;

10 Thus saith the Lord God; Behold, I am against the shepherds; and I will require my flock at their hand, and cause them to cease from feeding the flock; neither shall the shepherds feed themselves any more; for I will deliver my flock from

nec pascant amplius pastores semet ipsos et liberabo gregem meum de ore eorum et non erunt ultra eis in escam

11. quia haec dicit Dominus Deus ecce ego ipse requiram oves meas et visitabo eas

12. sicut visitat pastor gregem suum in die quando fuerit in medio ovium suarum dissipatarum sic visitabo oves meas et liberabo eas de omnibus locis quo dispersae fuerant in die nubis et caliginis

13. et educam eas de populis et congregabo eas de terris et inducam eas in terram suam et pascam eas in montibus Israhel in rivis et in cunctis sedibus terrae

14. in pascuis uberrimis pascam eas et in montibus excelsis Israhel erunt pascuae eorum ibi requiescent in herbis virentibus et in pascuis pinguibus pascentur super montes Israhel

15. ego pascam oves meas et ego eas accubare faciam dicit Dominus

their mouth, that they may not be meat for them.

11 For thus saith the Lord God; Behold, I, even I, will both search my sheep, and seek them out.

12 As a shepherd seeketh out his flock in the day that he is among his sheep that are scattered; so will I seek out my sheep, and will deliver them out of all places where they have been scattered in the cloudy and dark day.

13 And I will bring them out from the people, and gather them from the countries, and will bring them to their own land, and feed them upon the mountains of Israel by the rivers, and in all the inhabited places of the country.

14 I will feed them in a good pasture, and upon the high mountains of Israel shall their fold be: there shall they lie in a good fold, and in a fat pasture shall they feed upon the mountains of Israel.

15 I will feed my flock, and I will cause them to lie down, saith the Lord God.

16 I will seek that which was lost, and bring again that which was driven away, and

Deus
16. quod perierat requiram et quod abiectum erat reducam et quod confractum fuerat alligabo et quod infirmum erat consolidabo et quod pingue et forte custodiam et pascam illas in iudicio
17. vos autem greges mei haec dicit Dominus Deus ecce ego iudico inter pecus et pecus arietum et hircorum
18. nonne satis vobis erat pascuam bonam depasci insuper et reliquias pascuarum vestrarum conculcastis pedibus vestris et cum purissimam aquam biberetis reliquam pedibus vestris turbabatis
19. et oves meae his quae conculcata pedibus vestris fuerant pascebantur et quae pedes vestri turbaverant haec bibebant
20. propterea haec dicit Dominus Deus ad eos ecce ego ipse iudico inter pecus pingue et macilentum
21. pro eo quod lateribus

will bind up that which was broken, and will strengthen that which was sick: but I will destroy the fat and the strong; I will feed them with judgment.

17 And as for you, O my flock, thus saith the Lord God; Behold, I judge between cattle and cattle, between the rams and the he goats.

18 Seemeth it a small thing unto you to have eaten up the good pasture, but ye must tread down with your feet the residue of your pastures? and to have drunk of the deep waters, but ye must foul the residue with your feet?

19 And as for my flock, they eat that which ye have trodden with your feet; and they drink that which ye have fouled with your feet.

20 Therefore thus saith the Lord God unto them; Behold, I, even I, will judge between the fat cattle and between the lean cattle.

21 Because ye have thrust with side and with shoulder, and pushed all the diseased with your horns, till ye have scattered them abroad;

22 Therefore will I save my

et umeris inpingebatis et cornibus vestris ventilabatis omnia infirma pecora donec dispergerentur foras

22. salvabo gregem meum et non erit ultra in rapinam et iudicabo inter pecus et pecus

23. et suscitabo super ea pastorem unum qui pascat ea servum meum David ipse pascet ea et ipse erit eis in pastorem

24. ego autem Dominus ero eis in Deum et servus meus David princeps in medio eorum ego Dominus locutus sum

25. et faciam cum eis pactum pacis et cessare faciam bestias pessimas de terra et qui habitant in deserto securi dormient in saltibus

26. et ponam eos in circuitu collis mei benedictionem et deducam imbrem in tempore suo pluviae benedictionis erunt

27. et dabit lignum agri fructum suum et terra dabit germen suum et erunt in terra sua absque timore et scient quia ego

flock, and they shall no more be a prey; and I will judge between cattle and cattle.

23 And I will set up one shepherd over them, and he shall feed them, even my servant David; he shall feed them, and he shall be their shepherd.

24 And I the Lord will be their God, and my servant David a prince among them; I the Lord have spoken it.

25 And I will make with them a covenant of peace, and will cause the evil beasts to cease out of the land: and they shall dwell safely in the wilderness, and sleep in the woods.

26 And I will make them and the places round about my hill a blessing; and I will cause the shower to come down in his season; there shall be showers of blessing.

27 And the tree of the field shall yield her fruit, and the earth shall yield her increase, and they shall be safe in their land, and shall know that I am the Lord, when I have broken the bands of their yoke, and delivered them out of the hand of those that served themselves of them.

Dominus cum contrivero catenas iugi eorum et eruero eos de manu imperantium sibi

28. et non erunt ultra in rapinam gentibus neque bestiae terrae devorabunt eos sed habitabunt confidenter absque ullo terrore

29. et suscitabo eis germen nominatum et non erunt ultra inminuti fame in terra neque portabunt amplius obprobria gentium

30. et scient quia ego Dominus Deus eorum cum eis et ipsi populus meus domus Israhel ait Dominus Deus

31. vos autem greges mei greges pascuae meae homines estis et ego Dominus Deus vester dicit Dominus Deus

28 And they shall no more be a prey to the heathen, neither shall the beast of the land devour them; but they shall dwell safely, and none shall make them afraid.

29 And I will raise up for them a plant of renown, and they shall be no more consumed with hunger in the land, neither bear the shame of the heathen any more.

30 Thus shall they know that I the Lord their God am with them, and that they, even the house of Israel, are my people, saith the Lord God.

31 And ye my flock, the flock of my pasture, are men, and I am your God, saith the Lord God.

CHAPTER 35

CHAPTER 35

1. et factus est sermo Domini ad me dicens

2. fili hominis pone faciem tuam adversum montem Seir et prophetabis de eo et dices

MOREOVER the word of the Lord came unto me, saying,

2 Son of man, set thy face against mount Seir, and prophesy against it,

illi

3. haec dicit Dominus Deus ecce ego ad te mons Seir et extendam manum meam super te et dabo te desolatum atque desertum

4. urbes tuas demoliar et tu desertus eris et scies quia ego Dominus

5. eo quod fueris inimicus sempiternus et concluseris filios Israhel in manus gladii in tempore adflictionis eorum in tempore iniquitatis extremae

6. propterea vivo ego dicit Dominus Deus quoniam sanguini tradam te et sanguis te persequetur et cum sanguinem oderis sanguis persequetur te

7. et dabo montem Seir desolatum et desertum et auferam de eo euntem et redeuntem

8. et implebo montes eius occisorum suorum in collibus tuis et in vallibus tuis atque in torrentibus interfecti gladio cadent

9. in solitudines sempiternas tradam te et civitates tuae non habitabuntur et scietis

3 And say unto it, Thus saith the Lord God; Behold, O mount Seir, I am against thee, and I will stretch out mine hand against thee, and I will make thee most desolate.

4 I will lay thy cities waste, and thou shalt be desolate, and thou shalt know that I am the Lord.

5 Because thou hast had a perpetual hatred, and hast shed the blood of the children of Israel by the force of the sword in the time of their calamity, in the time that their iniquity had an end:

6 Therefore, as I live, saith the Lord God, I will prepare thee unto blood, and blood shall pursue thee: sith thou hast not hated blood, even blood shall pursue thee.

7 Thus will I make mount Seir most desolate, and cut off from it him that passeth out and him that returneth.

8 And I will fill his mountains with his slain men: in thy hills, and in thy valleys, and in all thy rivers, shall they fall that are slain with the sword.

9 I will make thee perpetual desolations, and thy cities shall not return: and ye shall

quoniam ego Dominus

10. eo quod dixeris duae gentes et duae terrae meae erunt et hereditate possidebo eas cum Dominus esset ibi

11. propterea vivo ego dicit Dominus Deus quia faciam iuxta iram tuam et secundum zelum tuum quem fecisti odio habens eos et notus efficiar per eos cum te iudicavero

12. et scies quia ego Dominus audivi universa obprobria tua quae locutus es de montibus Israhel dicens deserti nobis dati sunt ad devorandum

13. et insurrexistis super me ore vestro et rogastis adversum me verba vestra ego audivi

14. haec dicit Dominus Deus laetante universa terra in solitudinem te redigam

15. sicuti gavisus es super hereditatem domus Israhel eo quod fuerit dissipata sic faciam tibi dissipatus eris mons Seir et Idumea omnis et scient quia ego Dominus

know that I am the Lord.

10 Because thou hast said, These two nations and these two countries shall be mine, and we will possess it; whereas the Lord was there:

11 Therefore, as I live, saith the Lord God, I will even do according to thine anger, and according to thine envy which thou hast used out of thy hatred against them; and I will make myself known among them, when I have judged thee.

12 And thou shalt know that I am the Lord, and that I have heard all thy blasphemies which thou hast spoken against the mountains of Israel, saying, They are laid desolate, they are given us to consume.

13 Thus with your mouth ye have boasted against me, and have multiplied your words against me: I have heard them.

14 Thus saith the Lord God; When the whole earth rejoiceth, I will make thee desolate.

15 As thou didst rejoice at the inheritance of the house of Israel, because it was desolate, so will I do unto

185

thee: thou shalt be desolate, O mount Seir, and all Idumea, even all of it: and they shall know that I am the Lord.

CHAPTER 36

1. tu autem fili hominis propheta super montes Israhel et dices montes Israhel audite verbum Domini
2. haec dicit Dominus Deus eo quod dixerit inimicus de vobis euge altitudines sempiternae in hereditatem datae sunt nobis
3. propterea vaticinare et dic haec dicit Dominus Deus pro eo quod desolati estis et conculcati per circuitum et facti in hereditatem reliquis gentibus et ascendistis super labium linguae et obprobrium populi
4. propterea montes Israhel audite verbum Domini Dei haec dicit Dominus Deus montibus et collibus torrentibus vallibusque et desertis parietinis et urbibus

CHAPTER 36

ALSO, thou son of man, prophesy unto the mountains of Israel, and say, Ye mountains of Israel, hear the word of the Lord:

2 Thus saith the Lord God; Because the enemy hath said against you, Aha, even the ancient high places are ours in possession:

3 Therefore prophesy and say, Thus saith the Lord God; Because they have made you desolate, and swallowed you up on every side, that ye might be a possession unto the residue of the heathen, and ye are taken up in the lips of talkers, and are an infamy of the people:

4 Therefore, ye mountains of Israel, hear the word of the Lord God; Thus saith the Lord God to the mountains, and to the hills, to the rivers, and to the valleys, to the desolate wastes, and to the

derelictis quae depopulatae sunt et subsannatae a reliquis gentibus per circuitum

5. propterea haec dicit Dominus Deus quoniam in igne zeli mei locutus sum de reliquis gentibus et de Idumea universa qui dederunt terram meam sibi in hereditatem cum gaudio et toto corde ex animo et eiecerunt eam ut vastarent

6. idcirco vaticinare super humum Israhel et dices montibus et collibus iugis et vallibus haec dicit Dominus Deus ecce ego in zelo meo et in furore meo locutus sum eo quod confusionem gentium sustinueritis

7. idcirco haec dicit Dominus Deus ego levavi manum meam ut gentes quae in circuitu vestro sunt ipsae confusionem suam portent

8. vos autem montes Israhel ramos vestros germinetis et fructum vestrum adferatis populo meo Israhel prope est enim ut veniat

9. quia ecce ego ad vos et

cities that are forsaken, which became a prey and derision to the residue of the heathen that are round about;

5 Therefore thus saith the Lord God; Surely in the fire of my jealousy have I spoken against the residue of the heathen, and against all Idumea, which have appointed my land into their possession with the joy of all their heart, with despiteful minds, to cast it out for a prey.

6 Prophesy therefore concerning the land of Israel, and say unto the mountains, and to the hills, to the rivers, and to the valleys, Thus saith the Lord God; Behold, I have spoken in my jealousy and in my fury, because ye have borne the shame of the heathen:

7 Therefore thus saith the Lord God; I have lifted up mine hand, Surely the heathen that are about you, they shall bear their shame.

8 But ye, O mountains of Israel, ye shall shoot forth your branches, and yield your fruit to my people of Israel; for they are at hand to come.

convertar ad vos et arabimini et accipietis sementem

10. et multiplicabo in vobis homines omnemque domum Israhel et habitabuntur civitates et ruinosa instaurabuntur

11. et replebo vos hominibus et iumentis et multiplicabuntur et crescent et habitari vos faciam sicut a principio bonisque donabo maioribus quam habuistis ab initio et scietis quia ego Dominus

12. et adducam super vos homines populum meum Israhel et hereditate possidebunt te et eris eis in hereditatem et non addes ultra ut absque eis sis

13. haec dicit Dominus Deus pro eo quod dicunt de vobis devoratrix hominum es et suffocans gentem tuam

14. propterea homines non comedes amplius et gentem tuam non necabis ultra ait Dominus Deus

15. nec auditam faciam in te amplius confusionem

9 For, behold, I am for you, and I will turn unto you, and ye shall be tilled and sown:

10 And I will multiply men upon you, all the house of Israel, even all of it: and the cities shall be inhabited, and the wastes shall be builded:

11 And I will multiply upon you man and beast; and they shall increase and bring fruit: and I will settle you after your old estates, and will do better unto you than at your beginnings: and ye shall know that I am the Lord.

12 Yea, I will cause men to walk upon you, even my people Israel; and they shall possess thee, and thou shalt be their inheritance, and thou shalt no more henceforth bereave them of men.

13 Thus saith the Lord God; Because they say unto you, Thou land devourest up men, and hast bereaved thy nations;

14 Therefore thou shalt devour men no more, neither bereave thy nations any more, saith the Lord God.

15 Neither will I cause men to hear in thee the shame of the heathen any more, neither shalt thou bear the reproach

gentium et obprobrium populorum nequaquam portabis et gentem tuam non amittes amplius ait Dominus Deus

16. et factum est verbum Domini ad me dicens

17. fili hominis domus Israhel habitaverunt in humo sua et polluerunt eam in viis suis et in studiis suis iuxta inmunditiam menstruatae facta est via eorum coram me

18. et effudi indignationem meam super eos pro sanguine quem fuderunt super terram et in idolis suis polluerunt eam

19. et dispersi eos in gentes et ventilati sunt in terris iuxta vias eorum et adinventiones iudicavi eos

20. et ingressi sunt ad gentes ad quas introierunt et polluerunt nomen sanctum meum cum diceretur de eis populus Domini iste est et de terra eius egressi sunt

21. et peperci nomini meo sancto quod polluerat domus Israhel

of the people any more, neither shalt thou cause thy nations to fall any more, saith the Lord God.

16 Moreover the word of the Lord came unto me, saying,

17 Son of man, when the house of Israel dwelt in their own land, they defiled it by their own way and by their doings: their way was before me as the uncleanness of a removed woman.

18 Wherefore I poured my fury upon them for the blood that they had shed upon the land, and for their idols wherewith they had polluted it:

19 And I scattered them among the heathen, and they were dispersed through the countries: according to their way and according to their doings I judged them.

20 And when they entered unto the heathen, whither they went, they profaned my holy name, when they said to them, These are the people of the Lord, and are gone forth out of his land.

21 But I had pity for mine holy name, which the house of Israel had profaned among the heathen, whither they

in gentibus ad quas ingressi sunt

22. idcirco dices domui Israhel haec dicit Dominus Deus non propter vos ego faciam domus Israhel sed propter nomen sanctum meum quod polluistis in gentibus ad quas intrastis

23. et sanctificabo nomen meum magnum quod pollutum est inter gentes quod polluistis in medio earum ut sciant gentes quia ego Dominus ait Dominus exercituum cum sanctificatus fuero in vobis coram eis

24. tollam quippe vos de gentibus et congregabo de universis terris et adducam vos in terram vestram

25. et effundam super vos aquam mundam et mundabimini ab omnibus inquinamentis vestris et ab universis idolis vestris mundabo vos

26. et dabo vobis cor novum et spiritum novum ponam in medio vestri et auferam cor lapideum de carne vestra et dabo vobis cor carneum

went.

22 Therefore say unto the house of Israel, Thus saith the Lord God; I do not this for your sakes, O house of Israel, but for mine holy name's sake, which ye have profaned among the heathen, whither ye went.

23 And I will sanctify my great name, which was profaned among the heathen, which ye have profaned in the midst of them; and the heathen shall know that I am the Lord, saith the Lord God, when I shall be sanctified in you before their eyes.

24 For I will take you from among the heathen, and gather you out of all countries, and will bring you into your own land.

25 Then will I sprinkle clean water upon you, and ye shall be clean: from all your filthiness, and from all your idols, will I cleanse you.

26 A new heart also will I give you, and a new spirit will I put within you: and I will take away the stony heart out of your flesh, and I will give you an heart of flesh.

27 And I will put my spirit

27. et spiritum meum ponam in medio vestri et faciam ut in praeceptis meis ambuletis et iudicia mea custodiatis et operemini

28. et habitabitis in terra quam dedi patribus vestris et eritis mihi in populum et ego ero vobis in Deum

29. et salvabo vos ex universis inquinamentis vestris et vocabo frumentum et multiplicabo illud et non inponam in vobis famem

30. et multiplicabo fructum ligni et genimina agri ut non portetis ultra obprobrium famis in gentibus

31. et recordabimini viarum vestrarum pessimarum studiorumque non bonorum et displicebunt vobis iniquitates vestrae et scelera vestra

32. non propter vos ego faciam ait Dominus Deus notum sit vobis confundimini et erubescite super viis vestris domus Israhel

33. haec dicit Dominus

within you, and cause you to walk in my statutes, and ye shall keep my judgments, and do them.

28 And ye shall dwell in the land that I gave to your fathers; and ye shall be my people, and I will be your God.

29 I will also save you from all your uncleannesses: and I will call for the corn, and will increase it, and lay no famine upon you.

30 And I will multiply the fruit of the tree, and the increase of the field, that ye shall receive no more reproach of famine among the heathen.

31 Then shall ye remember your own evil ways, and your doings that were not good, and shall lothe yourselves in your own sight for your iniquities and for your abominations.

32 Not for your sakes do I this, saith the Lord God, be it known unto you: be ashamed and confounded for your own ways, O house of Israel.

33 Thus saith the Lord God; In the day that I shall have cleansed you from all your iniquities I will also cause

Deus in die qua mundavero vos ex omnibus iniquitatibus vestris et habitari fecero urbes et instauravero ruinosa

34. et terra deserta fuerit exculta quae quondam erat desolata in oculis omnis viatoris

35. dicent terra illa inculta facta est ut hortus voluptatis et civitates desertae et destitutae atque suffossae munitae sederunt

36. et scient gentes quaecumque derelictae fuerint in circuitu vestro quia ego Dominus aedificavi dissipata plantavique inculta ego Dominus locutus sum et fecerim

37. haec dicit Dominus Deus adhuc in hoc invenient me domus Israhel ut faciam eis multiplicabo eos sicut gregem hominum

38. ut gregem sanctum ut gregem Hierusalem in sollemnitatibus eius sic erunt civitates desertae plenaeque gregibus hominum et scient quia

you to dwell in the cities, and the wastes shall be builded.

34 And the desolate land shall be tilled, whereas it lay desolate in the sight of all that passed by.

35 And they shall say, This land that was desolate is become like the garden of Eden; and the waste and desolate and ruined cities are become fenced, and are inhabited.

36 Then the heathen that are left round about you shall know that I the Lord build the ruined places, and plant that that was desolate: I the Lord have spoken it, and I will do it.

37 Thus saith the Lord God; I will yet for this be inquired of by the house of Israel, to do it for them; I will increase them with men like a flock.

38 As the holy flock, as the flock of Jerusalem in her solemn feasts; so shall the waste cities be filled with flocks of men: and they shall know that I am the Lord.

ego Dominus

CHAPTER 37

1. facta est super me manus Domini et eduxit me in spiritu Domini et dimisit me in medio campi qui erat plenus ossibus
2. et circumduxit me per ea in gyro erant autem multa valde super faciem campi siccaque vehementer
3. et dixit ad me fili hominis putasne vivent ossa ista et dixi Domine Deus tu nosti
4. et dixit ad me vaticinare de ossibus istis et dices eis ossa arida audite verbum Domini
5. haec dicit Dominus Deus ossibus his ecce ego intromittam in vos spiritum et vivetis
6. et dabo super vos nervos et succrescere faciam super vos carnes et superextendam in vobis cutem et dabo vobis spiritum et vivetis et scietis quia ego Dominus
7. et prophetavi sicut

CHAPTER 37

THE hand of the Lord was upon me, and carried me out in the spirit of the Lord, and set me down in the midst of the valley which was full of bones,

2 And caused me to pass by them round about: and, behold, there were very many in the open valley; and, lo, they were very dry.

3 And he said unto me, Son of man, can these bones live? And I answered, O Lord God, thou knowest.

4 Again he said unto me, Prophesy upon these bones, and say unto them, O ye dry bones, hear the word of the Lord.

5 Thus saith the Lord God unto these bones; Behold, I will cause breath to enter into you, and ye shall live:

6 And I will lay sinews upon you, and will bring up flesh upon you, and cover you with skin, and put breath in you, and ye shall live; and ye shall know that I am the Lord.

praeceperat mihi factus
est autem sonitus
prophetante me et ecce
commotio et accesserunt
ossa ad ossa
unumquodque ad
iuncturam suam
8. et vidi et ecce super ea
nervi et carnes
ascenderunt et extenta est
in eis cutis desuper et
spiritum non habebant
9. et dixit ad me
vaticinare ad spiritum
vaticinare fili hominis et
dices ad spiritum haec
dicit Dominus Deus a
quattuor ventis veni
spiritus et insufla super
interfectos istos et
revivescant
10. et prophetavi sicut
praeceperat mihi et
ingressus est in ea spiritus
et vixerunt steteruntque
super pedes suos
exercitus grandis nimis
valde
11. et dixit ad me fili
hominis ossa haec
universa domus Israhel
est ipsi dicunt aruerunt
ossa nostra et periit spes
nostra et abscisi sumus
12. propterea vaticinare et
dices ad eos haec dicit

7 So I prophesied as I was
commanded: and as I
prophesied, there was a
noise, and behold a shaking,
and the bones came together,
bone to his bone.
8 And when I beheld, lo, the
sinews and the flesh came up
upon them, and the skin
covered them above: but
there was no breath in them.
9 Then said he unto me,
Prophesy unto the wind,
prophesy, son of man, and
say to the wind, Thus saith
the Lord God; Come from
the four winds, O breath, and
breathe upon these slain, that
they may live.
10 So I prophesied as he
commanded me, and the
breath came into them, and
they lived, and stood up upon
their feet, an exceeding great
army.
11 Then he said unto me,
Son of man, these bones are
the whole house of Israel:
behold, they say, Our bones
are dried, and our hope is
lost: we are cut off for our
parts.
12 Therefore prophesy and
say unto them, Thus saith the
Lord God; Behold, O my
people, I will open your

Dominus Deus ecce ego aperiam tumulos vestros et educam vos de sepulchris vestris populus meus et inducam vos in terram Israhel

13. et scietis quia ego Dominus cum aperuero sepulchra vestra et eduxero vos de tumulis vestris populus meus

14. et dedero spiritum meum in vobis et vixeritis et requiescere vos faciam super humum vestram et scietis quia ego Dominus locutus sum et feci ait Dominus Deus

15. et factus est sermo Domini ad me dicens

16. et tu fili hominis sume tibi lignum unum et scribe super illud Iudae et filiorum Israhel sociis eius et tolle lignum alterum et scribe super eum Ioseph lignum Ephraim et cunctae domui Israhel sociorumque eius

17. et adiunge illa unum ad alterum tibi in lignum unum et erunt in unionem in manu tua

18. cum autem dixerint ad te filii populi tui graves, and cause you to come up out of your graves, and bring you into the land of Israel.

13 And ye shall know that I am the Lord, when I have opened your graves, O my people, and brought you up out of your graves,

14 And shall put my spirit in you, and ye shall live, and I shall place you in your own land: then shall ye know that I the Lord have spoken it, and performed it, saith the Lord.

15 The word of the Lord came again unto me, saying,

16 Moreover, thou son of man, take thee one stick, and write upon it, For Judah, and for the children of Israel his companions: then take another stick, and write upon it, For Joseph, the stick of Ephraim, and for all the house of Israel his companions:

17 And join them one to another into one stick; and they shall become one in thine hand.

18 And when the children of thy people shall speak unto thee, saying, Wilt thou not shew us what thou meanest

loquentes nonne indicas nobis quid in his tibi velis 19. loqueris ad eos haec dicit Dominus Deus ecce ego adsumam lignum Ioseph quod est in manu Ephraim et tribus Israhel quae iunctae sunt ei et dabo eas pariter cum ligno Iuda et faciam eas in lignum unum et erunt unum in manu eius

20. erunt autem ligna super quae scripseris in manu tua in oculis eorum

21. et dices ad eos haec dicit Dominus Deus ecce ego adsumam filios Israhel de medio nationum ad quas abierunt et congregabo eos undique et adducam eos ad humum suam

22. et faciam eos gentem unam in terra in montibus Israhel et rex unus erit omnibus imperans et non erunt ultra duae gentes nec dividentur amplius in duo regna

23. neque polluentur ultra in idolis suis et abominationibus suis et in cunctis iniquitatibus suis et salvos eos faciam de universis sedibus suis

by these?

19 Say unto them, Thus saith the Lord God; Behold, I will take the stick of Joseph, which is in the hand of Ephraim, and the tribes of Israel his fellows, and will put them with him, even with the stick of Judah, and make them one stick, and they shall be one in mine hand.

20 And the sticks whereon thou writest shall be in thine hand before their eyes.

21 And say unto them, Thus saith the Lord God; Behold, I will take the children of Israel from among the heathen, whither they be gone, and will gather them on every side, and bring them into their own land:

22 And I will make them one nation in the land upon the mountains of Israel; and one king shall be king to them all: and they shall be no more two nations, neither shall they be divided into two kingdoms any more at all:

23 Neither shall they defile themselves any more with their idols, nor with their detestable things, nor with any of their transgressions: but I will save them out of all

in quibus peccaverunt et mundabo eos et erunt mihi populus et ego ero eis Deus

24. et servus meus David rex super eos et pastor unus erit omnium eorum in iudiciis meis ambulabunt et mandata mea custodient et facient ea

25. et habitabunt super terram quam dedi servo meo Iacob in qua habitaverunt patres vestri et habitabunt super eam ipsi et filii eorum et filii filiorum eorum usque in sempiternum et David servus meus princeps eorum in perpetuum

26. et percutiam illis foedus pacis pactum sempiternum erit eis et fundabo eos et multiplicabo et dabo sanctificationem meam in medio eorum in perpetuum

27. et erit tabernaculum meum in eis et ero eis Deus et ipsi erunt mihi populus

28. et scient gentes quia ego Dominus sanctificator Israhel cum

their dwellingplaces, wherein they have sinned, and will cleanse them: so shall they be my people, and I will be their God.

24 And David my servant shall be king over them; and they all shall have one shepherd: they shall also walk in my judgments, and observe my statutes, and do them.

25 And they shall dwell in the land that I have given unto Jacob my servant, wherein your fathers have dwelt; and they shall dwell therein, even they, and their children, and their children's children for ever: and my servant David shall be their prince for ever.

26 Moreover I will make a covenant of peace with them; it shall be an everlasting covenant with them: and I will place them, and multiply them, and will set my sanctuary in the midst of them for evermore.

27 My tabernacle also shall be with them: yea, I will be their God, and they shall be my people.

28 And the heathen shall know that I the Lord do

fuerit sanctificatio mea in medio eorum in perpetuum

sanctify Israel, when my sanctuary shall be in the midst of them for evermore.

CHAPTER 38

CHAPTER 38

1. et factus est sermo Domini ad me dicens
2. fili hominis pone faciem tuam contra Gog terram Magog principem capitis Mosoch et Thubal et vaticinare de eo
3. et dices ad eum haec dicit Dominus Deus ecce ego ad te Gog principem capitis Mosoch et Thubal
4. et circumagam te et ponam frenum in maxillis tuis et educam te et omnem exercitum tuum equos et equites vestitos loricis universos multitudinem magnam hastam et clypeum arripientium et gladium
5. Persae Aethiopes et Lybies cum eis omnes scutati et galeati
6. Gomer et universa agmina eius domus Thogorma latera aquilonis et totum robur eius populique multi tecum

AND the word of the Lord came unto me, saying,

2 Son of man, set thy face against Gog, the land of Magog, the chief prince of Meshech and Tubal, and prophesy against him,

3 And say, Thus saith the Lord God; Behold, I am against thee, O Gog, the chief prince of Meshech and Tubal:

4 And I will turn thee back, and put hooks into thy jaws, and I will bring thee forth, and all thine army, horses and horsemen, all of them clothed with all sorts of armour, even a great company with bucklers and shields, all of them handling swords:

5 Persia, Ethiopia, and Libya with them; all of them with shield and helmet:

6 Gomer, and all his bands; the house of Togarmah of the north quarters, and all his bands: and many people with

7. praepara et instrue te et omnem multitudinem tuam quae coacervata est ad te et esto eis in praeceptum

8. post dies multos visitaberis in novissimo annorum venies ad terram quae reversa est a gladio congregata est de populis multis ad montes Israhel qui fuerunt deserti iugiter haec de populis educta est et habitaverunt in ea confidenter universi

9. ascendens autem quasi tempestas venies et quasi nubes ut operias terram tu et omnia agmina tua et populi multi tecum

10. haec dicit Dominus Deus in die illa ascendent sermones super cor tuum et cogitabis cogitationem pessimam

11. et dices ascendam ad terram absque muro veniam ad quiescentes habitantesque secure omnes habitant sine muro vectes et portae non sunt eis

12. ut diripias spolia et invadas praedam ut inferas manum tuam super eos qui deserti

thee.

7 Be thou prepared, and prepare for thyself, thou, and all thy company that are assembled unto thee, and be thou a guard unto them.

8 After many days thou shalt be visited: in the latter years thou shalt come into the land that is brought back from the sword, and is gathered out of many people, against the mountains of Israel, which have been always waste: but it is brought forth out of the nations, and they shall dwell safely all of them.

9 Thou shalt ascend and come like a storm, thou shalt be like a cloud to cover the land, thou, and all thy bands, and many people with thee.

10 Thus saith the Lord God; It shall also come to pass, that at the same time shall things come into thy mind, and thou shalt think an evil thought:

11 And thou shalt say, I will go up to the land of unwalled villages; I will go to them that are at rest, that dwell safely, all of them dwelling without walls, and having neither bars nor gates,

12 To take a spoil, and to

fuerant et postea restituti et super populum qui est congregatus ex gentibus qui possidere coepit et esse habitator umbilici terrae

13. Seba et Dedan et negotiatores Tharsis et omnes leones eius dicent tibi numquid ad sumenda spolia tu venis ecce ad diripiendam praedam congregasti multitudinem tuam ut tollas argentum et aurum auferas supellectilem atque substantiam et diripias manubias infinitas

14. propterea vaticinare fili hominis et dices ad Gog haec dicit Dominus Deus numquid non in die illo cum habitaverit populus meus Israhel confidenter scies

15. et venies de loco tuo a lateribus aquilonis tu et populi multi tecum ascensores equorum universi coetus magnus et exercitus vehemens

16. et ascendes super populum meum Israhel quasi nubes ut operias terram in novissimis diebus eris et adducam te

take a prey; to turn thine hand upon the desolate places that are now inhabited, and upon the people that are gathered out of the nations, which have gotten cattle and goods, that dwell in the midst of the land.

13 Sheba, and Dedan, and the merchants of Tarshish, with all the young lions thereof, shall say unto thee, Art thou come to take a spoil? hast thou gathered thy company to take a prey? to carry away silver and gold, to take away cattle and goods, to take a great spoil?

14 Therefore, son of man, prophesy and say unto Gog, Thus saith the Lord God; In that day when my people of Israel dwelleth safely, shalt thou not know it?

15 And thou shalt come from thy place out of the north parts, thou, and many people with thee, all of them riding upon horses, a great company, and a mighty army:

16 And thou shalt come up against my people of Israel, as a cloud to cover the land; it shall be in the latter days,

super terram meam ut sciant gentes me cum sanctificatus fuero in te in oculis eorum o Gog

17. haec dicit Dominus Deus tu ergo ille es de quo locutus sum in diebus antiquis in manu servorum meorum prophetarum Israhel qui prophetaverunt in diebus illorum temporum ut adducerem te super eos

18. et erit in die illa in die adventus Gog super terram Israhel ait Dominus Deus ascendet indignatio mea in furore meo

19. et in zelo meo in igne irae meae locutus sum quia in die illa erit commotio magna super terram Israhel

20. et commovebuntur a facie mea pisces maris et volucres caeli et bestiae agri et omne reptile quod movetur super humum cunctique homines qui sunt super faciem terrae et subvertentur montes et cadent sepes et omnis murus in terra corruet

21. et convocabo adversum eum in cunctis

and I will bring thee against my land, that the heathen may know me, when I shall be sanctified in thee, O Gog, before their eyes.

17 Thus saith the Lord God; Art thou he of whom I have spoken in old time by my servants the prophets of Israel, which prophesied in those days many years that I would bring thee against them?

18 And it shall come to pass at the same time when Gog shall come against the land of Israel, saith the Lord God, that my fury shall come up in my face.

19 For in my jealousy and in the fire of my wrath have I spoken, Surely in that day there shall be a great shaking in the land of Israel;

20 So that the fishes of the sea, and the fowls of the heaven, and the beasts of the field, and all creeping things that creep upon the earth, and all the men that are upon the face of the earth, shall shake at my presence, and the mountains shall be thrown down, and the steep places shall fall, and every wall shall fall to the ground.

montibus meis gladium ait Dominus Deus gladius uniuscuiusque in fratrem suum dirigetur

22. et iudicabo eum peste et sanguine et imbre vehementi et lapidibus inmensis ignem et sulphur pluam super eum et super exercitum eius et super populos multos qui sunt cum eo

23. et magnificabor et sanctificabor et notus ero in oculis gentium multarum et scient quia ego Dominus

21 And I will call for a sword against him throughout all my mountains, saith the Lord God: every man's sword shall be against his brother.

22 And I will plead against him with pestilence and with blood; and I will rain upon him, and upon his bands, and upon the many people that are with him, an overflowing rain, and great hailstones, fire, and brimstone.

23 Thus will I magnify myself, and sanctify myself; and I will be known in the eyes of many nations, and they shall know that I am the Lord.

CHAPTER 39

CHAPTER 39

1. tu autem fili hominis vaticinare adversum Gog et dices haec dicit Dominus Deus ecce ego super te Gog principem capitis Mosoch et Thubal

2. et circumagam te et seducam te et ascendere faciam de lateribus aquilonis et adducam te super montes Israhel

3. et percutiam arcum tuum in manu sinistra tua

THEREFORE, thou son of man, prophesy against Gog, and say, Thus saith the Lord God; Behold, I am against thee, O Gog, the chief prince of Meshech and Tubal:

2 And I will turn thee back, and leave but the sixth part of thee, and will cause thee to come up from the north parts, and will bring thee upon the mountains of Israel:

3 And I will smite thy bow

et sagittas tuas de manu dextera tua deiciam

4. super montes Israhel cades tu et omnia agmina tua et populi qui sunt tecum feris avibus omnique volatili et bestiis terrae dedi te devorandum

5. super faciem agri cades quia ego locutus sum ait Dominus Deus

6. et emittam ignem in Magog et in his qui habitant in insulis confidenter et scient quia ego Dominus

7. et nomen sanctum meum notum faciam in medio populi mei Israhel et non polluam nomen sanctum meum amplius et scient gentes quia ego Dominus Sanctus Israhel

8. ecce venit et factum est ait Dominus Deus haec est dies de qua locutus sum

9. et egredientur habitatores de civitatibus Israhel et succendent et conburent arma clypeum et hastas arcum et sagittas et baculos manus et contos et succendent ea igne septem annis

out of thy left hand, and will cause thine arrows to fall out of thy right hand.

4 Thou shalt fall upon the mountains of Israel, thou, and all thy bands, and the people that is with thee: I will give thee unto the ravenous birds of every sort, and to the beasts of the field to be devoured.

5 Thou shalt fall upon the open field: for I have spoken it, saith the Lord God.

6 And I will send a fire on Magog, and among them that dwell carelessly in the isles: and they shall know that I am the Lord.

7 So will I make my holy name known in the midst of my people Israel; and I will not let them pollute my holy name any more: and the heathen shall know that I am the Lord, the Holy One in Israel.

8 Behold, it is come, and it is done, saith the Lord God; this is the day whereof I have spoken.

9 And they that dwell in the cities of Israel shall go forth, and shall set on fire and burn the weapons, both the shields and the bucklers, the bows

10. et non portabunt ligna de regionibus neque succident de saltibus quoniam arma succendent igne et depraedabuntur eos quibus praedae fuerant et diripient vastatores suos ait Dominus Deus

11. et erit in die illa dabo Gog locum nominatum sepulchrum in Israhel vallem Viatorum ad orientem maris quae obstupescere facit praetereuntes et sepelient ibi Gog et omnem multitudinem eius et vocabitur vallis Multitudinis Gog

12. et sepelient eos domus Israhel ut mundent terram septem mensibus

13. sepeliet autem omnis populus terrae et erit eis nominata dies in qua glorificatus sum ait Dominus Deus

14. et viros iugiter constituent lustrantes terram qui sepeliant et requirant eos qui remanserant super faciem terrae ut emundent eam post menses autem septem quaerere incipient

and the arrows, and the handstaves, and the spears, and they shall burn them with fire seven years:

10 So that they shall take no wood out of the field, neither cut down any out of the forests; for they shall burn the weapons with fire: and they shall spoil those that spoiled them, and rob those that robbed them, saith the Lord God.

11 And it shall come to pass in that day, that I will give unto Gog a place there of graves in Israel, the valley of the passengers on the east of the sea: and it shall stop the noses of the passengers: and there shall they bury Gog and all his multitude: and they shall call it The valley of Hamon-gog.

12 And seven months shall the house of Israel be burying of them, that they may cleanse the land.

13 Yea, all the people of the land shall bury them; and it shall be to them a renown the day that I shall be glorified, saith the Lord God.

14 And they shall sever out men of continual employment, passing through

15. et circumibunt peragrantes terram cumque viderint os hominis statuent iuxta illud titulum donec sepeliant illud pollinctores in valle Multitudinis Gog

16. nomen autem civitatis Amona et mundabunt terram

17. tu ergo fili hominis haec dicit Dominus Deus dic omni volucri et universis avibus cunctisque bestiis agri convenite properate concurrite undique ad victimam meam quam ego immolo vobis victimam grandem super montes Israhel ut comedatis carnes et bibatis sanguinem

18. carnes fortium comedetis et sanguinem principum terrae bibetis arietum agnorum et hircorum taurorumque altilium et pinguium omnium

19. et comedetis adipem in saturitate et bibetis sanguinem in ebrietate de victima quam ego immolabo vobis

the land to bury with the passengers those that remain upon the face of the earth, to cleanse it: after the end of seven months shall they search.

15 And the passengers that pass through the land, when any seeth a man's bone, then shall he set up a sign by it, till the buriers have buried it in the valley of Hamon-gog.

16 And also the name of the city shall be Hamonah. Thus shall they cleanse the land.

17 And, thou son of man, thus saith the Lord God; Speak unto every feathered fowl, and to every beast of the field, Assemble yourselves, and come; gather yourselves on every side to my sacrifice that I do sacrifice for you, even a great sacrifice upon the mountains of Israel, that ye may eat flesh, and drink blood.

18 Ye shall eat the flesh of the mighty, and drink the blood of the princes of the earth, of rams, of lambs, and of goats, of bullocks, all of them fatlings of Bashan.

19 And ye shall eat fat till ye be full, and drink blood till ye be drunken, of my

20. et saturabimini super mensam meam de equo et de equite forti et de universis viris bellatoribus ait Dominus Deus

21. et ponam gloriam meam in gentibus et videbunt omnes gentes iudicium meum quod fecerim et manum meam quam posuerim super eos

22. et scient domus Israhel quia ego Dominus Deus eorum a die illa et deinceps

23. et scient gentes quoniam in iniquitate sua capta sit domus Israhel eo quod reliquerint me et absconderim faciem meam ab eis et tradiderim eos in manu hostium et ceciderint in gladio universi

24. iuxta inmunditiam eorum et scelus feci eis et abscondi faciem meam ab illis

25. propterea haec dicit Dominus Deus nunc reducam captivitatem Iacob et miserebor omnis domus Israhel et adsumam zelum pro nomine sancto meo

sacrifice which I have sacrificed for you.

20 Thus ye shall be filled at my table with horses and chariots, with mighty men, and with all men of war, saith the Lord God.

21 And I will set my glory among the heathen, and all the heathen shall see my judgment that I have executed, and my hand that I have laid upon them.

22 So the house of Israel shall know that I am the Lord their God from that day and forward.

23 And the heathen shall know that the house of Israel went into captivity for their iniquity: because they trespassed against me, therefore hid I my face from them, and gave them into the hand of their enemies: so fell they all by the sword.

24 According to their uncleanness and according to their transgressions have I done unto them, and hid my face from them.

25 Therefore thus saith the Lord God; Now will I bring again the captivity of Jacob, and have mercy upon the whole house of Israel, and

26. et portabunt confusionem suam et omnem praevaricationem quam praevaricati sunt in me cum habitaverint in terra sua confidenter neminem formidantes

27. et reduxero eos de populis et congregavero de terris inimicorum suorum et sanctificatus fuero in eis in oculis gentium plurimarum

28. et scient quia ego Dominus Deus eorum eo quod transtulerim eos in nationes et congregavero eos super terram suam et non dereliquerim quemquam ex eis ibi

29. et non abscondam ultra faciem meam ab eis eo quod effuderim spiritum meum super omnem domum Israhel ait Dominus Deus

will be jealous for my holy name;

26 After that they have borne their shame, and all their trespasses whereby they have trespassed against me, when they dwelt safely in their land, and none made them afraid.

27 When I have brought them again from the people, and gathered them out of their enemies' lands, and am sanctified in them in the sight of many nations;

28 Then shall they know that I am the Lord their God, which caused them to be led into captivity among the heathen: but I have gathered them unto their own land, and have left none of them any more there.

29 Neither will I hide my face any more from them: for I have poured out my spirit upon the house of Israel, saith the Lord God.

CHAPTER 40

CHAPTER 40

1. in vicesimo et quinto anno transmigrationis nostrae in exordio anni decima mensis

IN the five and twentieth year of our captivity, in the beginning of the year, in the tenth day of the month, in the

quartodecimo anno postquam percussa est civitas in ipsa hac die facta est super me manus Domini et adduxit me illuc

2. in visionibus Dei adduxit me in terram Israhel et dimisit me super montem excelsum nimis super quem erat quasi aedificium civitatis vergentis ad austrum

3. et introduxit me illuc et ecce vir cuius erat species quasi species aeris et funiculus lineus in manu eius et calamus mensurae in manu eius stabat autem in porta

4. et locutus est ad me idem vir fili hominis vide oculis tuis et auribus tuis audi et pone cor tuum in omnia quae ego ostendam tibi quia ut ostendantur tibi adductus es huc adnuntia omnia quae tu vides domui Israhel

5. et ecce murus forinsecus in circuitu domus undique et in manu viri calamus mensurae sex cubitorum et palmo et mensus est latitudinem aedificii

fourteenth year after that the city was smitten, in the selfsame day the hand of the Lord was upon me, and brought me thither.

2 In the visions of God brought he me into the land of Israel, and set me upon a very high mountain, by which was as the frame of a city on the south.

3 And he brought me thither, and, behold, there was a man, whose appearance was like the appearance of brass, with a line of flax in his hand, and a measuring reed; and he stood in the gate.

4 And the man said unto me, Son of man, behold with thine eyes, and hear with thine ears, and set thine heart upon all that I shall shew thee; for to the intent that I might shew them unto thee art thou brought hither: declare all that thou seest to the house of Israel.

5 And behold a wall on the outside of the house round about, and in the man's hand a measuring reed of six cubits long by the cubit and an hand breadth: so he measured the breadth of the building, one reed; and the

calamo uno altitudinem quoque calamo uno

6. et venit ad portam quae respiciebat viam orientalem et ascendit per gradus eius et mensus est limen portae calamo uno latitudinem id est limen unum calamo uno in latitudine

7. et thalamum uno calamo in longum et uno calamo in latum et inter thalamos quinque cubitos

8. et limen portae iuxta vestibulum portae intrinsecus calamo uno

9. et mensus est vestibulum portae octo cubitorum et frontem eius duobus cubitis vestibulum autem portae erat intrinsecus

10. porro thalami portae ad viam orientalem tres hinc et tres inde mensura una trium et mensura una frontium ex utraque parte

11. et mensus est latitudinem liminis portae decem cubitorum et longitudinem portae tredecim cubitorum

12. et marginem ante thalamos cubiti unius et cubitus unus finis

height, one reed.

6 Then came he unto the gate which looketh toward the east, and went up the stairs thereof, and measured the threshold of the gate, which was one reed broad; and the other threshold of the gate, which was one reed broad.

7 And every little chamber was one reed long, and one reed broad; and between the little chambers were five cubits; and the threshold of the gate by the porch of the gate within was one reed.

8 He measured also the porch of the gate within, one reed.

9 Then measured he the porch of the gate, eight cubits; and the posts thereof, two cubits; and the porch of the gate was inward.

10 And the little chambers of the gate eastward were three on this side, and three on that side; they three were of one measure: and the posts had one measure on this side and on that side.

11 And he measured the breadth of the entry of the gate, ten cubits; and the length of the gate, thirteen cubits.

utrimque thalami autem sex cubitorum erant hinc et inde

13. et mensus est portam a tecto thalami usque ad tectum eius latitudinem viginti et quinque cubitorum ostium contra ostium

14. et fecit frontes per sexaginta cubitos et ad frontem atrium portae undique per circuitum

15. et ante faciem portae quae pertingebat usque ad faciem vestibuli portae interioris quinquaginta cubitos

16. et fenestras obliquas in thalamis et in frontibus eorum quae erant intra portam undique per circuitum similiter autem erant et in vestibulis fenestrae per gyrum intrinsecus et ante frontes pictura palmarum

17. et eduxit me ad atrium exterius et ecce gazofilacia et pavimentum stratum lapide in atrio per circuitum triginta gazofilacia in circuitu pavimenti

18. et pavimentum in

12 The space also before the little chambers was one cubit on this side, and the space was one cubit on that side: and the little chambers were six cubits on this side, and six cubits on that side.

13 He measured then the gate from the roof of one little chamber to the roof of another: the breadth was five and twenty cubits, door against door.

14 He made also posts of threescore cubits, even unto the post of the court round about the gate.

15 And from the face of the gate of the entrance unto the face of the porch of the inner gate were fifty cubits.

16 And there were narrow windows to the little chambers, and to their posts within the gate round about, and likewise to the arches: and windows were round about inward: and upon each post were palm trees.

17 Then brought he me into the outward court, and, lo, there were chambers, and a pavement made for the court round about: thirty chambers were upon the pavement.

18 And the pavement by the

fronte portarum secundum longitudinem portarum erat inferius

19. et mensus est latitudinem a facie portae inferioris usque ad frontem atrii interioris extrinsecus centum cubitos ad orientem et ad aquilonem

20. portam quoque quae respiciebat viam aquilonis atrii exterioris mensus est tam in longitudine quam in latitudine

21. et thalamos eius tres hinc et tres inde et frontem eius et vestibulum eius secundum mensuram portae prioris quinquaginta cubitorum longitudinem eius et latitudinem viginti quinque cubitorum

22. fenestrae autem eius et vestibulum et scalpturae secundum mensuram portae quae respiciebat ad orientem et septem graduum erat ascensus eius et vestibulum ante eam

23. et porta atrii interioris contra portam aquilonis

side of the gates over against the length of the gates was the lower pavement.

19 Then he measured the breadth from the forefront of the lower gate unto the forefront of the inner court without, an hundred cubits eastward and northward.

20 And the gate of the outward court that looked toward the north, he measured the length thereof, and the breadth thereof.

21 And the little chambers thereof were three on this side and three on that side; and the posts thereof and the arches thereof were after the measure of the first gate: the length thereof was fifty cubits, and the breadth five and twenty cubits.

22 And their windows, and their arches, and their palm trees, were after the measure of the gate that looketh toward the east; and they went up unto it by seven steps; and the arches thereof were before them.

23 And the gate of the inner court was over against the gate toward the north, and toward the east; and he measured from gate to gate

et orientalem et mensus est a porta usque ad portam centum cubitos

24. et duxit me ad viam australem et ecce porta quae respiciebat ad austrum et mensus est frontem eius et vestibulum eius iuxta mensuras superiores

25. et fenestras eius et vestibula in circuitu sicut fenestras ceteras quinquaginta cubitorum longitudine et latitudine viginti quinque cubitorum

26. et in gradibus septem ascendebatur ad eam et vestibulum ante fores eius et celatae palmae erant una hinc et altera inde in fronte eius

27. et porta atrii interioris in via australi et mensus est a porta usque ad portam in via australi centum cubitos

28. et introduxit me in atrium interius ad portam australem et mensus est portam iuxta mensuras superiores

29. thalamum eius et frontem eius et vestibulum eius hisdem mensuris et fenestras eius

an hundred cubits.

24 After that he brought me toward the south, and behold a gate toward the south: and he measured the posts thereof and the arches thereof according to these measures.

25 And there were windows in it and in the arches thereof round about, like those windows: the length was fifty cubits, and the breadth five and twenty cubits.

26 And there were seven steps to go up to it, and the arches thereof were before them: and it had palm trees, one on this side, and another on that side, upon the posts thereof.

27 And there was a gate in the inner court toward the south: and he measured from gate to gate toward the south an hundred cubits.

28 And he brought me to the inner court by the south gate: and he measured the south gate according to these measures;

29 And the little chambers thereof, and the posts thereof, and the arches thereof, according to these measures: and there were windows in it and in the arches thereof

et vestibulorum eius in circuitu quinquaginta cubitos longitudinis et latitudinis viginti quinque cubitos

30. et vestibulum per gyrum longitudine viginti quinque cubitorum et latitudine quinque cubitorum

31. et vestibulum eius ad atrium exterius et palmas eius in fronte et octo gradus erant quibus ascendebatur per eam

32. et introduxit me in atrium interius per viam orientalem et mensus est portam secundum mensuras superiores

33. thalamum eius et frontem eius et vestibula eius sicut supra et fenestras eius et vestibuli eius in circuitu longitudine quinquaginta cubitorum et latitudine viginti quinque cubitorum

34. et vestibulum eius id est atrii exterioris et palmae celatae in fronte eius hinc et inde et in octo gradibus ascensus eius

35. et introduxit me ad portam quae respiciebat

round about: it was fifty cubits long, and five and twenty cubits broad.

30 And the arches round about were five and twenty cubits long, and five cubits broad.

31 And the arches thereof were toward the utter court; and palm trees were upon the posts thereof: and the going up to it had eight steps.

32 And he brought me into the inner court toward the east: and he measured the gate according to these measures.

33 And the little chambers thereof, and the posts thereof, and the arches thereof, were according to these measures: and there were windows therein and in the arches thereof round about: it was fifty cubits long, and five and twenty cubits broad.

34 And the arches thereof were toward the outward court; and palm trees were upon the posts thereof, on this side, and on that side: and the going up to it had eight steps.

35 And he brought me to the north gate, and measured it according to these measures;

ad aquilonem et mensus est secundum mensuras superiores

36. thalamum eius frontem eius vestibulum eius et fenestras eius per circuitum longitudine quinquaginta cubitorum et latitudine viginti quinque cubitorum

37. vestibulum eius in atrium exterius et celatura palmarum in fronte illius hinc et inde et in octo gradibus ascensus eius

38. et per singula gazofilacia ostium in frontibus portarum ibi lavabunt holocaustum

39. et in vestibulo portae duae mensae hinc et duae mensae inde ut immoletur super eas holocaustum et pro peccato et pro delicto

40. et ad latus exterius quod ascendit ad ostium portae quae pergit ad aquilonem duae mensae et ad latus alterum ante vestibulum portae duae mensae

41. quattuor mensae hinc et quattuor mensae inde per latera portae octo mensae erunt super quas immolabunt

36 The little chambers thereof, the posts thereof, and the arches thereof, and the windows to it round about: the length was fifty cubits, and the breadth five and twenty cubits.

37 And the posts thereof were toward the utter court; and palm trees were upon the posts thereof, on this side, and on that side: and the going up to it had eight steps.

38 And the chambers and the entries thereof were by the posts of the gates, where they washed the burnt offering.

39 And in the porch of the gate were two tables on this side, and two tables on that side, to slay thereon the burnt offering and the sin offering and the trespass offering.

40 And at the side without, as one goeth up to the entry of the north gate, were two tables; and on the other side, which was at the porch of the gate, were two tables.

41 Four tables were on this side, and four tables on that side, by the side of the gate; eight tables, whereupon they slew their sacrifices.

42 And the four tables were of hewn stone for the burnt

42. quattuor autem mensae ad holocaustum de lapidibus quadris extructae longitudine cubiti unius et dimidii et latitudine cubiti unius et dimidii et altitudine cubiti unius super quas ponant vasa in quibus immolatur holocaustum et victima

43. et labia earum palmi unius reflexa intrinsecus per circuitum super mensas autem carnes oblationis

44. et extra portam interiorem gazofilacia cantorum in atrio interiori quod erat in latere portae respicientis ad aquilonem et facies eorum contra viam australem una ex latere portae orientalis quae respiciebat ad viam aquilonis

45. et dixit ad me hoc est gazofilacium quod respicit viam meridianam sacerdotum qui excubant in custodiis templi

46. porro gazofilacium quod respicit ad viam aquilonis sacerdotum erit qui excubant ad ministerium altaris isti sunt filii Sadoc qui

offering, of a cubit and an half long, and a cubit and an half broad, and one cubit high: whereupon also they laid the instruments wherewith they slew the burnt offering and the sacrifice.

43 And within were hooks, an hand broad, fastened round about: and upon the tables was the flesh of the offering.

44 And without the inner gate were the chambers of the singers in the inner court, which was at the side of the north gate; and their prospect was toward the south: one at the side of the east gate having the prospect toward the north.

45 And he said unto me, This chamber, whose prospect is toward the south, is for the priests, the keepers of the charge of the house.

46 And the chamber whose prospect is toward the north is for the priests, the keepers of the charge of the altar: these are the sons of Zadok among the sons of Levi, which come near to the Lord to minister unto him.

47 So he measured the court,

accedunt de filiis Levi ad Dominum ut ministrent ei 47. et mensus est atrium longitudine centum cubitorum et latitudine centum cubitorum per quadrum et altare ante faciem templi

48. et introduxit me in vestibulum templi et mensus est vestibulum quinque cubitis hinc et quinque cubitis inde et latitudinem portae trium cubitorum hinc et trium cubitorum inde

49. longitudinem autem vestibuli viginti cubitorum et latitudinem undecim cubitorum et octo gradibus ascendebatur ad eam et columnae erant in frontibus una hinc et altera inde

an hundred cubits long, and an hundred cubits broad, foursquare; and the altar that was before the house.

48 And he brought me to the porch of the house, and measured each post of the porch, five cubits on this side, and five cubits on that side: and the breadth of the gate was three cubits on this side, and three cubits on that side.

49 The length of the porch was twenty cubits, and the breadth eleven cubits; and he brought me by the steps whereby they went up to it: and there were pillars by the posts, one on this side, and another on that side.

CHAPTER 41

1. et introduxit me in templum et mensus est frontes sex cubitos latitudinis hinc et sex cubitos latitudinis inde latitudinem tabernaculi

2. et latitudo portae

CHAPTER 41

AFTERWARD he brought me to the temple, and measured the posts, six cubits broad on the one side, and six cubits broad on the other side, which was the breadth of the tabernacle.

decem cubitorum erat et latera portae quinque cubitis hinc et quinque cubitis inde et mensus est longitudinem eius quadraginta cubitorum et latitudinem viginti cubitorum

3. et introgressus intrinsecus mensus est in fronte portae duos cubitos et portam sex cubitorum et latitudinem portae septem cubitorum

4. et mensus est longitudinem eius viginti cubitorum et latitudinem viginti cubitorum ante faciem templi et dixit ad me hoc est sanctum sanctorum

5. et mensus est parietem domus sex cubitorum et latitudinem lateris quattuor cubitorum undique per circuitum domus

6. latera autem latus ad latus bis triginta tria et erant eminentia quae ingrederentur per parietem domus in lateribus per circuitum ut continerent et non adtingerent parietem templi

2 And the breadth of the door was ten cubits; and the sides of the door were five cubits on the one side, and five cubits on the other side: and he measured the length thereof, forty cubits: and the breadth, twenty cubits.

3 Then went he inward, and measured the post of the door, two cubits; and the door, six cubits; and the breadth of the door, seven cubits.

4 So he measured the length thereof, twenty cubits; and the breadth, twenty cubits, before the temple: and he said unto me, This is the most holy place.

5 After he measured the wall of the house, six cubits; and the breadth of every side chamber, four cubits, round about the house on every side.

6 And the side chambers were three, one over another, and thirty in order; and they entered into the wall which was of the house for the side chambers round about, that they might have hold, but they had not hold in the wall of the house.

7 And there was an

7. et platea erat in rotundum ascendens sursum per cocleam et in cenaculum templi deferebat per gyrum idcirco latius erat templum in superioribus et sic de inferioribus ascendebatur ad superiora in medium

8. et vidi in domo altitudinem per circuitum fundata latera ad mensuram calami sex cubitorum spatio

9. et latitudinem per parietem lateris forinsecus quinque cubitorum et interior domus in lateribus domus

10. et inter gazofilacia latitudinem viginti cubitorum in circuitu domus undique

11. et ostium lateris ad orationem ostium unum ad viam aquilonis et ostium unum ad viam australem et latitudinem loci ad orationem quinque cubitorum in circuitu

12. et aedificium quod erat separatum versumque ad viam respicientem ad mare

enlarging, and a winding about still upward to the side chambers: for the winding about of the house went still upward round about the house: therefore the breadth of the house was still upward, and so increased from the lowest chamber to the highest by the midst.

8 I saw also the height of the house round about: the foundations of the side chambers were a full reed of six great cubits.

9 The thickness of the wall, which was for the side chamber without, was five cubits: and that which was left was the place of the side chambers that were within.

10 And between the chambers was the wideness of twenty cubits round about the house on every side.

11 And the doors of the side chambers were toward the place that was left, one door toward the north, and another door toward the south: and the breadth of the place that was left was five cubits round about.

12 Now the building that was before the separate place at the end toward the west was

latitudinis septuaginta cubitorum paries autem aedificii quinque cubitorum latitudinis per circuitum et longitudo eius nonaginta cubitorum

13. et mensus est domus longitudinem centum cubitorum et quod separatum erat aedificium et parietes eius longitudinis centum cubitorum

14. latitudo autem ante faciem domus et eius quod erat separatum contra orientem centum cubitorum

15. et mensus est longitudinem aedificii contra faciem eius quod erat separatum ad dorsum ekthetas ex utraque parte centum cubitorum et templum interius et vestibula atrii

16. limina et fenestras obliquas et ekthetas in circuitu per tres partes contra uniuscuiusque limen stratumque ligno per gyrum in circuitu terra autem usque ad fenestras et fenestrae clausae super ostia

17. et usque ad domum

seventy cubits broad; and the wall of the building was five cubits thick round about, and the length thereof ninety cubits.

13 So he measured the house, an hundred cubits long; and the separate place, and the building, with the walls thereof, an hundred cubits long;

14 Also the breadth of the face of the house, and of the separate place toward the east, an hundred cubits.

15 And he measured the length of the building over against the separate place which was behind it, and the galleries thereof on the one side and on the other side, an hundred cubits, with the inner temple, and the porches of the court;

16 The door posts, and the narrow windows, and the galleries round about on their three stories, over against the door, cieled with wood round about, and from the ground up to the windows, and the windows were covered;

17 To that above the door, even unto the inner house, and without, and by all the wall round about within and

interiorem et forinsecus per omnem parietem in circuitu intrinsecus et forinsecus ad mensuram

18. et fabrefacta cherubin et palmae et palma inter cherub et cherub duasque facies habebat cherub

19. faciem hominis iuxta palmam ex hac parte et faciem leonis iuxta palmam ex alia parte expressam per omnem domum in circuitu

20. de terra usque ad superiora portae cherubin et palmae celatae erant in pariete templi

21. limen quadrangulum et facies sanctuarii aspectus contra aspectum

22. altaris lignei trium cubitorum altitudo et longitudo eius duo cubitorum et anguli eius et longitudo eius et parietes eius lignei et locutus est ad me haec est mensa coram Domino

23. et duo ostia erant in templo et in sanctuario

24. et in duobus ostiis ex utraque parte bina erant ostiola quae in se invicem plicabantur bina enim ostia erant ex utraque

without, by measure.

18 And it was made with cherubims and palm trees, so that a palm tree was between a cherub and a cherub; and every cherub had two faces;

19 So that the face of a man was toward the palm tree on the one side, and the face of a young lion toward the palm tree on the other side: it was made through all the house round about.

20 From the ground unto above the door were cherubims and palm trees made, and on the wall of the temple.

21 The posts of the temple were squared, and the face of the sanctuary; the appearance of the one as the appearance of the other.

22 The altar of wood was three cubits high, and the length thereof two cubits; and the corners thereof, and the length thereof, and the walls thereof, were of wood: and he said unto me, This is the table that is before the Lord.

23 And the temple and the sanctuary had two doors.

24 And the doors had two leaves apiece, two turning

parte ostiorum

25. et celata erant in ipsis ostiis templi cherubin et scalptura palmarum sicut in parietibus quoque expressa erat quam ob rem erant et grossiora ligna in vestibuli fronte forinsecus

26. super quae fenestrae obliquae et similitudo palmarum hinc atque inde in umerulis vestibuli secundum latera domus latitudinemque parietum

leaves; two leaves for the one door, and two leaves for the other door.

25 And there were made on them, on the doors of the temple, cherubims and palm trees, like as were made upon the walls; and there were thick planks upon the face of the porch without.

26 And there were narrow windows and palm trees on the one side and on the other side, on the sides of the porch, and upon the side chambers of the house, and thick planks.

CHAPTER 42

1. et eduxit me in atrium exterius per viam ducentem ad aquilonem et eduxit me in gazofilacium quod erat contra separatum aedificium et contra aedem vergentem ad aquilonem

2. in facie longitudinis centum cubitos ostii aquilonis et latitudinis quinquaginta cubitos

3. contra viginti cubitos atrii interioris et contra

CHAPTER 42

THEN he brought me forth into the utter court, the way toward the north: and he brought me into the chamber that was over against the separate place, and which was before the building toward the north.

2 Before the length of an hundred cubits was the north door, and the breadth was fifty cubits.

3 Over against the twenty cubits which were for the inner court, and over against

pavimentum stratum lapide atrii exterioris ubi erat porticus iuncta porticui triplici

4. et ante gazofilacia deambulatio decem cubitorum latitudinis ad interiora respiciens viae cubiti unius et ostia earum ad aquilonem

5. ubi erant gazofilacia in superioribus humiliora quia subportabant porticus quae ex illis eminebant de inferioribus et de mediis aedificii

6. tristega enim erant et non habebant columnas sicut erant columnae atriorum propterea eminebant de inferioribus et de mediis a terra

7. et peribolus exterior secundum gazofilacia quae erant in via atrii exterioris ante gazofilacia longitudo eius quinquaginta cubitorum

8. quia longitudo erat gazofilaciorum atrii exterioris quinquaginta cubitorum et longitudo ante faciem templi centum cubitorum

9. et erat subter gazofilacia haec introitus

the pavement which was for the utter court, was gallery against gallery in three stories.

4 And before the chambers was a walk of ten cubits breadth inward, a way of one cubit; and their doors toward the north.

5 Now the upper chambers were shorter: for the galleries were higher than these, than the lower, and than the middlemost of the building.

6 For they were in three stories, but had not pillars as the pillars of the courts: therefore the building was straitened more than the lowest and the middlemost from the ground.

7 And the wall that was without over against the chambers, toward the utter court on the forepart of the chambers, the length thereof was fifty cubits.

8 For the length of the chambers that were in the utter court was fifty cubits: and, lo, before the temple were an hundred cubits.

9 And from under these chambers was the entry on the east side, as one goeth into them from the utter

ab oriente ingredientium in ea de atrio exteriori

10. in latitudine periboli atrii quod erat contra viam orientalem in facie aedificii separati et erant ante aedificium gazofilacia

11. et via ante faciem eorum iuxta similitudinem gazofilaciorum quae erant in via aquilonis secundum longitudinem eorum sic et latitudo eorum et omnis introitus eorum et similitudines et ostia eorum

12. secundum ostia gazofilaciorum quae erant in via respiciente ad notum ostium in capite viae quae via erat ante vestibulum separatum per viam orientalem ingredientibus

13. et dixit ad me gazofilacia aquilonis et gazofilacia austri quae sunt ante aedificium separatum haec sunt gazofilacia sancta in quibus vescuntur sacerdotes qui adpropinquant ad Dominum in sancta court.

10 The chambers were in the thickness of the wall of the court toward the east, over against the separate place, and over against the building.

11 And the way before them was like the appearance of the chambers which were toward the north, as long as they, and as broad as they: and all their goings out were both according to their fashions, and according to their doors.

12 And according to the doors of the chambers that were toward the south was a door in the head of the way, even the way directly before the wall toward the east, as one entereth into them.

13 Then said he unto me, The north chambers and the south chambers, which are before the separate place, they be holy chambers, where the priests that approach unto the Lord shall eat the most holy things: there shall they lay the most holy things, and the meat offering, and the sin offering, and the trespass offering; for the place is holy.

14 When the priests enter

sanctorum ibi ponent sancta sanctorum et oblationem pro peccato et pro delicto locus enim sanctus est

14. cum autem ingressi fuerint sacerdotes non egredientur de sanctis in atrium exterius et ibi reponent vestimenta sua in quibus ministrant quia sancta sunt vestienturque vestimentis aliis et sic procedent ad populum

15. cumque conplesset mensuras domus interioris eduxit me per viam portae quae respiciebat ad viam orientalem et mensus est eam undique per circuitum

16. mensus autem est contra ventum orientalem calamo mensurae quingentos calamos in calamo mensurae per circuitum

17. et mensus est contra ventum aquilonem quingentos calamos in calamo mensurae per gyrum

18. et ad ventum australem mensus est quingentos calamos in

therein, then shall they not go out of the holy place into the utter court, but there they shall lay their garments wherein they minister; for they are holy; and shall put on other garments, and shall approach to those things which are for the people.

15 Now when he had made an end of measuring the inner house, he brought me forth toward the gate whose prospect is toward the east, and measured it round about.

16 He measured the east side with the measuring reed, five hundred reeds, with the measuring reed round about.

17 He measured the north side, five hundred reeds, with the measuring reed round about.

18 He measured the south side, five hundred reeds, with the measuring reed.

19 He turned about to the west side, and measured five hundred reeds with the measuring reed.

20 He measured it by the four sides: it had a wall round about, five hundred reeds long, and five hundred broad, to make a separation between the sanctuary and

calamo mensurae per circuitum

19. et ad ventum occidentalem mensus est quingentos calamos in calamo mensurae

20. per quattuor ventos mensus est illud murum eius undique per circuitum longitudine quingentorum cubitorum et latitudine quingentorum cubitorum dividentem inter sanctuarium et vulgi locum

the profane place.

CHAPTER 43

1. et duxit me ad portam quae respiciebat ad viam orientalem

2. et ecce gloria Dei Israhel ingrediebatur per viam orientalem et vox erat ei quasi vox aquarum multarum et terra splendebat a maiestate eius

3. et vidi visionem secundum speciem quam videram quando venit ut disperderet civitatem et species secundum aspectum quem videram

CHAPTER 43

AFTERWARD he brought me to the gate, even the gate that looketh toward the east:

2 And, behold, the glory of the God of Israel came from the way of the east: and his voice was like a noise of many waters: and the earth shined with his glory.

3 And it was according to the appearance of the vision which I saw, even according to the vision that I saw when I came to destroy the city: and the visions were like the vision that I saw by the river

iuxta fluvium Chobar et cecidi super faciem meam

4. et maiestas Domini ingressa est templum per viam portae quae respiciebat ad orientem

5. et levavit me spiritus et introduxit me in atrium interius et ecce repleta erat gloria Domini domus

6. et audivi loquentem ad me de domo et vir qui stabat iuxta me

7. dixit ad me fili hominis locus solii mei et locus vestigiorum pedum meorum ubi habito in medio filiorum Israhel in aeternum et non polluent ultra domus Israhel nomen sanctum meum ipsi et reges eorum in fornicationibus suis et in ruinis regum suorum et in excelsis

8. qui fabricati sunt limen suum iuxta limen meum et postes suos iuxta postes meos et murus erat inter me et eos et polluerunt nomen sanctum meum in abominationibus quas fecerunt propter quod consumpsi eos in ira mea

Chebar; and I fell upon my face.

4 And the glory of the Lord came into the house by the way of the gate whose prospect is toward the east.

5 So the spirit took me up, and brought me into the inner court; and, behold, the glory of the Lord filled the house.

6 And I heard him speaking unto me out of the house; and the man stood by me.

7 And he said unto me, Son of man, the place of my throne, and the place of the soles of my feet, where I will dwell in the midst of the children of Israel for ever, and my holy name, shall the house of Israel no more defile, neither they, nor their kings, by their whoredom, nor by the carcases of their kings in their high places.

8 In their setting of their threshold by my thresholds, and their post by my posts, and the wall between me and them, they have even defiled my holy name by their abominations that they have committed: wherefore I have consumed them in mine anger.

9 Now let them put away

9. nunc ergo repellant procul fornicationem suam et ruinas regum suorum a me et habitabo in medio eorum semper

10. tu autem fili hominis ostende domui Israhel templum et confundantur ab iniquitatibus suis et metiantur fabricam

11. et erubescant ex omnibus quae fecerunt figuram domus et fabricae eius exitus et introitus et omnem descriptionem eius et universa praecepta eius cunctumque ordinem eius et omnes leges eius ostende eis et scribes in oculis eorum et custodiant omnes descriptiones eius et praecepta illius et faciant ea

12. ista est lex domus in summitate montis omnes fines eius in circuitu sanctum sanctorum est haec ergo est lex domus

13. istae autem mensurae altaris in cubito verissimo qui habebat cubitum et palmum in sinu eius erat cubitus et cubitus in latitudine et definitio

their whoredom, and the carcases of their kings, far from me, and I will dwell in the midst of them for ever.

10 Thou son of man, shew the house to the house of Israel, that they may be ashamed of their iniquities: and let them measure the pattern.

11 And if they be ashamed of all that they have done, shew them the form of the house, and the fashion thereof, and the goings out thereof, and the comings in thereof, and all the forms thereof, and all the ordinances thereof, and all the forms thereof, and all the laws thereof: and write it in their sight, that they may keep the whole form thereof, and all the ordinances thereof, and do them.

12 This is the law of the house; Upon the top of the mountain the whole limit thereof round about shall be most holy. Behold, this is the law of the house.

13 And these are the measures of the altar after the cubits: The cubit is a cubit and an hand breadth; even the bottom shall be a cubit, and the breadth a cubit, and

usque ad labium eius in circuitu palmus unus haec quoque erat fossa altaris

14. et de sinu terrae usque ad crepidinem novissimam duo cubiti et latitudo cubiti unius et a crepidine maiori usque ad crepidinem minorem quattuor cubiti et latitudo unius cubiti

15. ipse autem arihel quattuor cubitorum et ab arihel usque sursum cornua quattuor

16. et arihel duodecim cubitorum in longitudine per duodecim cubitos latitudinis quadrangulatum aequis lateribus

17. et crepido quattuordecim cubitorum longitudinis per quattuordecim latitudinis in quattuor angulis eius et corona in circuitu eius dimidii cubitus et sinus eius unius cubiti per circuitum gradus autem eius versi ad orientem

18. et dixit ad me fili hominis haec dicit Dominus Deus hii sunt ritus altaris in quacumque die fuerit fabricatum ut

the border thereof by the edge thereof round about shall be a span: and this shall be the higher place of the altar.

14 And from the bottom upon the ground even to the lower settle shall be two cubits, and the breadth one cubit; and from the lesser settle even to the greater settle shall be four cubits, and the breadth one cubit.

15 So the altar shall be four cubits; and from the altar and upward shall be four horns.

16 And the altar shall be twelve cubits long, twelve broad, square in the four squares thereof.

17 And the settle shall be fourteen cubits long and fourteen broad in the four squares thereof; and the border about it shall be half a cubit; and the bottom thereof shall be a cubit about; and his stairs shall look toward the east.

18 And he said unto me, Son of man, thus saith the Lord God; These are the ordinances of the altar in the day when they shall make it, to offer burnt offerings thereon, and to sprinkle

offeratur super illud holocaustum et effundatur sanguis

19. et dabis sacerdotibus Levitis qui sunt de semine Sadoc qui accedunt ad me ait Dominus Deus ut offerant mihi vitulum de armento pro peccato

20. et adsumens de sanguine eius pones super quattuor cornua eius et super quattuor angulos crepidinis et super coronam in circuitu et mundabis illud et expiabis

21. et tolles vitulum qui oblatus fuerit pro peccato et conbures illum in separato loco domus extra sanctuarium

22. et in die secunda offeres hircum caprarum inmaculatum pro peccato et expiabunt altare sicut expiaverunt in vitulo

23. cumque conpleveris expians illud offeres vitulum de armento inmaculatum et arietem de grege inmaculatum

24. et offeres eos in conspectu Domini et mittent sacerdotes super

blood thereon.

19 And thou shalt give to the priests the Levites that be of the seed of Zadok, which approach unto me, to minister unto me, saith the Lord God, a young bullock for a sin offering.

20 And thou shalt take of the blood thereof, and put it on the four horns of it, and on the four corners of the settle, and upon the border round about: thus shalt thou cleanse and purge it.

21 Thou shalt take the bullock also of the sin offering, and he shall burn it in the appointed place of the house, without the sanctuary.

22 And on the second day thou shalt offer a kid of the goats without blemish for a sin offering; and they shall cleanse the altar, as they did cleanse it with the bullock.

23 When thou hast made an end of cleansing it, thou shalt offer a young bullock without blemish, and a ram out of the flock without blemish.

24 And thou shalt offer them before the Lord, and the priests shall cast salt upon them, and they shall offer

229

eos sal et offerent eos holocaustum Domino

25. septem diebus facies hircum pro peccato cotidie et vitulum de armento et arietem de pecoribus inmaculatos offerent

26. septem diebus expiabunt altare et mundabunt illud et implebunt manum eius

27. expletis autem diebus in die octava et ultra facient sacerdotes super altare holocausta vestra et quae pro pace offerunt et placatus ero vobis ait Dominus Deus

them up for a burnt offering unto the Lord.

25 Seven days shalt thou prepare every day a goat for a sin offering: they shall also prepare a young bullock, and a ram out of the flock, without blemish.

26 Seven days shall they purge the altar and purify it; and they shall consecrate themselves.

27 And when these days are expired, it shall be, that upon the eighth day, and so forward, the priests shall make your burnt offerings upon the altar, and your peace offerings; and I will accept you, saith the Lord God.

CHAPTER 44

CHAPTER 44

1. et convertit me ad viam portae sanctuarii exterioris quae respiciebat ad orientem et erat clausa

2. et dixit Dominus ad me porta haec clausa erit non aperietur et vir non transiet per eam quoniam Dominus Deus Israhel ingressus est per eam

THEN he brought me back the way of the gate of the outward sanctuary which looketh toward the east; and it was shut.

2 Then said the Lord unto me; This gate shall be shut, it shall not be opened, and no man shall enter in by it; because the Lord, the God of Israel, hath entered in by it,

eritque clausa

3. principi princeps ipse sedebit in ea ut comedat panem coram Domino per viam vestibuli portae ingredietur et per viam eius egredietur

4. et adduxit me per viam portae aquilonis in conspectu domus et vidi et ecce implevit gloria Domini domum Domini et cecidi in faciem meam

5. et dixit ad me Dominus fili hominis pone cor tuum et vide oculis tuis et auribus tuis audi omnia quae ego loquor ad te de universis caerimoniis domus Domini et de cunctis legibus eius et pones cor tuum in viis templi per omnes exitus sanctuarii

6. et dices ad exasperantem me domum Israhel haec dicit Dominus Deus sufficiant vobis omnia scelera vestra domus Israhel

7. eo quod inducitis filios alienos incircumcisos corde et incircumcisos carne ut sint in sanctuario meo et polluant domum meam et offertis panes

therefore it shall be shut.

3 It is for the prince; the prince, he shall sit in it to eat bread before the Lord; he shall enter by the way of the porch of that gate, and shall go out by the way of the same.

4 Then brought he me the way of the north gate before the house: and I looked, and, behold, the glory of the Lord filled the house of the Lord: and I fell upon my face.

5 And the Lord said unto me, Son of man, mark well, and behold with thine eyes, and hear with thine ears all that I say unto thee concerning all the ordinances of the house of the Lord, and all the laws thereof; and mark well the entering in of the house, with every going forth of the sanctuary.

6 And thou shalt say to the rebellious, even to the house of Israel, Thus saith the Lord God; O ye house of Israel, let it suffice you of all your abominations,

7 In that ye have brought into my sanctuary strangers, uncircumcised in heart, and uncircumcised in flesh, to be in my sanctuary, to pollute it,

meos adipem et sanguinem et dissolvitis pactum meum in omnibus sceleribus vestris

8. et non servastis praecepta sanctuarii mei et posuistis custodes observationum mearum in sanctuario meo vobismet ipsis

9. haec dicit Dominus Deus omnis alienigena incircumcisus corde et incircumcisus carne non ingredietur sanctuarium meum omnis filius alienus qui est in medio filiorum Israhel

10. sed et Levitae qui longe recesserunt a me in errore filiorum Israhel et erraverunt a me post idola sua et portaverunt iniquitatem suam

11. erunt in sanctuario meo aeditui et ianitores portarum domus et ministri domus ipsi mactabunt holocaustosin et victimas populi et ipsi stabunt in conspectu eorum ut ministrent eis

12. pro eo quod ministraverunt illis in conspectu idolorum suorum et facti sunt

even my house, when ye offer my bread, the fat and the blood, and they have broken my covenant because of all your abominations.

8 And ye have not kept the charge of mine holy things: but ye have set keepers of my charge in my sanctuary for yourselves.

9 Thus saith the Lord God; No stranger, uncircumcised in heart, nor uncircumcised in flesh, shall enter into my sanctuary, of any stranger that is among the children of Israel.

10 And the Levites that are gone away far from me, when Israel went astray, which went astray away from me after their idols; they shall even bear their iniquity.

11 Yet they shall be ministers in my sanctuary, having charge at the gates of the house, and ministering to the house: they shall slay the burnt offering and the sacrifice for the people, and they shall stand before them to minister unto them.

12 Because they ministered unto them before their idols, and caused the house of Israel to fall into iniquity;

domui Israhel in offendiculum iniquitatis idcirco levavi manum meam super eos dicit Dominus Deus et portaverunt iniquitatem suam

13. et non adpropinquabunt ad me ut sacerdotio fungantur mihi neque accedent ad omne sanctuarium meum iuxta sancta sanctorum sed portabunt confusionem suam et scelera sua quae fecerunt

14. et dabo eos ianitores domus in omni ministerio eius et universis quae fiunt in ea

15. sacerdotes autem Levitae filii Sadoc qui custodierunt caerimonias sanctuarii mei cum errarent filii Israhel a me ipsi accedent ad me ut ministrent mihi et stabunt in conspectu meo ut offerant mihi adipem et sanguinem ait Dominus Deus

16. ipsi ingredientur sanctuarium meum et ipsi accedent ad mensam meam ut ministrent mihi et custodiant caerimonias

therefore have I lifted up mine hand against them, saith the Lord God, and they shall bear their iniquity.

13 And they shall not come near unto me, to do the office of a priest unto me, nor to come near to any of my holy things, in the most holy place: but they shall bear their shame, and their abominations which they have committed.

14 But I will make them keepers of the charge of the house, for all the service thereof, and for all that shall be done therein.

15 But the priests the Levites, the sons of Zadok, that kept the charge of my sanctuary when the children of Israel went astray from me, they shall come near to me to minister unto me, and they shall stand before me to offer unto me the fat and the blood, saith the Lord God:

16 They shall enter into my sanctuary, and they shall come near to my table, to minister unto me, and they shall keep my charge.

17 And it shall come to pass, that when they enter in at the gates of the inner court, they

meas

17. cumque ingredientur portas atrii interioris vestibus lineis induentur nec ascendet super eos quicquam laneum quando ministrant in portis atrii interioris et intrinsecus

18. vittae lineae erunt in capitibus eorum et feminalia linea erunt in lumbis eorum et non accingentur in sudore

19. cumque egredientur atrium exterius ad populum exuent se vestimenta sua in quibus ministraverunt et reponent ea in gazofilacio sanctuarii et vestient se vestimentis aliis et non sanctificabunt populum in vestibus suis

20. caput autem suum non radent neque comam nutrient sed tondentes adtondent capita sua

21. et vinum non bibet omnis sacerdos quando ingressurus est atrium interius

22. et viduam et repudiatam non accipient uxores sed virgines de semine domus Israhel sed et viduam quae fuerit

shall be clothed with linen garments; and no wool shall come upon them, whiles they minister in the gates of the inner court, and within.

18 They shall have linen bonnets upon their heads, and shall have linen breeches upon their loins; they shall not gird themselves with any thing that causeth sweat.

19 And when they go forth into the utter court, even into the utter court to the people, they shall put off their garments wherein they ministered, and lay them in the holy chambers, and they shall put on other garments; and they shall not sanctify the people with their garments.

20 Neither shall they shave their heads, nor suffer their locks to grow long; they shall only poll their heads.

21 Neither shall any priest drink wine, when they enter into the inner court.

22 Neither shall they take for their wives a widow, nor her that is put away: but they shall take maidens of the seed of the house of Israel, or a widow that had a priest before.

vidua a sacerdote accipient

23. et populum meum docebunt quid sit inter sanctum et pollutum et inter mundum et inmundum ostendent eis

24. et cum fuerit controversia stabunt in iudiciis meis et iudicabunt leges meas et praecepta mea in omnibus sollemnitatibus meis custodient et sabbata mea sanctificabunt

25. et ad mortuum hominem non ingredientur ne polluantur nisi ad patrem et matrem et filium et filiam et fratrem et sororem quae alterum virum non habuit in quibus contaminabuntur

26. et postquam fuerit emundatus septem dies numerabuntur ei

27. et in die introitus sui in sanctuarium ad atrium interius ut ministret mihi in sanctuario offeret pro peccato suo ait Dominus Deus

28. erit autem eis hereditas ego hereditas

23 And they shall teach my people the difference between the holy and profane, and cause them to discern between the unclean and the clean.

24 And in controversy they shall stand in judgment; and they shall judge it according to my judgments: and they shall keep my laws and my statutes in all mine assemblies; and they shall hallow my sabbaths.

25 And they shall come at no dead person to defile themselves: but for father, or for mother, or for son, or for daughter, for brother, or for sister that hath had no husband, they may defile themselves.

26 And after he is cleansed, they shall reckon unto him seven days.

27 And in the day that he goeth into the sanctuary, unto the inner court, to minister in the sanctuary, he shall offer his sin offering, saith the Lord God.

28 And it shall be unto them for an inheritance: I am their inheritance: and ye shall give them no possession in Israel: I am their possession.

eorum et possessionem non dabitis eis in Israhel ego enim possessio eorum

29. victimam et pro peccato et pro delicto ipsi comedent et omne votum in Israhel ipsorum erit

30. et primitiva omnium primogenitorum et omnia libamenta ex omnibus quae offeruntur sacerdotum erunt et primitiva ciborum vestrorum dabitis sacerdoti ut reponat benedictionem domui suae

31. omne morticinum et captum a bestia de avibus et de pecoribus non comedent sacerdotes

29 They shall eat the meat offering, and the sin offering, and the trespass offering; and every dedicated thing in Israel shall be theirs.

30 And the first of all the firstfruits of all things, and every oblation of all, of every sort of your oblations, shall be the priest's: ye shall also give unto the priest the first of your dough, that he may cause the blessing to rest in thine house.

31 The priests shall not eat of any thing that is dead of itself, or torn, whether it be fowl or beast.

CHAPTER 45

CHAPTER 45

1. cumque coeperitis terram dividere sortito separate primitias Domino sanctificatum de terra longitudine viginti quinque milia et latitudine decem milia sanctificatum erit in omni termino eius per circuitum

MOREOVER, when ye shall divide by lot the land for inheritance, ye shall offer an oblation unto the Lord, an holy portion of the land: the length shall be the length of five and twenty thousand reeds, and the breadth shall be ten thousand. This shall be holy in all the borders thereof

2. et erit ex omni parte sanctificatum quingentos per quingentos quadrifariam per circuitum et quinquaginta cubitis in suburbana eius per gyrum

3. et a mensura ista mensurabis longitudinem viginti quinque milium et latitudinem decem milium et in ipso erit templum sanctumque sanctorum

4. sanctificatum de terra erit sacerdotibus ministris sanctuarii qui accedunt ad ministerium Domini et erit eis locus in domos et in sanctuarium sanctitatis

5. viginti quinque autem milia longitudinis et decem milia latitudinis erunt Levitis qui ministrant domui ipsi possidebunt viginti gazofilacia

6. et possessionem civitatis dabitis quinque milia latitudinis et longitudinis viginti quinque milia secundum separationem sanctuarii omni domui Israhel

7. principi quoque hinc et inde in separationem

round about.

2 Of this there shall be for the sanctuary five hundred in length, with five hundred in breadth, square round about; and fifty cubits round about for the suburbs thereof.

3 And of this measure shalt thou measure the length of five and twenty thousand, and the breadth of ten thousand: and in it shall be the sanctuary and the most holy place.

4 The holy portion of the land shall be for the priests the ministers of the sanctuary, which shall come near to minister unto the Lord: and it shall be a place for their houses, and an holy place for the sanctuary.

5 And the five and twenty thousand of length, and the ten thousand of breadth, shall also the Levites, the ministers of the house, have for themselves, for a possession for twenty chambers.

6 And ye shall appoint the possession of the city five thousand broad, and five and twenty thousand long, over against the oblation of the holy portion: it shall be for

sanctuarii et in possessionem civitatis contra faciem separationis sanctuarii et contra faciem possessionis urbis a latere maris usque ad mare et a latere orientis usque ad orientem longitudinem autem iuxta unamquamque partium a termino occidentali usque ad terminum orientalem

8. de terra erit ei possessio in Israhel et non depopulabuntur ultra principes populum meum sed terram dabunt domui Israhel secundum tribus eorum

9. haec dicit Dominus Deus sufficiat vobis principes Israhel iniquitatem et rapinas intermittite et iudicium et iustitiam facite separate confinia vestra a populo meo ait Dominus Deus

10. statera iusta et oephi iustum et batus iustus erit vobis

11. oephi et batus aequalia et unius mensurae erunt ut capiat decimam partem chori batus et decimam partem

the whole house of Israel.

7 And a portion shall be for the prince on the one side and on the other side of the oblation of the holy portion, and of the possession of the city, before the oblation of the holy portion, and before the possession of the city, from the west side westward, and from the east side eastward: and the length shall be over against one of the portions, from the west border unto the east border.

8 In the land shall be his possession in Israel: and my princes shall no more oppress my people; and the rest of the land shall they give to the house of Israel according to their tribes.

9 Thus saith the Lord God; Let it suffice you, O princes of Israel: remove violence and spoil, and execute judgment and justice, take away your exactions from my people, saith the Lord God.

10 Ye shall have just balances, and a just ephah, and a just bath.

11 The ephah and the bath shall be of one measure, that the bath may contain the

chori oephi iuxta mensuram chori erit aequa libratio eorum

12. siclus autem viginti obolos habeat porro viginti sicli et viginti quinque sicli et quindecim sicli minam facient

13. et haec sunt primitiae quas tolletis sextam partem oephi de choro frumenti et sextam partem oephi de choro hordei

14. mensura quoque olei batus olei decima pars chori est et decem bati chorum faciunt quia decem bati implent chorum

15. et arietem unum de grege ducentorum de his quae nutriunt Israhel in sacrificium et in holocaustum et in pacifica ad expiandum pro eis ait Dominus Deus

16. omnis populus terrae tenebitur primitiis his principi in Israhel

17. et super principem erunt holocausta et sacrificium et libamina in sollemnitatibus et in kalendis et in sabbatis in

tenth part of an homer, and the ephah the tenth part of an homer: the measure thereof shall be after the homer.

12 And the shekel shall be twenty gerahs: twenty shekels, five and twenty shekels, fifteen shekels, shall be your maneh.

13 This is the oblation that ye shall offer; the sixth part of an ephah of an homer of wheat, and ye shall give the sixth part of an ephah of an homer of barley:

14 Concerning the ordinance of oil, the bath of oil, ye shall offer the tenth part of a bath out of the cor, which is an homer of ten baths; for ten baths are an homer:

15 And one lamb out of the flock, out of two hundred, out of the fat pastures of Israel; for a meat offering, and for a burnt offering, and for peace offerings, to make reconciliation for them, saith the Lord God.

16 All the people of the land shall give this oblation for the prince in Israel.

17 And it shall be the prince's part to give burnt offerings, and meat offerings, and drink offerings, in the

universis sollemnitatibus domus Israhel ipse faciat pro peccato sacrificium et holocaustum et pacifica ad expiandum pro domo Israhel

18. haec dicit Dominus Deus in primo mense una mensis sumes vitulum de armento inmaculatum et expiabis sanctuarium

19. et tollet sacerdos de sanguine quod erit pro peccato et ponet in postibus domus et in quattuor angulis crepidinis altaris et in postibus portae atrii interioris

20. et sic facies in septima mensis pro unoquoque qui ignoravit et errore deceptus est et expiabitis pro domo

21. in primo mense quartadecima die mensis erit vobis paschae sollemnitas septem diebus azyma comedentur

22. et faciet princeps in die illa pro se et pro universo populo terrae vitulum pro peccato

23. et in septem dierum sollemnitate faciet holocaustum Domino

feasts, and in the new moons, and in the sabbaths, in all solemnities of the house of Israel: he shall prepare the sin offering, and the meat offering, and the burnt offering, and the peace offerings, to make reconciliation for the house of Israel.

18 Thus saith the Lord God; In the first month, in the first day of the month, thou shalt take a young bullock without blemish, and cleanse the sanctuary:

19 And the priest shall take of the blood of the sin offering, and put it upon the posts of the house, and upon the four corners of the settle of the altar, and upon the posts of the gate of the inner court.

20 And so thou shalt do the seventh day of the month for every one that erreth, and for him that is simple: so shall ye reconcile the house.

21 In the first month, in the fourteenth day of the month, ye shall have the passover, a feast of seven days; unleavened bread shall be eaten.

22 And upon that day shall

septem vitulos et septem arietes inmaculatos cotidie septem diebus et pro peccato hircum caprarum cotidie

24. et sacrificium oephi per vitulum et oephi per arietem faciet et olei hin per singula oephi

25. septimo mense quintadecima die mensis in sollemnitate faciet sicut supra dicta sunt per septem dies tam pro peccato quam pro holocausto et in sacrificio et in oleo

the prince prepare for himself and for all the people of the land a bullock for a sin offering.

23 And seven days of the feast he shall prepare a burnt offering to the Lord, seven bullocks and seven rams without blemish daily the seven days; and a kid of the goats daily for a sin offering.

24 And he shall prepare a meat offering of an ephah for a bullock, and an ephah for a ram, and an hin of oil for an ephah.

25 In the seventh month, in the fifteenth day of the month, shall he do the like in the feast of the seven days, according to the sin offering, according to the burnt offering, and according to the meat offering, and according to the oil.

CHAPTER 46

CHAPTER 46

1. haec dicit Dominus Deus porta atrii interioris quae respicit ad orientem erit clausa sex diebus in quibus opus fit die autem sabbati aperietur sed et in die kalendarum aperietur

THUS saith the Lord God; The gate of the inner court that looketh toward the east shall be shut the six working days; but on the sabbath it shall be opened, and in the day of the new moon it shall

2. et intrabit princeps per viam vestibuli portae de foris et stabit in limine portae et facient sacerdotes holocaustum eius et pacifica eius et adorabit super limen portae et egredietur porta autem non claudetur usque ad vesperam

3. et adorabit populus terrae ad ostium portae illius in sabbatis et in kalendis coram Domino

4. holocaustum autem hoc offeret princeps Domino in die sabbati sex agnos inmaculatos et arietem inmaculatum

5. et sacrificium oephi per arietem agnis autem sacrificium quod dederit manus eius et olei hin per singula oephi

6. in die autem kalendarum vitulum de armento inmaculatum et sex agni et arietes inmaculati erunt

7. et oephi per vitulum oephi quoque per arietem faciet sacrificium agnis autem sicut invenerit manus eius et olei hin per singula oephi

8. cumque ingressurus est

be opened.

2 And the prince shall enter by the way of the porch of that gate without, and shall stand by the post of the gate, and the priests shall prepare his burnt offering and his peace offerings, and he shall worship at the threshold of the gate: then he shall go forth; but the gate shall not be shut until the evening.

3 Likewise the people of the land shall worship at the door of this gate before the Lord in the sabbaths and in the new moons.

4 And the burnt offering that the prince shall offer unto the Lord in the sabbath day shall be six lambs without blemish, and a ram without blemish.

5 And the meat offering shall be an ephah for a ram, and the meat offering for the lambs as he shall be able to give, and an hin of oil to an ephah.

6 And in the day of the new moon it shall be a young bullock without blemish, and six lambs, and a ram: they shall be without blemish.

7 And he shall prepare a meat offering, an ephah for a

princeps per viam
vestibuli portae
ingrediatur et per eandem
viam exeat

9. et cum intrabit populus
terrae in conspectu
Domini in sollemnitatibus
qui ingreditur per portam
aquilonis ut adoret
egrediatur per viam
portae meridianae porro
qui ingreditur per viam
portae meridianae
egrediatur per viam
portae aquilonis non
revertetur per viam portae
per quam ingressus est
sed e regione illius
egredietur

10. princeps autem in
medio eorum cum
ingredientibus ingredietur
et cum egredientibus
egredietur

11. et in nundinis et in
sollemnitatibus erit
sacrificium oephi per
vitulum et oephi per
arietem agnis autem erit
sacrificium sicut invenerit
manus eius et olei hin per
singula oephi

12. cum autem fecerit
princeps spontaneum
holocaustum aut pacifica
voluntaria Domino

bullock, and an ephah for a
ram, and for the lambs
according as his hand shall
attain unto, and an hin of oil
to an ephah.

8 And when the prince shall
enter, he shall go in by the
way of the porch of that gate,
and he shall go forth by the
way thereof.

9 But when the people of the
land shall come before the
Lord in the solemn feasts, he
that entereth in by the way of
the north gate to worship
shall go out by the way of the
south gate; and he that
entereth by the way of the
south gate shall go forth by
the way of the north gate: he
shall not return by the way of
the gate whereby he came in,
but shall go forth over
against it.

10 And the prince in the
midst of them, when they go
in, shall go in; and when they
go forth, shall go forth.

11 And in the feasts and in
the solemnities the meat
offering shall be an ephah to
a bullock, and an ephah to a
ram, and to the lambs as he is
able to give, and an hin of oil
to an ephah.

12 Now when the prince

aperietur ei porta quae respicit ad orientem et faciet holocaustum suum et pacifica sua sicut fieri solet in die sabbati et egredietur claudeturque porta postquam exierit

13. et agnum eiusdem anni inmaculatum faciet holocaustum cotidie Domino semper mane faciet illud

14. et sacrificium faciet super eo cata mane mane sextam partem oephi et de oleo tertiam partem hin ut misceatur similae sacrificium Domino legitimum iuge atque perpetuum

15. faciet agnum et sacrificium et oleum cata mane mane holocaustum sempiternum

16. haec dicit Dominus Deus si dederit princeps donum alicui de filiis suis hereditas eius filiorum suorum erit possidebunt ea hereditarie

17. si autem dederit legatum de hereditate sua uni servorum suorum erit illius usque ad annum remissionis et revertetur ad principem hereditas

shall prepare a voluntary burnt offering or peace offerings voluntarily unto the Lord, one shall then open him the gate that looketh toward the east, and he shall prepare his burnt offering and his peace offerings, as he did on the sabbath day: then he shall go forth; and after his going forth one shall shut the gate.

13 Thou shalt daily prepare a burnt offering unto the Lord of a lamb of the first year without blemish: thou shalt prepare it every morning.

14 And thou shalt prepare a meat offering for it every morning, the sixth part of an ephah, and the third part of an hin of oil, to temper with the fine flour; a meat offering continually by a perpetual ordinance unto the Lord.

15 Thus shall they prepare the lamb, and the meat offering, and the oil, every morning for a continual burnt offering.

16 Thus saith the Lord God; If the prince give a gift unto any of his sons, the inheritance thereof shall be his sons'; it shall be their possession by inheritance.

autem eius filiis eius erit

18. et non accipiet princeps de hereditate populi per violentiam et de possessione eorum sed de possessione sua hereditatem dabit filiis suis ut non dispergatur populus meus unusquisque a possessione sua

19. et introduxit me per ingressum qui erat ex latere portae in gazofilacia sanctuarii ad sacerdotes quae respiciebant ad aquilonem et erat ibi locus vergens ad occidentem

20. et dixit ad me iste est locus ubi coquent sacerdotes pro delicto et pro peccato ubi coquent sacrificium ut non efferant in atrio exteriori et sanctificetur populus

21. et eduxit me in atrium exterius et circumduxit me per quattuor angulos atrii et ecce atriolum erat in angulo atrii atriola singula per angulos atrii

22. in quattuor angulos atrii atriola disposita quadraginta cubitorum

17 But if he give a gift of his inheritance to one of his servants, then it shall be his to the year of liberty; after it shall return to the prince: but his inheritance shall be his sons' for them.

18 Moreover the prince shall not take of the people's inheritance by oppression, to thrust them out of their possession; but he shall give his sons inheritance out of his own possession: that my people be not scattered every man from his possession.

19 After he brought me through the entry, which was at the side of the gate, into the holy chambers of the priests, which looked toward the north: and, behold, there was a place on the two sides westward.

20 Then said he unto me, This is the place where the priests shall boil the trespass offering and the sin offering, where they shall bake the meat offering; that they bear them not out into the utter court, to sanctify the people.

21 Then he brought me forth into the utter court, and caused me to pass by the four corners of the court; and,

per longum et triginta per latum mensurae unius quattuor erant

23. et paries per circuitum ambiens quattuor atriola et culinae fabricatae erant subter porticus per gyrum

24. et dixit ad me haec est domus culinarum in qua coquent ministri domus Domini victimas populi

behold, in every corner of the court there was a court.

22 In the four corners of the court there were courts joined of forty cubits long and thirty broad: these four corners were of one measure.

23 And there was a row of building round about in them, round about them four, and it was made with boiling places under the rows round about.

24 Then said he unto me, These are the places of them that boil, where the ministers of the house shall boil the sacrifice of the people.

CHAPTER 47

1. et convertit me ad portam domus et ecce aquae egrediebantur subter limen domus ad orientem facies enim domus respiciebat ad orientem aquae autem descendebant in latus templi dextrum ad meridiem altaris

2. et eduxit me per viam portae aquilonis et convertit me ad viam foras portam exteriorem

CHAPTER 47

AFTERWARD he brought me again unto the door of the house; and, behold, waters issued out from under the threshold of the house eastward: for the forefront of the house stood toward the east, and the waters came down from under from the right side of the house, at the south side of the altar.

2 Then brought he me out of the way of the gate northward, and led me about

viam quae respiciebat ad orientem et ecce aquae redundantes a latere dextro

3. cum egrederetur vir ad orientem qui habebat funiculum in manu sua et mensus est mille cubitos et transduxit me per aquam usque ad talos

4. rursumque mensus est mille et transduxit me per aquam usque ad genua

5. et mensus est mille et transduxit me per aquam usque ad renes et mensus est mille torrentem quem non potui pertransire quoniam intumuerant aquae profundae torrentis qui non potest transvadari

6. et dixit ad me certe vidisti fili hominis et duxit me et convertit ad ripam torrentis

7. cumque me convertissem ecce in ripa torrentis ligna multa nimis ex utraque parte

8. et ait ad me aquae istae quae egrediuntur ad tumulos sabuli orientalis et descendunt ad plana deserti intrabunt mare et exibunt et sanabuntur aquae

the way without unto the utter gate by the way that looketh eastward; and, behold, there ran out waters on the right side.

3 And when the man that had the line in his hand went forth eastward, he measured a thousand cubits, and he brought me through the waters; the waters were to the ancles.

4 Again he measured a thousand, and brought me through the waters; the waters were to the knees. Again he measured a thousand, and brought me through; the waters were to the loins.

5 Afterward he measured a thousand; and it was a river that I could not pass over: for the waters were risen, waters to swim in, a river that could not be passed over.

6 And he said unto me, Son of man, hast thou seen this? Then he brought me, and caused me to return to the brink of the river.

7 Now when I had returned, behold, at the bank of the river were very many trees on the one side and on the other.

9. et omnis anima vivens quae serpit quocumque venerit torrens vivet et erunt pisces multi satis postquam venerint illuc aquae istae et sanabuntur et vivent omnia ad quae venerit torrens

10. vivent et stabunt super illa piscatores ab Engaddi usque ad Engallim siccatio sagenarum erunt plurimae species erunt piscium eius sicut pisces maris magni multitudinis nimiae

11. in litoribus autem eius et in palustribus non sanabuntur quia in salinas dabuntur

12. et super torrentem orietur in ripis eius ex utraque parte omne lignum pomiferum non defluet folium ex eo et non deficiet fructus eius per singulos menses adferet primitiva quia aquae eius de sanctuario egredientur et erunt fructus eius in cibum et folia eius ad medicinam

13. haec dicit Dominus Deus hic est terminus in quo possidebitis terram in

8 Then said he unto me, These waters issue out toward the east country, and go down into the desert, and go into the sea: which being brought forth into the sea, the waters shall be healed.

9 And it shall come to pass, that every thing that liveth, which moveth, whithersoever the rivers shall come, shall live: and there shall be a very great multitude of fish, because these waters shall come thither: for they shall be healed; and every thing shall live whither the river cometh.

10 And it shall come to pass, that the fishers shall stand upon it from En-gedi even unto En-eglaim; they shall be a place to spread forth nets; their fish shall be according to their kinds, as the fish of the great sea, exceeding many.

11 But the miry places thereof and the marishes thereof shall not be healed; they shall be given to salt.

12 And by the river upon the bank thereof, on this side and on that side, shall grow all trees for meat, whose leaf shall not fade, neither shall

duodecim tribubus Israhel quia Ioseph duplicem funiculum habet

14. possidebitis autem eam singuli aeque ut frater suus quam levavi manum meam ut darem patribus vestris et cadet terra haec vobis in possessionem

15. hic est autem terminus terrae ad plagam septentrionalem a mari magno via Bethalon venientibus Sadada

16. Emath Berotha Sabarim quae est inter terminum Damasci et confinium Emath domus Atticon quae est iuxta terminos Auran

17. et erit terminus a mari usque ad atrium Aenon terminus Damasci et ab aquilone ad aquilonem et terminus Emath plaga autem septentrionalis

18. porro plaga orientalis de medio Auran et de medio Damasci et de medio Galaad et de medio terrae Israhel Iordanis disterminans ad mare orientale metiemini etiam plagam orientalem

19. plaga autem australis

the fruit thereof be consumed: it shall bring forth new fruit according to his months, because their waters they issued out of the sanctuary: and the fruit thereof shall be for meat, and the leaf thereof for medicine.

13 Thus saith the Lord God; This shall be the border, whereby ye shall inherit the land according to the twelve tribes of Israel: Joseph shall have two portions.

14 And ye shall inherit it, one as well as another: concerning the which I lifted up mine hand to give it unto your fathers: and this land shall fall unto you for inheritance.

15 And this shall be the border of the land toward the north side, from the great sea, the way of Hethlon, as men go to Zedad;

16 Hamath, Berothah, Sibraim, which is between the border of Damascus and the border of Hamath; Hazar-hatticon, which is by the coast of Hauran.

17 And the border from the sea shall be Hazar-enan, the border of Damascus, and the north northward, and the

249

meridiana a Thamar usque ad aquas Contradictionis Cades et torrens usque ad mare magnum et plaga ad meridiem australis

20. et plaga maris mare magnum a confinio per directum donec venias Emath haec est plaga maris

21. et dividetis terram istam vobis per tribus Israhel

22. et mittetis eam in hereditatem vobis et advenis qui accesserint ad vos qui genuerint filios in medio vestrum et erunt vobis sicut indigenae inter filios Israhel vobiscum divident possessionem in medio tribuum Israhel

23. in tribu autem quacumque fuerit advena ibi dabitis possessionem illi ait Dominus Deus

border of Hamath. And this is the north side.

18 And the east side ye shall measure from Hauran, and from Damascus, and from Gilead, and from the land of Israel by Jordan, from the border unto the east sea. And this is the east side.

19 And the south side southward, from Tamar even to the waters of strife in Kadesh, the river to the great sea. And this is the south side southward.

20 The west side also shall be the great sea from the border, till a man come over against Hamath. This is the west side.

21 So shall ye divide this land unto you according to the tribes of Israel.

22 And it shall come to pass, that ye shall divide it by lot for an inheritance unto you, and to the strangers that sojourn among you, which shall beget children among you: and they shall be unto you as born in the country among the children of Israel; they shall have inheritance with you among the tribes of Israel.

23 And it shall come to pass,

that in what tribe the stranger sojourneth, there shall ye give him his inheritance, saith the Lord God.

CHAPTER 48

1. et haec nomina tribuum a finibus aquilonis iuxta viam Aethlon pergentibus Emath atrium Aenon terminus Damasci ad aquilonem iuxta Emath et erit ei plaga orientalis mare Dan una
2. et ad terminum Dan a plaga orientali usque ad plagam maris Aser una
3. et super terminum Aser a plaga orientali usque ad plagam maris Nepthalim una
4. et super terminum Nepthalim a plaga orientali usque ad plagam maris Manasse una
5. et super terminum Manasse a plaga orientali usque ad plagam maris Ephraim una
6. et super terminum Ephraim a plaga orientali usque ad plagam maris Ruben una

CHAPTER 48

NOW these are the names of the tribes. From the north end to the coast of the way of Hethlon, as one goeth to Hamath, Hazar-enan, the border of Damascus northward, to the coast of Hamath; for these are his sides east and west; a portion for Dan.

2 And by the border of Dan, from the east side unto the west side, a portion for Asher.

3 And by the border of Asher, from the east side even unto the west side, a portion for Naphtali.

4 And by the border of Naphtali, from the east side unto the west side, a portion for Manasseh.

5 And by the border of Manasseh, from the east side unto the west side, a portion for Ephraim.

6 And by the border of Ephraim, from the east side

7. et super terminum Ruben a plaga orientali usque ad plagam maris Iuda una

8. et super terminum Iuda a plaga orientali usque ad plagam maris erunt primitiae quas separabitis viginti quinque milibus latitudinis et longitudinis sicuti singulae partes a plaga orientali usque ad plagam maris et erit sanctuarium in medio eius

9. primitiae quas separastis Domino longitudo viginti quinque milibus et latitudo decem milibus

10. hae autem erunt primitiae sanctuarii sacerdotum ad aquilonem viginti quinque milia et ad mare latitudinis decem milia sed et ad orientem latitudinis decem milia et ad meridiem longitudinis viginti quinque milia et erit sanctuarium Domini in medio eius

11. sacerdotibus sanctuarium erit de filiis Sadoc qui custodierunt caerimonias meas et non erraverunt cum errarent

even unto the west side, a portion for Reuben.

7 And by the border of Reuben, from the east side unto the west side, a portion for Judah.

8 And by the border of Judah, from the east side unto the west side, shall be the offering which ye shall offer of five and twenty thousand reeds in breadth, and in length as one of the other parts, from the east side unto the west side: and the sanctuary shall be in the midst of it.

9 The oblation that ye shall offer unto the Lord shall be of five and twenty thousand in length, and of ten thousand in breadth.

10 And for them, even for the priests, shall be this holy oblation; toward the north five and twenty thousand in length, and toward the west ten thousand in breadth, and toward the east ten thousand in breadth, and toward the south five and twenty thousand in length: and the sanctuary of the Lord shall be in the midst thereof.

11 It shall be for the priests that are sanctified of the sons

filii Israhel sicut erraverunt et Levitae

12. et erunt eis primitiae de primitiis terrae sanctum sanctorum iuxta terminum Levitarum

13. sed et Levitis similiter iuxta fines sacerdotum viginti quinque milia longitudinis et latitudinis decem milia omnis longitudo viginti et quinque milium et latitudo decem milium

14. et non venundabunt ex eo neque mutabunt nec transferentur primitiae terrae quia sanctificatae sunt Domino

15. quinque milia autem quae supersunt in latitudine per viginti quinque milia profana erunt urbis in habitaculum et in suburbana et erit civitas in medio eius

16. et heae mensurae eius ad plagam septentrionalem quingenti et quattuor milia et ad plagam meridianam quingenti et quattuor milia et ad plagam orientalem quingenti et quattuor milia et ad

of Zadok; which have kept my charge, which went not astray when the children of Israel went astray, as the Levites went astray.

12 And this oblation of the land that is offered shall be unto them a thing most holy by the border of the Levites.

13 And over against the border of the priests the Levites shall have five and twenty thousand in length, and ten thousand in breadth: all the length shall be five and twenty thousand, and the breadth ten thousand.

14 And they shall not sell of it, neither exchange, nor alienate the firstfruits of the land: for it is holy unto the Lord.

15 And the five thousand, that are left in the breadth over against the five and twenty thousand, shall be a profane place for the city, for dwelling, and for suburbs: and the city shall be in the midst thereof.

16 And these shall be the measures thereof; the north side four thousand and five hundred, and the south side four thousand and five hundred, and on the east side

plagam occidentalem quingenti et quattuor milia

17. erunt autem suburbana civitatis ad aquilonem ducenti quinquaginta et in meridie ducenti quinquaginta et ad orientem ducenti quinquaginta et ad mare ducenti quinquaginta

18. quod autem reliquum fuerit in longitudine secundum primitias sanctuarii decem milia in orientem et decem milia ad occidentem erunt sicut primitiae sanctuarii et erunt fruges eius in panes his qui serviunt civitati

19. servientes autem civitati operabuntur ex omnibus tribubus Israhel

20. omnes primitiae viginti quinque milium per viginti quinque milia in quadrum separabuntur in primitias sanctuarii et possessionem civitatis

21. quod autem reliquum fuerit principis erit ex omni parte primitiarum sanctuarii et possessionis civitatis e regione viginti quinque milium

four thousand and five hundred, and the west side four thousand and five hundred.

17 And the suburbs of the city shall be toward the north two hundred and fifty, and toward the south two hundred and fifty, and toward the east two hundred and fifty, and toward the west two hundred and fifty.

18 And the residue in length over against the oblation of the holy portion shall be ten thousand eastward, and ten thousand westward: and it shall be over against the oblation of the holy portion; and the increase thereof shall be for food unto them that serve the city.

19 And they that serve the city shall serve it out of all the tribes of Israel.

20 All the oblation shall be five and twenty thousand by five and twenty thousand: ye shall offer the holy oblation foursquare, with the possession of the city.

21 And the residue shall be for the prince, on the one side and on the other of the holy oblation, and of the possession of the city, over

primitiarum usque ad terminum orientalem sed et ad mare e regione viginti quinque milium usque ad terminum maris similiter in partibus principis erit et erunt primitiae sanctuarii et sanctuarium templi in medio eius

22. de possessione autem Levitarum et de possessione civitatis in medio partium principis erit inter terminum Iuda et inter terminum Beniamin et ad principem pertinebit

23. et reliquis tribubus a plaga orientali usque ad plagam occidentalem Beniamin una

24. et contra terminum Beniamin a plaga orientali usque ad plagam occidentalem Symeon una

25. et super terminum Symeonis a plaga orientali usque ad plagam occidentis Isachar una

26. et super terminum Isachar a plaga orientali usque ad plagam occidentalem Zabulon una

against the five and twenty thousand of the oblation toward the east border, and westward over against the five and twenty thousand toward the west border, over against the portions for the prince: and it shall be the holy oblation; and the sanctuary of the house shall be in the midst thereof.

22 Moreover from the possession of the Levites, and from the possession of the city, being in the midst of that which is the prince's, between the border of Judah and the border of Benjamin, shall be for the prince.

23 As for the rest of the tribes, from the east side unto the west side, Benjamin shall have a portion.

24 And by the border of Benjamin, from the east side unto the west side, Simeon shall have a portion.

25 And by the border of Simeon, from the east side unto the west side, Issachar a portion.

26 And by the border of Issachar, from the east side unto the west side, Zebulun a portion.

27 And by the border of

27. et super terminum Zabulon a plaga orientali usque ad plagam maris Gad una

28. et super terminum Gad ad plagam austri in meridiem et erit finis de Thamar usque ad aquas Contradictionis Cades hereditas contra mare magnum

29. haec est terra quam mittetis in sortem tribubus Israhel et hae partitiones earum ait Dominus Deus

30. et hii egressus civitatis a plaga septentrionali quingentos et quattuor milia mensurabis

31. et portae civitatis in nominibus tribuum Israhel portae tres a septentrione porta Ruben una porta Iudae una porta Levi una

32. et ad plagam orientalem quingentos et quattuor milia et portae tres porta Ioseph una porta Beniamin una porta Dan una

33. et ad plagam meridianam quingentos et quattuor milia metieris

Zebulun, from the east side unto the west side, Gad a portion.

28 And by the border of Gad, at the south side southward, the border shall be even from Tamar unto the waters of strife in Kadesh, and to the river toward the great sea.

29 This is the land which ye shall divide by lot unto the tribes of Israel for inheritance, and these are their portions, saith the Lord God.

30 And these are the goings out of the city on the north side, four thousand and five hundred measures.

31 And the gates of the city shall be after the names of the tribes of Israel: three gates northward; one gate of Reuben, one gate of Judah, one gate of Levi.

32 And at the east side four thousand and five hundred: and three gates; and one gate of Joseph, one gate of Benjamin, one gate of Dan.

33 And at the south side four thousand and five hundred measures: and three gates; one gate of Simeon, one gate of Issachar, one gate of Zebulun.

portam Symeonis unam
portam Isachar unam
portam Zabulon unam

34. et ad plagam
occidentalem quingenti et
quattuor milia portae
eorum tres porta Gad una
porta Aser una porta
Nepthalim una

35. per circuitum decem
et octo milia et nomen
civitatis ex illa die
Dominus ibidem

34 At the west side four
thousand and five hundred,
with their three gates; one
gate of Gad, one gate of
Asher, one gate of Naphtali.

35 It was round about
eighteen thousand measures:
and the name of the city from
that day shall be, The Lord is
there.

Printed in Great Britain
by Amazon